SOCIAL DEVIANCE

SOCIAL
DEVIANCE
Perspectives
and Prospects

CHARLES S. SUCHAR
DePaul University

Holt, Rinehart and Winston

New York   Chicago   San Francisco   Dallas

Montreal   Toronto   London   Sydney

For Edith and David

Copyright © 1978 by Holt, Rinehart and Winston
All rights reserved

Library of Congress Cataloging in Publication Data

Suchar, Charles.
    Social Deviance: Perspectives and Prospects

    Bibliography: p. 267
    Includes index.
    1. Deviant behavior. I. Title.
HM291.S86   301.6'2   77-89740
ISBN 0-03-015521-5

Printed in the United States of America
890   090   987654321

FOREWORD

The theoretical sources of the specialized field called the sociology of deviance can be traced most directly to Durkheim's statements on the conditions of social order in *The Rules of Sociological Method, The Division of Labor in Society, Suicide,* and other works. However, Durkheim's influence was not clearly evident in the work of the early sociologists, who were less interested in theory than in investigating the myriad social conditions that developed in the wake of industrialization and urbanization. Indeed, the diversity of subject matter—ranging from legally defined and controled crime, suicide, and divorce to the more informally sanctioned forms of behavior, such as alcoholism, pauperism, and illegitimate births—effectively obscured the theoretical and methodological problems that lay unexamined beneath the ad hoc character of that research. This was perhaps inevitable in a field that early in its development attracted all manner of social reformer, each intent on documenting the harmful social consequences of the particular conditions that epitomized their concerns. The sociologists who crowded this field of specialization during the first decades of the twentieth century were animated by a passionate moral vision, a research stance that sought to appreciate the grinding social conditions in which their subjects lived, and the liberal's faith in the ameliorative effects of social reform and individual rehabilitation. Although ad hoc theory and research no longer dominates the field, this legacy of the early "social pathologists" persists as a minor theme, particularly in textbook treatments of "social problems."

Durkheim's influence on the remarkable developments in the sociology of deviance over the past 35 years is explicit and clear in two works that distinctively shaped that development. Merton's landmark paper "Social Structure and Anomie" drew conceptually and methodologically on Durkheim's *Suicide,* linking forms of deviant behavior to social structures through an analysis of the distribution of the rates of deviant behavior among social categories. The large body of research stimulated by Merton's paper focused on the "structural pressures" impinging on persons differentially situated in the social structure to account for the etiology of deviant behavior.

Almost 25 years later, Kai T. Erikson published "Notes on the Sociology of Deviance," citing Durkheim's *Rules of Sociological Method* to direct attention to what has become known as the societal reaction to deviance. The so-called labeling theory of deviance with which Erikson's work is commonly associated developed as a critique of the definitions of deviant behavior that are presupposed in etiological research on deviance. Erikson stated the issue simply and succinctly:

> In short, the "anomie theory" may help us appreciate the various ways in which people respond to conditions of strain, but it does not help us differentiate between those people who infringe the letter of the norm without attracting any notice and those who excite so much alarm that they earn a deviant reputation in society and are committed to special institutions like prisons and hospitals.

These two papers, then, are dialectically related in the contemporary controversies that engage sociologists of deviance. They reflect a basic theoretical tension between the focus on the social psychology of deviant behavior and the sociology of social control that has marked the development of this field. In his discussion of the theoretical and methodological developments in the sociology of deviance, Charles Suchar has deftly managed to find and to follow the sometimes thin and tenuous threads of logic that connect these two lines of investigation. His task has been made even more challenging by the intramural debates generated by various statements of the labeling perspective. The recent convergence of several theoretical orientations in the sociology of deviance—symbolic interactionism, ethnomethodology, phenomenological and, most recently, Marxist sociology—has added further complexities to his effort to present a coherent account of the issues that animate the controversies in this field.

The reader will find that Suchar's treatment of the sociologists whose works are described and examined in this book—among them Becker, Cicourel, Gibbs, Gove, Hirschi, Lemert, Matza, and McHugh —is informed and judicious. He has provided us a useful review and analysis of the theoretical issues underlying the major developments in the sociology of deviance. Some may disagree with this analysis, even more with his views on the problems and prospects of future development. But in so volatile a field, this is as it should be.

John I. Kitsuse

PREFACE

For centuries, scholars have sought to explain nonconforming behavior and the nonconformist. The focus of attention had been placed on specific forms of deviance—murder, theft, madness, adultery, homosexuality, heresy, and so on. The goal of discourse and analysis had usually been to discover the causes of such behavior, ostensibly for the purposes of control or correction. Contemporary sociologists, concerned with developing a theoretical perspective on the role, function, and meaning of deviation in society, have attempted to discover features common or general to such divergent forms of behavior.

In this book, I shall try to trace the historical development of thought that has led to the many contemporary sociological debates on social deviance. I am particularly concerned with explaining the emergence of subjectivist perspectives on deviance as reactions to perspectives that seek to demonstrate factors said to predispose an individual toward deviant behavior.

With the development of symbolic interaction as a basic perspective within sociology and as a principal vantage point from which to view social deviance, sociologists initiated the analysis of the *learning* of deviant behavior and the study of deviance as an *evaluative* reality. The latter emphasis, best known as the *labeling* approach, has come under fire in recent years. In this book, I review the advantages and shortcomings of this perspective, as well as trace the development of contending perspectives in the field.

The goal of this book is to offer students a historical review of major explanatory models of social deviance; to clarify the line of theoretical investigation initiated by subjectivist analysts; and to locate themes and topics derived from a subjectivist model in need of empirical investigation and theoretical reformulation.

I wish to take this opportunity to thank the many persons who have helped to make this book possible. First, to my teachers at Northwestern University, John I. Kitsuse and Howard S. Becker, for leading me to the study of social deviance; to the many students in my social deviance courses at DePaul University who have helped me hone some of these conceptual tools for analyzing deviance; to Ray Ashton and Jim Bergin at Holt, Rinehart and Winston for their support of this project; to Robert Heidel for his copyediting; and to the many reviewers who commented on early drafts of the manuscript—I am grateful to all of you for your help. I owe a special debt of gratitude to my friend and colleague Rosemary S. Bannan for her detailed commentary on the manuscript and her good advice. I also wish to thank my wife, Edith, for her help and encouragement during this project.

C.S.S.

CONTENTS

SELECTED APPLICATIONS   261

CHAPTER 1

INTRODUCTION

Students are often suspicious of the concept *"social deviation."* To many, it is a loaded term. What could sociologists tell us about behavior the establishment defines as "deviant"? When students discover that the course includes such topics as drug use, homosexuality, prostitution, mental illness, and transvestism, their initial reactions vary considerably. Why should the social scientist be concerned with behavior and individuals that students define as "weird," "immoral," "unjustly persecuted," "better left alone," or "perfectly normal"? Will we spend an entire semester bemoaning the terrible social problems that persons labeled as deviant are causing our society? Or will we go to the other extreme of offering excuses for, or glamorizing, persons whom we believe "society" has wronged?

These are understandable and legitimate concerns. Social deviation, after all, includes just those types of phenomena that will unsettle people, for whatever reason. Either they feel uncomfortable with it because they share the establishment's concerns about it, or they feel that to discuss such topics as drug use and homosexuality under the rubric of "deviant behavior" prejudges the issue and is unfair to the activities and persons in question. Most of us have our own views on such topics and sometimes vehemently defend them when confronted by opposing views. As we shall see, evaluation, disagreement, and social reactions of various kinds are the stuff that the study of social deviation is made of.

Social deviation is problematic because of this widespread disagreement, not only among the proverbial people on the street but also among professional analysts, whose task is to understand systematically what behavior and persons so defined are really like. There

1

are, in fact, few areas of sociological analysis in which so many conflicting lay and professional theories have been espoused. Although social deviation has not been as popular a topic for polite conversation as politics, people have always been concerned with those who they feel have not met the groups' expectations for acceptable behavior.

The problematic nature of social deviation is also considered a primary reason for its questionable popularity. Colleagues and students alike have often felt that social deviation has a natural attraction for students (perhaps once their initial concerns have been allayed): "it deals with the exotic"; "it appeals to prurient interests"; "the kinky subject matter almost teaches itself"; and so on. Although students do soon develop a strong curiosity about what drug users, homosexuals, prostitutes, and "crazy" people are really like, it is not true that the sociology of social deviation is therefore an easier subject matter to teach or learn.

In addition to the sheer number of available explanations for social deviation, the confusing nature of the particular explanations makes the subject matter a difficult one to study. This field of sociological inquiry contains so many ideas that are not well integrated and that seem to beg to be tied together so that a more unitary model of social deviation can be constructed. The goal of this book is to help students understand the major perspectives on social deviation and to specify the significant differences and consistencies in theoretical and conceptual frameworks on social deviation.

This book offers students an organizing conceptual framework, which facilitates the comparative analysis of perspectives on social deviation. It also gives students an understanding of the historical development of these perspectives. In doing so, it traces how and why both scholars and laymen have changed their views on social deviation. In particular, this book traces the development of a subjectivist perspective on deviant behavior and deviance. It analyzes how persons learn behavior others define as deviant and the analysis of the evaluative reality of deviance itself—how value judgments are made about particular persons and behavior. For centuries, scholars and laymen alike were concerned with the objective causes and conditions of deviant behavior and deviants. They paid little attention to the more dynamic characteristics underlying the development of behavior and to the judgmental processes that were integral to determinations of deviance.

In recent years, there has been much confusion about the value of a subjectivist orientation to social deviation. This book hopes to shed some light on the sources of this confusion and to indicate the need for a refocusing of theoretical and empiricial work that takes a subjectivist stance toward social deviation.

WHY STUDY SOCIAL DEVIATION?

A basic question that new students to the field ought to confront is *why* sociologists study social deviation. These topics have more commonly been discussed in popular literature by journalists and novelists. However, social scientists also study such behavior and individuals because they are concerned with discovering the basis for social *order* and *disorder.*

Sociology, like every science, must impose some orderliness and regularity upon what it attempts to analyze. Physical scientists, such as chemists, have sought to discover the regularity of chemicals and chemical reactions to determine the rules that govern these phenomena. The natural and physical sciences have developed from the premise that natural laws concerning these phenomena exist, and that the goal of science is to discover them. Sociology has also searched for the rules that govern social behavior and the functioning of social institutions. These rules, however, are created by men and women living in groups.

The creation of rules—or "norms," as social scientists have called them—has not always been a conscious, formal process. "Social convention"—doing things in a certain way because that is how people seem to agree they "ought" to be done or how they have been done for a long time—has its roots in seemingly unknown traditions, beliefs, practices, and extenuating circumstances. Yet they are powerful determinants of what people *will do.* They offer members of a group the expectations for acceptable behavior and facilitate social interaction and human relationship. Whether we call these rules folkways, mores, or (more generally) "norms," they form the broad structure of social relationships. How people interpret or define these rules and apply them to situations in which they are participants will help determine subsequent behavior—both theirs and others'.

If the normative order is the veritable backbone of a society or social group, the study of norms and the control they exercise over the behavior of people is one of the fundamental tasks of sociology. At whatever level these rules are found in the social order, we as sociologists should be concerned with how group members impart significance to the observance of various social rules or conventions. How dear are these rules to them? It should be apparent that one of the best ways of understanding this is to see what societal or individual reactions occur when these rules are violated. The defined severity of the violation and the reactions to it should tell us how significant these rules are to the group members. It should also tell us whether there is any variability in the observance of these rules. Do people always hold the observance of the rule in high esteem? Under what conditions does the reaction come about? For what individuals? With what consequences?

To study the normal and normative functioning of social institutions and human interaction, we must also study social deviance: situations in which some members of the social group have defined a person and action to be in violation of a social rule or convention.[1]* Sociologists thus study social deviation because it can tell us much about both the regularity and the irregularity of human social behavior.

There are other, equally important reasons for studying social deviation. As many observers have pointed out, deviation is an everyday feature of social life. The daily reports in our news media well attest to this fact. As the next chapter will show, some leading analysts have gone so far as to say that it is indeed a "normal" or "natural" feature of societies. For this reason alone it deserves the same in-depth analysis as other so-called normal societal features.

A more practical reason for studying social deviation is that since some persons will define an activity and an individual as a social problem, and will act toward the individual accordingly, there will be significant consequences for the parties involved, and in particular for the person defined as deviant. Lifestyles, lifechances, and future participations in the social order can be implicated by the actions of deviation and by the reactions to it. Time, money, personnel, institutional policy, friendship networks, family stability, popular culture, and more are affected by these actions and reactions. Their impact on the social system is proportionate to their significance as reflectors of the normative or rule-guided order of society.

RELATING SOCIAL DEVIATION TO OTHER FIELDS OF SOCIOLOGICAL INVESTIGATION

The study of the violation of social norms, or rule breaking, is certainly not the exclusive domain of the subfield of social deviation. Several other subfields within sociology are equally interested in these phenomena. The areas of analysis that sociologists have labelled "social problems" and "criminology" display especially strong interest in these matters. What makes their analysis or subject matter different from that of social deviation? We can best answer this by diagraming the relationship among these three fields (see Figure 1-1).

As the figure indicates, social problems is the most general area

*Notes fall at ends of chapters.

Figure 1-1 Related Areas of Study in Sociology

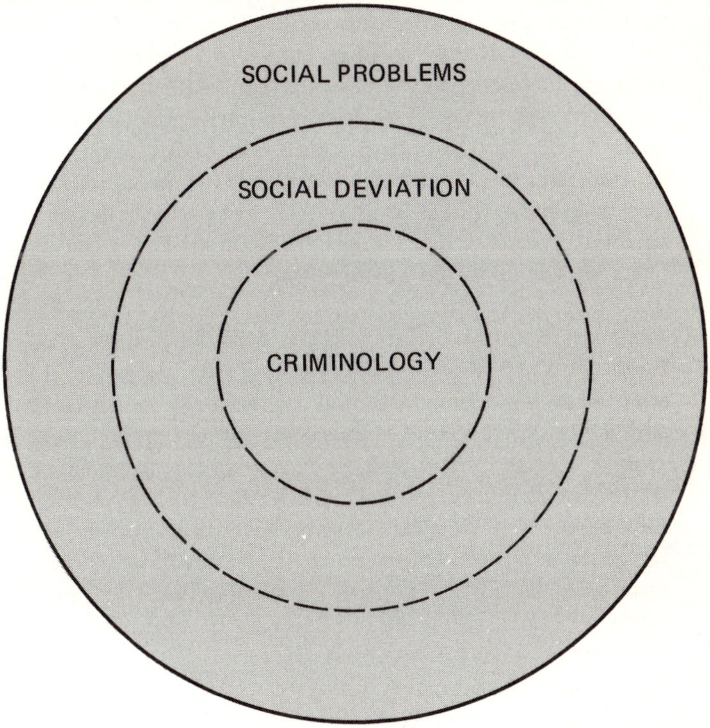

of investigation and includes within it the subfields of social deviation and criminology. Social problems are social issues for which various persons offer opposing explanations or resolutions, or that they consider problematic for or injurious to the welfare of a group. Social problems are usually marked by conflicting claims made by various persons and interest groups over the significance of such issues. This field includes such issues as air pollution, juvenile delinquency, abortion, consumer fraud, racial and ethnic discrimination, the treatment of rape victims by police and courts, unemployment, and political corruption.

An important characteristic of a social problem is its extensiveness, the number of persons it affects. However, it is often very difficult to tell how widespread are such social problems as the mistreatment of rape victims or racial discrimination or, in fact, what constitutes their being "widespread." To some, a handful of cases might constitute a social menace, while to others thousands of cases might not seem too significant.

Although social deviations are by definition social problems, some social problems are not clearly deviations—situations in which social rules have been broken. Recently the rise in the cost of physicians' malpractice insurance has been proclaimed as a grave social problem.[2] Yet here, specific rules have not been violated; we have only the physicians' feelings that the insurance industry and their patients have conspired against them. Another interesting difference is that for many social problems, a particular "offender" or scapegoat cannot be found. The previous example is a good illustration of this. In the case of alleged social deviation on the other hand, an offender can usually be found or assumed. Very often the offender in a social problem is said to be a category of individuals, a network of organizations, or a societal "condition" itself.

Social deviation includes within it the subspecialty of criminology. Just as social deviation is the study of behavior and of those who have been defined as rule breakers, criminology is the study of persons who have been defined as violators of institutionalized rules called "laws." A crime is therefore an act that is perceived to be in violation of the criminal law. It is a special form of deviant behavior that is formally and officially proscribed by a governmental authority. Many types of deviant behavior are not criminal, but all criminal behavior is by definition deviant.[3] Mental illness, student radicalism, excessive drinking, and unwed motherhood are good examples of deviant behavior that are not necessarily criminal.

Sociologists who work in the areas of social deviation and criminology have a good deal in common. In fact, many study both criminal and noncriminal forms of deviant behavior. Researchers in both fields have been concerned with the sources of deviant behavior, the formation of deviant groups and subcultures, the analysis of the reactions of significant individuals and institutions to deviant behavior and the deviant, and socialization into deviant roles. While although there have historically been different theoretical traditions and understandings of what issues needed to be studied in both social deviation and criminology, there have also been a great many similarities. As we will see in later chapters, leading scholars in the study of social deviation have often used criminological data to illustrate the theoretical properties of deviant behavior in general.

There has been a healthy cross-fertilizaton of ideas in social deviation and criminology, although much more is needed. Some sociologists have treated social deviation as the more theoretical handmaiden of criminology and as the more general study of social problems. Others would prefer to see the development of theoretical perspectives and conceptual models that were more peculiar to the separate phenomena studied by each of these disciplines. It is this author's opinion that some of the most significant theoretical advances in the last several decades have been made in the sociology of deviation and that their application to the understanding of issues in social problems and criminology has been both possible and profitable.

Like other subfields within sociology, the study of social deviation has also contributed to the understanding of more basic characteristics of societies and human behavior. Because of its focus, it has led to the understanding of *variations* in the normal features of everyday life: variations in patterns of socialization, role playing, group affiliation, group organization, intergroup relations, lifestyle, attitudes, values, family life, social control, social change—that is, the fundamental components of society and behavior of concern to all sociologists. As we will show, the field of social deviation has also been a testing ground for general theoretical and methodological debates in sociology. Its students have been in the forefront of innovations in thought and technique, the benefits of which have gone to many other areas of sociological investigation, as well.

SOCIAL DEVIATION

Rule breaking, rule breakers, and those who have considered it their responsibility to react against these have undergone many changes in the history of human societies. There probably have always existed persons and behavior that have not completely met the expectations of other members of the social group. In the history of mankind the powerful have always been able to decide which behaviors and individuals were "deviant." What has changed from epoch to epoch, society to society, have been: (1), the acts considered deviant; (2) the types of persons accused of these acts; (3) the type of authority empowered to react to the "deviant"; (4) the types of reactions to the "deviant"; (5) the rationales used to justify the reactions; and (6) the consequences of these reactions.

The acts or behaviors that have been labeled deviant have varied greatly. In Pilgrim America of the 1600s, a wife who defied the wishes of her husband could be placed in the pillory on public display. Today, labeling the husband a "male chauvinist pig" would be only one of several possible responses to a husband who treated his wife in any such manner. What is labeled deviant often seems to be riding the crest of a trend. Smoking in Elizabethan England was considered a "vile and filthy habit," and within the last 15 years a similar sentiment has grown even though people are smoking more and more. In the early 1960s long hair on males often caused violent and severe reactions, but soon came to be the "norm" among members of the youth culture. In some societies homosexuality has been accepted and homosexuals have even been accorded special privileges and high social status.[4] In our own society, although attitudes have been changing, homosexuality remains stigmatized.

Not all members of a society are subject to its proscriptions. Some individuals have always, for various reasons, escaped censure for behavior otherwise labeled as deviant. In many cases, reactions are very different for different individuals. This can clearly be seen in some ancient codes of law in which reactions have been formalized. Chambliss commenting on the *Code of Hammurabi,* the Babylonian code of law discovered by French archeologists in 1901, notes:

> If a man struck a superior, he might be given sixty strokes with an ox-tail whip in public, whereas the penalty for an assault on an inferior was a fine scaled according to the status of the victim. It cost considerably more to break the bone of a freeman than of a slave. To knock out the tooth of a man of one's own rank cost a tooth in return, but an aristocrat could knock out the tooth of a commoner for the small sum of twenty shekels.
>
> On the other hand, merchants, officials, and men of wealth were expected to act honorably; if they failed to do so, a much heavier penalty fell on them than upon those of whom less was expected, because of their lower social status.[5]

In our own society, black males are more likely to be apprehended by the police on "suspicion," are more likely to be arrested and convicted, and are more likely to receive severe punishments than are their white male counterparts.[6] A wealthy man, wandering around the park in old clothes and talking to the birds, bushes, and trees, would most likely be called eccentric and tolerated, while his impoverished counterpart might have his mental health questioned and his freedom restricted. Two women in their 30s or 40s sharing an apartment together do not meet with the same suspicions as two males doing the same thing. In short, *who you are* has often been a more significant factor in bringing about societal disapproval than *what you have done.*[7]

In most societies the family and peer group have been the first lines of control to secure and safeguard individual and group welfare. As societies become complex, the function of control is extended to other social agents and institutions: religious, educational, work, and political or governmental institutions establish formal and informal controls over the members of society. Social problems or deviations that are felt to require *special* consideration and societal reaction (such as crime and mental illness) develop their own institutional orders in which processing is more formal and uniform. In determining social deviance, *who does the reacting* is often just as significant as who has engaged in the activity. While there are similarities in the styles and patterns of social control among village priests, peer-group leaders, psychiatrists, teachers, and local constables, there are also very significant differences; and the societal reactions of each to the person considered deviant may lead to different consequences for all concerned.

One of the variants both within and between categories of societal reaction is the nature of the reaction and the explanations given for the reactions. Reactions for similar types of deviations can vary from mild rebukes, to curtailment of social interaction with the deviant, to death. Individuals who today would be defined as mentally or emotionally ill have in various societies and historical periods been tortured, drowned, hung, cloistered in religious institutions, placed in prisons, sold into slavery, as well as treated in a variety of more favorable ways.[8] Explanations for such treatment have included such varied epithets as saving the souls of the unfortunates, protecting the interests or welfare of society, preserving or reestablishing the health of the individual, an eye for an eye, and spare the rod and spoil the child.

Finally, one of the most significant variants of social deviation has been the consequences of the deviation for the future of the deviant. In some societies it has been possible to neutralize the stigma attached to the deviant, and the deviation and reaction to it have not unduly influenced the persons later life. In other societies and historical periods, neutralization or eradication has not been possible, and the life chances of the deviant have been drastically curtailed or eliminated. Often, it has prevented the deviant from engaging in various activities, participating within various groups, and forming certain types of associational and interpersonal ties. For example, possessing a criminal record or a record of hospitalization in a mental institution has often impeded the search for employment.

Sociologists have been concerned with analyzing all these variants or variables of social deviation. The early analysts, as well as contemporary scholars, share the basic interests of the layman: how do these behaviors come about and, with what results for the deviants and for the social group as a whole? In the following chapters we will explore the many answers offered by both sociologists and others for the behaviors and individuals in question. We will examine the trends in explanation that have led to the contemporay formulations of the 1960s and 1970s. To do so, we have organized the chapter materials to reflect the many similarities of interest, styles of explanation, and "explanatory logics" of leading theoreticians and empirical analysts in the field.

EXPLANATIONS FOR SOCIAL DEVIATION

The second chapter of this book examines one of the first major sociological statements on the nature of social deviation—or *social pathology,* as its author, Emile Durkheim, called it. Among the many characterizations that Durkheim made of social deviation, the most significant was that the essence of deviation—its defining attributes— were not to be found within the *actor* or in the *act* of deviation. Durkheim believed that social pathologies, like crime, are social facts whose existence could only be explained by other social facts or societal influences.[9] This view of social deviation was in opposition to two traditional categories of explanation—theories of moral depravity and biophysiological, causal theories of predisposition. These two types posited the predisposing factors as residing (respectively) within the act or the deviant.

Theories of moral depravity (see Chapter 3) are legalistic–moralistic theories that stem from a priori values. These theories view the act of deviation itself as being inherently deviant. They assume that certain behaviors are always to be considered as wrong or bad, and that individuals who willfully engage in such activities are morally depraved. For the most part these are distinctively noncausal explanations of deviant behavior—their authors are less concerned with the cause of deviant behavior than with the threat posed to God's ordained laws, the natural rights of man, or the moral imperatives without which society cannot exist.

Causal theories of predisposition (Chapter 3) have in common the following "logic" of explanation: an attribute *within* the individual predisposes him toward a particular type of deviation. The attributes that have been singled out are indeed numerous. The earliest ones were spirits and demons. In addition, excesses, deprivation, or imbalances of certain "humors" (body fluids) were believed to lead to immoral or illegal acts. Attached to these theories were various explanations which identified individuals who possessed or were possessed by these attributes. The well-known trials—by fire, drowning, combat, torture, and so on—were used to assess the presence of these attributes and ostensibly to prove guilt.

The biophysiological, causal theories of predisposition are the more contemporary versions of this type of explanation. These were prominent in the eighteenth and nineteenth centuries, but they exist in various forms to this day. Such predisposing factors as skull type, body shape, temperament, feeblemindedness, hormonal imbalance, and, much more recently, the XYY chromosome anomaly have been singled out as deserving careful investigation.

Durkheim's formulation, although a major departure from these explanations of social deviation, was similar in one important respect. While denying the significance of individualistic or psychological factors and underscoring the significance of social factors, Durkheim's model of social pathology was also conducive to a causal analysis of predisposing factors. The only difference being that the predisposing factors were now located in the social environment or "social structure."

The *sociological theories of predisposition* (see Chapter 4), formulated in the 1930s, 1940s, and 1950s, were the descendants of the Durkheim tradition. In the search for the causes of deviant behavior, these theories emphasized such factors as ecological and cultural area, population density, and migration. Sociologists who were perhaps more faithful to the point of view of the great French sociologist looked for the causes of societal instability or disorganization. They were concerned with the role of *anomie* (a state of normlessness in which societal constraint is lacking) in producing this disorganization. They focused their attention on group and class conflict and generally maintained that an individual's disadvantaged position in the social structure was a major factor predisposing him toward social deviation. Such factors as economic deprivation, differential opportunities, and value conflict and dissensus were used to explain social deviations like crime.

A MAJOR SHIFT IN PERSPECTIVE

A major change in the behavioral-science analysis of social deviation occurred in the first several decades of this century. In psychology and especially in sociology, scholars became concerned with how deviant behavior was *actualized,* or learned. They were dissatisfied with causal theories of predisposition, which rarely, if ever, directly confronted the vital behavioral process of *learning.* In sociology, the social-psychological perspective of *symbolic interaction* (see Chapter 5) offered a conceptual framework that was adopted by a number of sociologists and applied to the study of social deviation. The early proponents of this perspective stressed both the evaluative nature of social deviation—the fact that it is subject to the interpretations, perceptions, and actions of other individuals (deviance)—and the process by which individuals learn to engage in *behavior* that others define as deviant.

This dual focus on the learning of deviant behavior and the actualization of deviance is exemplified in the work of William I. Thomas, Edwin Sutherland and Frank Tannenbaum. Thomas and Sutherland were concerned with how deviant behavior was learned. Both concentrated on the role of learned definitions of reality in supporting participation in deviant or criminal activities. Tannenbaum, on the other hand, was interested in the impact of community evaluations and reactions on the behavior of those who are perceived as rule breakers. He drew attention to the influence of the "dramatization of evil" on the commitment to deviant behavior.

A major consequence of the work of these early proponents of an interactionist perspective was the pronounced investigation of deviance as a judgmental reality—the examination of "labeling" (see Chapter 6). Sociologists became interested in aspects of the societal reaction to deviants. Of particular concern was the process of stigmatization and its present and future impact on those processed by formal control agents and agencies. These "labeling" sociologists studied the basis of control-agent decision making, the influence of bureaucratic structure and practice on determinations of deviance, and "secondary deviation"—the impact of the societal reaction on commitment to deviant role playing. The labeling perspective, in the mid- and late 1960s became one of the leading, though extremely controversial, perspectives on the study of social deviation.

THE REACTION TO LABELING

A considerable portion of the literature on deviation in the 1970s has been directed at either demonstrating or depreciating the value of a labeling approach to deviance. Chapter 7 examines the basic themes that recur in the theoretical debates. The issues of causal versus noncausal analysis, secondary deviation, and structural versus symbolic interactionist analysis are particularly significant.

Several major new perspectives on social deviation came to prominence through their critiques of labeling. One of these perspectives, the "phenomenological" approach, has much in common with those that emphasize how the judgment of deviance comes about.[10] The phenomenological perspective, as we will see, focuses on the social world as directly experienced by members of society. It is interested in the common-sense understandings that members develop about their social worlds, including such phenomena as social deviance.

Sociologists who take the phenomenological perspective are particularly interested in describing the "routine grounds of everyday activities," such as social deviation, and also the interpretive schemes by which people arrive at determinations of social deviation. Like the interactionist, they focus on the "micro-order" of deviation: the social construction of meanings of deviation and the negotiation processes whereby these meanings are established. This is all very helpful in comprehending how individuals who engage in deviant behavior construct their own social worlds and lines of action. It also helps us to understand how others react to them and their behavior.

Thus, the phenomenological and the interactionist approaches share a basic perspective on methodological approaches to the study of social deviance. In this respect they are quite different from the methodological orientations of the inheritors of the Durkheimian sociological perspective. They also differ on theoretical and methodological grounds from orientations like behavioristic psychology, which also focuses on the learning of behavior.

Another influential perspective in the field of social deviation is the Neo-Marxist, or "New Criminology," perspective (see Chapter 7). Its proponents maintain that an explanation of deviance must begin with the role of the social structure in influencing the social arrangements within which deviant behavior and deviance occur. These sociologists claim that crime and other forms of deviation are due to inequalities of wealth and power, property, and life chances. They propose a model of deviation analysis that begins with politicoeconomic explanations and combines these with a social-psychological approach to social deviation.

Chapter 8 will examine questions of the future of the subjectivist approach to the study of social deviation; specifically what major issues must be investigated, and what theoretical problems must be solved for the advancement of this perspective?

Finally, consideration is given to the policy implications of the perspectives discussed in Chapters 5, 6, and 7.

The study of social deviation offers students an insight into the very substance of societal organization and human interaction. It allows us to see the normative or rule-bound substructure of society in operation. More than giving us a glimpse of society's "other side," it also lets us see to the very core of ourselves. It is a reflection of our society's concern with the appropriate, the just, the moral, the ethical —that is, *with what should be.* For this reason alone, social deviation is a fundamental area of sociological investigation.

Students are sometimes perplexed by the need to study theories, conceptual frameworks, and typologies of social deviation. Why make something so naturally interesting, exotic, and curious into something so very complex by weighing down its analysis with seemingly confusing ideas? The only answer to objections of this sort is that the analysis of these perspectives makes the understanding of social deviation all the more rewarding and intellectually satisfying. They allow us to see how scholars and laymen with varying degrees of insight have penetrated very complex social phenomena. It is the goal of this book to guide students through the issues, debates, and ideas that make the sociology of social deviation the fascinating discipline it is.

¹See Howard S. Becker, *Outsiders*. New York: The Free Press, 1963, pp. 8–9 for a discussion of the definition of social deviance. Also see Edwin M. Schur, *Labeling Deviant Behavior*. New York: Harper & Row, 1971, pp. 23–27.

²See, for example, *Time*, May 19, 1975, p. 38, and *Time*, May 5, 1975, p. 82.

³Some would argue that there are situations of labeled criminality that even those who do the labeling do not really define as "deviant"; for example, the glorification or romanticizing of criminals who commit million-dollar bank robberies or who are very gifted confidence artists. These individuals often become "folk heroes." In such relatively rare cases, the societal reaction is very difficult to evaluate. In any case, for our purposes these will also be considered as examples of social deviance.

⁴See, for example, Wainwright Churchill, *Homosexual Behavior among Males*. New York: Hawthorn Books, 1967, pp. 15–35, 70–88.

⁵Rollin Chambliss, *Social Thought*. New York: Holt, Rinehart and Winston, 1954, p. 24.

⁶Edwin Sutherland and Donald Cressey, *Criminology*, 9th ed. Philadelphia: Lippincott, 1974, Ch. 7.

⁷See, for example, Becker's discussion of this in *Outsiders*, pp. 124–26.

⁸See Michel Foucault, *Madness in Civilization*, trans. by Richard Howard. New York: Pantheon, 1965.

⁹See Chapter 2 in this text for an explanation of "social facts."

¹⁰See, for example, Schur, *Labeling*, pp. 115–36, and Jack Douglas, ed., *Deviance and Respectability*. New York: Basic Books, 1970. Also see Douglas's article "Deviance and Respectability: The Social Construction of Moral Meanings" in same book.

SELECTED READINGS

1963   Howard S. Becker, *Outsiders*. New York: The Free Press, Ch. 1.

1973   Earl Rubington and Martin S. Weinberg, *Deviance: The Interactionist Perspective*. New York: Macmillan, pp. 1-10.

1974   Marshall Clinard, *Sociology of Deviant Behavior*, 4th ed. New York: Holt, Rinehart and Winston, Ch. 1.

CHAPTER 2

SOCIAL PATHOLOGY:
The Durkheimian
Watershed

Occasionally, in the development of our thought about the social world and the problems and issues that we have perceived within it, there appears a major departure from previous understandings and a redirection of intellectual effort. It is certainly true that such advances in knowledge are often judged to be "quantum" leaps forward only many years after their initial pronouncements. Rare indeed are the ideas that are acclaimed intellectual breakthroughs in their own time. As Kuhn has indicated, scientific revolutions or paradigm shifts often take generations to accomplish. There is a gradual realization among groups of scholars that a certain theory or set of explanations is more suitable than those that have come before it.[1]

Emile Durkheim (1858-1917), the French philosopher, academician, and sociologist, was responsible for many intellectual breakthroughs. His contributions to the sociological understanding of religion, economic institutions, education, and the family are impressive. His influence on the development of the "structural–functional" theoretical perspective in sociology has been widely acknowledged. It is Durkheim's analysis of what he termed *social pathology* that interests us here; and, as in other areas to which he directed his attention and analytic skills, his contributions in this field have been highly significant. To understand the nature of this contribution and at the same time to see the extent of his departure from previous points of view, we must trace the development of his argument, as well as its intellectual sources. Durkheim's conception of social pathology can serve as a model with which other perspectives on social deviation, both ancient and modern, can be compared. To a large extent Durkheim's formulation was designed to counter the prevalent common-sense conceptions of the man on the street, of the academicians in the newly founded social-behavioral sciences, and of the bureaucrat-practitioners who had to contend with the social problems and "pathologies" of an industrialized, urban society.

IN SEARCH OF A SOCIOLOGICAL EXPLANATION
FOR SOCIAL DEVIATION

H. Stuart Hughes, the historian of social philosophy and social science, has indicated that the 40 years from 1890 to 1930 were marked by an extraordinary wealth of reflection on the study of society and the individual's role within it.[2] To the "generation of the 1890s" as Hughes has labeled this cluster of remarkable intellects, belong such names as Freud, Weber, Pareto, Croce, Mosca, Michels, and Durkheim—all scholars of international reputation. In addition, when we add names like Spengler, Bergson, Wittgenstein, and Gramsci to the list of those who published significant works during this 40-year period, the group becomes quite formidable indeed.

It is difficult to say why some periods in history produce so many scholars of great imagination and creative ability. For sociology, which, in its relative infancy, seemed to be searching for significant guides and guidelines, the time and conditions were probably optimal. Basic questions had to be asked. What were the best methods for investigating the social world? Were there unique subject matters for disciplines like sociology, political science, psychology, and history, or were they all reducible to some common set of elements or ideas? How different were the social sciences from the natural sciences? What were the relationships of various social philosophies to the empirical social-behavioral sciences? To answer these and many other plaguing questions, many adherents to new schools of thought or disciplines during this period wrote various types of "manifestos." These were treatises that attempted to explain both to disciples and interested outsiders the proper substantive domains, responsibilities, assumptions, logics of inquiry, methods of analysis, moral imperatives, and first principles of the neophyte disciplines.

In sociology, Durkheim's *The Rules of Sociological Method* was one attempt along these lines.[3] He sought to clearly establish sociology as an independent discipline. This work was meant to be a guidebook for sociologists on the rules by which they could determine the characteristics of phenomena deemed worthy of analysis by the new discipline; and on how best to proceed in observing, classifying, and explaining "social facts" and establishing sociological "proofs."

A major goal of Durkheim's manifesto was to establish sociological territorality: to make sociology a unique area of scholarly investigation. This is apparent in the very first chapter, entitled "What Is a Social Fact?" Durkheim answers that a social fact (1) is external to the individual and (2) exercises a constraining power over the individual. Later he added that one social fact can only be explained by another social fact. In this way, Durkheim hoped to clearly differentiate social facts from individual or psychological facts and thus sociology from psychology. If social facts are nonreducible to individual representations of it and are therefore a reality sui generis (a reality unto itself) and if social facts cannot ultimately be explained by psychological or philosophical speculative facts, then the analysis of social facts is truly unique.

Thus, social facts like crime rates are not reducible to individualistic or psychological explanations. They are explicable only by *other* social facts. One of the most significant realizations for the development of a new discipline is that the system of ideas, facts, or phenomena that it has cut off for itself can only be explained from within that system. In sociology, this means that similarities or differences in social behavior are due to elements of *social* influence. We can call this type of intellectually ethnocentric view *sociologism.* Certainly Durkheim, in *The Rules of Sociological Method,* was advocating a very strong sociologistic position.

This theoretical stance had particular ramifications for the analysis of social deviation. In fact, the only substantive field of inquiry that Durkheim discusses in *The Rules* is the distinguishing features of "social pathology" and "social normality." This particular stance toward the study of social deviation is taken again (as we shall see) two years later (1897), with the publication of Durkheim's three-book monograph on *Suicide,* which many have acclaimed as the first modern piece of empirical research in sociology.[4]

THE CHARACTERISTICS OF SOCIAL PATHOLOGY

What especially concerns us as students of social deviation is Chapter 3 of *The Rules,* "Rules for Distinguishing between the Normal and the Pathological." Here Durkheim proposes one of the earliest and most significant characterizations of social deviation, or (as he chose to call it) "social pathology." According to Durkheim, social pathologies share three essential characteristics with other social facts; they are (1) *relative,* (2) *normal,* and (3) *functional* (useful).[5]

To claim that social pathologies like crime are relative, normal, and functional seems to contradict the conventional wisdoms of our own culture, as it did for the conventional understandings of Durkheim's contemporaries. How could murder, suicide, or rape be considered normal and useful forms of human behavior? Are not these acts *always* wrong and thus *universal* and not *relative* phenomena? Are they not basic negations of man's humanity? To be sure, for most inheritors of the Judeo-Christian ethical tradition, these acts are violations of God's ordained commandments, and are assuredly purposeless and to be universally condemned as immoral. But, alas, leave it to the sociologist to question conventional wisdom or to offer alternative ways of looking at the role of social institutions, conventions, and behavior. The sociologist, then as now, *appears* to be profaning beliefs that many hold as sacred or unquestionable. In Durkheim's case, however, all is not what it appears to be.

SOCIAL PATHOLOGY AS A RELATIVE REALITY

Throughout his discussion of the distinguishing characteristics of the normal and pathological, Durkheim made use of the "organic analogy": the likening of society, culture, and social institutions to functioning biological organisms. This allowed Durkheim to view society as composed of a variety of substructures and internal processes, which, while in balance and harmony with each other, serve to maintain the larger organism, society. Indeed, he saw it as sociology's main task to study the functioning of these substructures toward maintaining societal balance, or *"homeostasis."* It is the language of the biological or organismic analogy that Durkheim uses to characterize the *relative* nature of social pathology.

> It is clear that a condition can be defined as pathological only in relation to a given species. The conditions of health and morbidity cannot be defined in the abstract and absolutely. This rule is not denied in biology; it has never occurred to anyone to assume that what is normal for a mollusk is normal also for a vertebrate. Each species has a health of its own because it has an average type of its own. . . . The same principle applies to sociology, although it is often misunderstood here. One should completely abandon the still-too-widespread habit of judging an institution, a practice or a moral standard as if it were good or bad in and by itself, for all social types indiscriminately.[6]

Durkheim, like the more contemporary students of social deviation, was also well aware of the defining role that society played in
determining social deviance:

> Thus, since there cannot be a society for which the individuals
> do not differ more or less from the collective type, it is also
> inevitable that among these divergences, there are some with a
> criminal character. What confers this character upon them is
> not the intrinsic quality of a given act but that definition which
> the collective conscience leads them.[7]

To be more specific, what our society deems pathological or
deviant may be considered normal in another society or in the same
society at a different era. There is indeed no single act of deviation
that has received condemnation in all societies and in all historical
epochs. Murder is only a category for disapproved killings. Exactly
the same behavior under battlefield conditions is considered a service
to one's country. Infanticide is now anathema to the average American or European, but was not always so, and it is still an accepted
practice in some remote areas of the world.

The American sociologist William Graham Sumner very aptly
characterized the source of the variability and relativity of the normal
and pathological. In his discussion of the evolution of the normative
social order from folkways to mores to laws, he indicated: "Mores can
make anything right and prevent condemnation of anything."[8] Since
a culture's mores are said to reflect the needs of the members of that
culture, and since these vary in many different ways, it is not surprising that the definitions of the normal and the pathological are equally
variable and relative.

When we combine this characteristic of the normal and pathological with Durkheim's sociologistic premise that a social fact (such as
social pathology) can only be explained by another social fact, we have
a major departure from classical, as well as many contemporary, understandings of social deviation.

Before Durkheim, the essence of social deviation was posited as
existing in either the *actor* or in the *act* of deviation itself. Explanations
of deviant behavior usually characterized the act as inherently deviant
and the actor as deviant because of some inherent feature of his
physiological, biological, chemical, and moral (or psychological)
makeup. As the next few chapters will attest, these theories held sway
for hundreds of years and gave very little attention to societal influences. To this day many common-sense understandings of social deviation fail to consider the role of social factors in such behavior. To
most persons, homosexuality, mental illness, drug use, murder, and

suicide are psychologically rooted and explicable problems. Some are willing to entertain biological or physiological explanations for such behaviors. If they are permitted, social factors are usually given a secondary or tertiary role in the production of these social pathologies.

Durkheim was certainly one of the first students of social deviation to point away from the act and the actor themselves as sources of explanation for this type of behavior. For Durkheim, the conditions of the sociocultural order were responsible for social facts like crime and suicide. To focus on the psychological basis of crime merely ignored the fact that the *collective representations* of crime were not reducible to individualistic variables. For Durkheim, the collective representations were to be found in the statistical *rates* of a phenomena in a given population. This is a very important point. Durkheim never really concerns himself with individual cases of social pathology. He firmly believed that sociology's task is to explain social facts, independent of their individual manifestations.[9] For this reason, Durkheim insisted that the sociologist analyze the "average types" that all social facts are said to have. He seems to have meant that all social facts had average collective representations or average rates. It was precisely these average rates of social pathology that could not be explained by biological, psychological, or physiological factors. They were realities unto themselves, in need of their own unique explanations.

The relatively of social pathology also implied that the search for knowledge about its social character could not be focused on the act's inherent characteristics. To view killing as inherently pathological failed to understand the variable meaning that objectively similar acts of killing had in different cultures or in the same culture under different conditions. The characterization of deviant behavior as a relative phenomenon had one fundamental implication for sociological analysis: it made the sociologist look to the functional requirements of the normative order for explanations of crime, suicide, and other deviant behaviors. The collective representations of social pathology needed to be linked with the collective *needs* of the members of society, which were ostensibly reflected in the normative order. Again, both Durkheim's theoretical stance toward the explanation of social facts and his characterization of social facts as relative phenomena made him look beyond the act and the actor for his explanation of social pathology.

Durkheim's concern with the study of "average types" and the collective representations of human behavior led to a second characterization of social pathology—one that has drawn much more criticism and spirited debate than his contention that social pathology was a relative phenomenon.

SOCIAL PATHOLOGY AS A NORMAL REALITY

At first glance, to call social pathology "normal" appears to be a contradiction in terms. A thoughtful reader of *The Rules* might ask, why be concerned with rules for distinguishing between the normal and the pathological if, in the end, the pathological is said to be normal? Characterizing the pathological as normal appears less contradictory (though still controversial) if we understand that, for Durkheim, the pathological was normal under *certain* conditions.

What makes social pathologies like crime and suicide normal? For Durkheim, the universal existence and distribution of social pathology were principal reasons for its "normal" status:

> In the first place crime is normal because a society exempt from it is utterly impossible. . . .
>
> No doubt it is possible that crime itself will have abnormal forms, as for example, when its rate is unusually high. This excess is, indeed, undoubtedly morbid in nature. What is normal, simply, is the existence of criminality provided that it attains and does not exceed, for each social type, a certain level. . . .
>
> Crime is present not only in the majority of societies of one particular species but in all societies of all types. There is no society that is not confronted with the problem of criminality. Its form changes, the acts thus characterized are not the same everywhere, but, everywhere and always, there have been men who have behaved in such a way as to draw upon themselves penal repression. . . .
>
> Crime, for its part, must no longer be conceived as an evil that cannot be too much suppressed. There is no occasion for self-congratulation when the crime rate drops noticeably below the average level, for we may be certain that this apparent progress is associated with some social disorder.
>
> In order that sociology may be a true science of things the generality of phenomena must be taken as the criterion of their normality.[10]

This view of crime as a normal reality can best be called a *statistical model* or *explanation*. Its premise is that deviant behaviors, such as murder, rape, and suicide, have an average statistical distribution within a given society or community. Every society has its own average, and therefore its pathology relative to others is very difficult to assess. What is truly pathological is a decrease or increase in the rate of a particular deviant behavior relative to its average, from one specified time period to the next. The mere existence of social deviation is not pathological, for it need not hamper the overall functioning of the social unit.

According to Durkheim, the existence of social deviation is not accidental but is tied to the fundamental character of society. Only a drastic change in the average rate of a particular social deviation can be an indication of societal disorganization. However, Durkheim never specifies how much of a deviation from the average rate is necessary for societal disorganization to be indicated. Also he never clearly indicates how these deviations affect the institutional order of the society such that social disorganization is said to exist. Nevertheless, deviations from the average statistical rates of social facts are seen as pathological, and societal disorganization is synonymous with these statistical deviations.

Durkheim's claim that we should not congratulate ourselves when the crime rate falls strikes contemporary members of crime-plagued societies like our own as outrageous, if not downright foolish. Any contemporary sociologist who publicly took such a position might have his mental health seriously questioned. Should not the goal of criminology be to find the means by which crime rates could constantly be decreased? Durkheim might have agreed that we ought to find ways of decreasing rates that were deviations from the "healthy" or normal average for our society. However, is it not a logical derivation of Durkheim's position that we should also to try to *increase* the rate when it drops precipitously? One problem with this, of course, is to find the average or normal rate of a crime like murder. Durkheim certainly is not helpful in this regard.

Finding our society's normal rate of murder is highly problematic. Why should these averages represent the "healthy" state of the social organism? Ethical philosophers and theologians would indicate that this position is too accepting of our inhumanity to our fellows and therefore dangerously nihilistic. It seems to say that a certain number of murders ought to be expected. Durkheim seems to be saying that (as outrageous as it might seem to some) the average in society is our best indication of the natural characteristics of that society.

In addition, Durkheim claimed that any tampering with that natural order would ultimately be destructive to a precarious societal balance. This position has been referred to as a basically laissez-faire attitude toward social problems. Durkheim, however, is not the only classical sociologist who has been "accused" of this kind of stance. There is a strongly conservative ideological base to Durkheim's sociological model, as there was for early sociologists like the Englishman Herbert Spencer and the American William Graham Sumner.[11]

The sociological model that Durkheim helped develop—one of the most basic in sociology—is called the *structural–functional perspec-*

tive. Essentially it sees society as being composed of numerous substructures which have their corresponding functions. The principle function that each substructure shares with others is the maintenance of the larger social order. Under normal conditions, that social order exists in a state of balance. All of these substructures, taking care of the various primary functions or needs of the society, will allow the society to maintain itself. This model and its attached assumptions are largely responsible for Durkheim's characterizations about social deviation.

If a certain social institution, practice, or behavior has been in existence for a long time and has not put the social system out of balance or caused societal disorganization, then it must be a normal feature of the society. If every society that we know of has some type of social deviation, and if deviations (at least in some proportions) have always existed, then social deviation is normal. This particular assumption of the model, however, leads to another, perhaps even more controversial assumption. Durkheim insisted that everything that was normal in society must also be functional or useful. Translated back to the illustration that we have been using and that Durkheim himself used, this means that social deviations like crime or suicide can be functional or useful to the maintenance of the social order! This characterization needs more careful analysis.

SOCIAL PATHOLOGY AS A FUNCTIONAL REALITY

In *The Rules,* Durkheim makes the following observations:

> Crime is, then, necessary; it is bound up with the fundamental conditions of all social life, and by that very fact it is useful, because these conditions of which it is a part are themselves indispensable to the normal evolution of morality and law. . . .
>
> Aside from this indirect utility, it happens that crime itself plays a useful role in this evolution. Crime implies not only that the way remains open to necessary changes but that in certain cases it directly prepares these changes. Where crime exists, collective sentiments are sufficiently flexible to take on a new form, and crime sometimes helps to determine the form they will take. . . .
>
> From this point of view the fundamental facts of criminality present themselves to us in an entirely new light. Contrary to current ideas, the criminal no longer seems a totally unsociable being, a sort of parasitic element, a strange and unassuma-

> ble body, introduced into the midst of society. On the contrary, he plays a definite role in social life.[12]

The position that Durkheim takes with regard to the functionality of social deviation has, for many, been more difficult to accept than his other characterizations. To those who view social deviation in the purely moral terms of disapproval, the belief that crime or suicide could in any way be useful to maintaining societal balance seems to go well beyond the pale of reason. Durkheim's functionalist view that the normal should have some purposeful role in the gradual evolution of the social collective, as well as in its system maintenance, might seem to lead to questionable characterizations when applied to evils like murder, rape, and suicide.

Durkheim claimed that social deviations like crime had a *boundary-maintaining* function. They, along with the societal reactions to them, helped reinforce the boundaries of acceptable and nonacceptable social behavior. They are indications to the populace that the violation of certain norms will bring down the wrath of the collective sentiments, while the violations of others will bring about less severe reactions or none at all. A society's penal law, according to Durkheim, can acquire a sway over the public conscience of a community only if violations of them are made more vivid. He says:

> For murderers to disappear, the horror of bloodshed must become greater in those social strata from which murderers are recruited; but, first it must become greater throughout the entire society. Moreover, the very absence of crime would directly contribute to produce this horror; because any sentiment seems much more respectable when it is always and uniformly respected.[13]

For this reason in small, nonliterate societies, hangings, floggings, and other public punishments were very effective ways of reinforcing the collective sentiments of the community. In a way, the headlines and news stories of our own communication media serve a similar function. The reports of serious crimes, political corruption, and social upheavals around the world serve to indicate the normative standards that the community ought to maintain.

If we agree with Durkheim's premise that all societies have social deviation as normal features, and accept his structural–functional assumption that the average or normal must be useful, we can see how he came to the idea of boundary maintenance. Such boundary-maintaining devices are not, however, very effective in complex urban societies that experience almost annual rises in the crime rate. The argument that social forms like criminal activity only adequately perform such boundary-maintaining functions when they are in a normal statistical state only serves to make the Durkheimian position rather tenuous at best. It is a self-defeating argument.

Like his claim that crime is a normal phenomenon, Durkheim's depiction of crime as useful *seems* overly tolerant of such behavior. On this point, however, Durkheim is quite clear in his other writings:

> *Whatever is an indispensible condition of life cannot fail to be useful, unless life itself is not useful.* The proposition is inescapable and we have actually shown how crime may be of service. But it serves only when reproved and repressed. The mere fact of cataloging it among the phenomena of normal sociology has been wrongly thought to imply its absolution. If it is normal that there should be crimes, it is normal that they should be punished. Punishment and crime are two terms of an inseparable pair. One is indispensable as the other. Every abnormal relaxation of the system of repression results in stimulating criminality and giving it an abnormal intensity.[14]

Beyond the fact that social deviations like crime and reactions to crime are boundary-maintaining factors, Durkheim also believed that they are occasionally responsible for significant social change, including change in the moral order. As an example, he used Socrates' death to show that what was once considered a crime (the independence of Socrates' thought) can be viewed as a great leap forward in man's quest for intellectual freedom.[15] Similar arguments have been made for various types of political crimes, especially when moral–legal doctrines have been directly challenged and shown to rest on less firm moral or practical foundations than was generally presumed. A good deal of civil-rights and human-rights legislation, as well as public sentiment, has been influenced by the behavior of those whose actions were originally judged to be in violation of the law or accepted moral convention. Today's crime or disapproved behavior may be tomorrow's tolerated if not well-accepted conventional behavior, and might lead to the acceptance of other behaviors that society currently condemns.

Aside from boundary maintenance and the prompting of social change, Durkheim does not attribute any other primary functions to social deviations like crime. We could argue that even these two functions are frought with so many exceptions that his claim appears contrived to meet the demands of the theoretical assumptions with which he began. The theoretical position that widely distributed social behavior could not have survived the struggle for existence unless it played a useful role in maintaining the social order makes one search for utility where, perhaps, not much can be found. In any case, this characterization, along with the other two, was a major departure from previous understandings of social deviation. Durkheim, through his analysis of the normal and pathological, was able to question the conventional wisdoms of lay and professional analysts concerning what were thought to be well-understood, unusual, and intolerable societal problems.

SUICIDE AS A CASE IN POINT

Two years after the publication of *The Rules of Sociological Method,* Durkheim published his empirical study entitled *Suicide* (1897). This highly acclaimed and controversial book can be seen as a continuation of Durkheim's effort to outline the unique territoriality of sociological investigation. Here, too, he stressed sociology's independence from other disciplines, as well as its ability to offer social-structural explanations for behavior that had earlier been explained in decidedly psychological, economic, moralistic, and biological terms. *Suicide* is also a direct continuation of Durkheim's fascination with the relationship between normality and social pathology.

From a theoretical viewpoint, suicide is a particularly interesting form of social deviation.[16] Since it is as individualistic a form of behavior as one could find, Durkheim saw its explanation by social rather than psychological facts as a crucial demonstration of the power of sociological theory and methodology. Likewise, Durkheim was interested in demonstrating the power of sociological explanations for a type of social deviation that had always been viewed as a moral problem not easily reducible to a positivistic or statistically based empirical investigation to determine its causes. The philosophical debates over suicide had centered on issues such as the rights of individuals versus the authority of society to limit behavior it deemed objectionable, and individual responsibility and determinism versus free will. Durkheim was interested in revealing suicide as a collective representation of social-structural conditions that could be explained without reference to moral-philosophical debates, theories of psychopathy, or other psychological processes.

After studying the relationship between the rates of insanity and the rates for suicide in a number of European countries, as well as the relationship of alcoholism to suicide rates, Durkheim concludes:

> Thus no psychopathic state bears a regular and indisputable relation to suicide. Society does not depend for its number of suicides on having more or fewer neuropaths or alcoholics.[17]

In a like manner, Durkheim "disproves" causal theories based on "normal psychological states" (very questionable racial and hereditary characteristics linked with personality characteristics), "cosmic factors" (climatic conditions, seasonal variations, temperature, time of day), and the psychological process of imitation, which Gabriel Tarde had considered the main source of all collective or social life. In each case, Durkheim's analysis is marked by a comparison of official statistics having a bearing on these variables.

Forms of Suicide

In Book II, Durkheim outlines the social causes of suicide. He immediately points out that since there are a number of different causes of suicide, there are also a number of different types. However, each is related to a very significant structural variable: the degree of social integration—the extent to which members of society are attached to the normative order of the society and develop ties to that society as a result. He designates three major forms of suicide:

1. *Egoistic suicide* results from a lack of involvement in social or collective activities that impart meaning and purposefulness to life. "The more weakened the groups to which he belongs, [and] the less he depends on them, the more he consequently depends only on himself and recognizes no other rules of conduct than what are founded on his private interests. . . . We may call egoistic the special type of suicide springing from excessive individualism. . . . When, therefore, we have no other object than ourselves, we cannot avoid the thought that our efforts will finally end in nothingness, since we ourselves disappear." In contrast, Durkheim indicated, "When society is strongly integrated, it holds individuals under its control, considers them at its service and thus forbids them to dispose willfully of themselves."[18]

2. *Altruistic suicide* results from too strict a subordination of the individual to the group. In some cases the suicide is the fulfillment of the person's obligation toward the collective, or is an option held in some esteem by the group. According to Durkheim, several religions have supported this type of suicide—among them, Hinduism, Buddism, and Jainism. These religious beliefs held in common that "what reality there is in the individual is foreign to his nature, that the soul which animates him is not his own and that consequently he has no personal

existence." The person in these societies sees his own essence in the group. Durkheim says: "We actually see the individual in all these cases [of suicide] seek to strip himself of his personal being in order to be engulfed in something which he regards as his true essence." To those of us who have grown up with films about World War II, the image of the Japanese Kamikaze pilot nose-diving into the enemy ship out of a sense of duty to country and emperor is perhaps the best contemporary example of altruistic suicide.[19]

3. *Anomic suicide* results when the society is incapable of exercising constraint over the individual, especially in times of crisis or disaster. When this control is lost, the standards used to judge one's own behavior, and others, become unclear or lose meaning. When social institutions become disorganized, the individuals affected by them no longer know what is possible or impossible, acceptable or unacceptable, just or unjust. Under these circumstances, aspirations go well beyond readily attainable goals. Durkheim believed that both domestic disorganization (such as divorce) and economic disorganization are significant causes of anomic suicide. Marriage and the economic institution are responsible for setting the limits or standards for acceptable goals. Durkheim tried to show that when these institutions lose the power to define such limits and standards, suicide becomes a possibility.[20]

It is important to note that for each of these types of suicide, Durkheim is primarily concerned with explaining variations in the "collective representations"—rates—of that suicide. These rates are the social facts that need to be explained by other social facts. As the descriptions of the three types of suicide given above will indicate, Durkheim was convinced that the extent of the individual's integration into society is the most important social variable for explaining fluctuations in suicide rates. He states:

> The conclusion from all these facts is that the social suicide rate can be explained only sociologically. At any given moment the moral constitution of society establishes the contingent of voluntary deaths. There is, therefore, for each people a collective force of a definite amount of energy impelling men to self-destruction. The victim's acts which at first seem to express only his personal temperament are really the supplement and proclamation of a social condition which they express externally. . . . Each social group has a collective inclination for the

> act, quite its own, and the *source* of all individual inclination, rather than their result. It is made up of the currents of egoism, altruism or anomy running through the society under consideration with the tendencies to languorous melancholy, active renunciation or exasperated weariness derivative from these currents. These tendencies of the whole social body, by affecting individuals, cause them to commit suicide.[21]

This passage also indicates Durkheim's belief that, like other social facts, suicide was a relative phenomena—each society has its own "collective forces" impelling men toward suicide. As he indicates, these collective forces are the trends toward egoism, altruism, or anomy that are present within the society. He was also convinced that suicide, in its usual statistical state, was not morbid or pathological but normal. An important question was whether the statistical rates of suicide in his own French society, as well as in other contemporary societies, were normal. After a lengthy analysis, he concludes that modern societies are witnessing a pathological increase in suicide rates. The very fact that suicide has always been a feature of industrial societies is enough for someone of Durkheim's theoretical bent to label it normal:

> At any rate, it is certain that suicidogenetic currents of different intensity, depending on the historical period, have always existed among the peoples of Europe; statistics prove ever since the last century, and juridical monuments prove it for earlier periods. Suicide is therefore an element of their normal constitution, and even, probably, of any social constitution.[22]

In a like manner, Durkheim also points to the functionality of suicide, but here he hedges somewhat. He claims that the forces that lead to suicide (egoism, altruism, anomy) are useful: "But not only are these excesses in one or the other direction necessary; they have their uses."[23] He seems, however, to stop short of clearly stating that suicides that are brought about by these forces are likewise necessary or useful. In fact, to this author at least, it appears that Durkheim cannot bring himself to this logical conclusion of his theoretical assumptions. Perhaps he had not much more utility to point to than the somewhat vague claims that social pathologies like suicide maintain the boundaries of the acceptable and nonacceptable or that they are potential agents for social change.

DURKHEIM'S INFLUENCE ON OTHER SCHOLARS

The theoretical understanding of social deviation took a decisive leap forward with Durkheim's formulations. For the first time, there was a strong call for an analysis of social deviation based on a radical sociologistic perspective: from the analysis of social forces to the explanation of social pathology in their collective representations—this was the directive that Durkheim gave to contemporary sociological analysts and the legacy he left for future generations of sociologists. For European and American scholars, he was very influential in establishing the theoretical frame of analysis for the study of social problems, social deviance, and criminology. The 1930s and 1940s saw the development of various functionalist orientations that have direct roots in Durkheim's writings. These perspectives will be analyzed in Chapter 4. Suffice it to say here that the major theories of juvenile delinquency, the emergence of delinquent subcultures, adult criminality, prostitutions, drug use, and other social deviations published in the decades of the 1930s and 1940s were heavily influenced by Durkheim's theoretical assumptions and his methods of inquiry.

Sociologists of the 1920s and 1930s who wished to build on Durkheim's ideas had an uphill fight on their hands. For soon after Durkheim died, the psychological explanations for social deviation were given added impetus by the flowering of the theories and practices of psychoanalysis and psychiatry. In some cases, sociologists attempted to integrate the understandings gained through the Durkheimian perspective with those of the newly developed psychoanalytic frameworks. Many others shunned such attempts and remained purist disciples of the Durkheimian legacy, adhering to the credo that "society is reality sui generis."

Durkheim's insistence that the reality of social deviation was to be found outside of the actor and the act of deviance was also a significant break with other causal theories that had dominated intellectual thought for centuries and that were developing their own twentieth-century versions. Chief among these were the biophysiological theories of social deviation, which had been developing for several centuries and had made a strong appearance on the intellectual scene (albeit in a new guise) only a few years before Durkheim's initial analysis of social pathology. Durkheim was as well aware of these biophysiological theories as he was of the psychological, and was equally disdainful of their relative merits. The disciples of Durkheim, along with other contemporary sociologists, are to this day wary of such explanations. They have united in their rejection of the more recent hormonal-imbalance or chromosome-anomaly theories of homosexuality and criminal behavior, respectively. These theories will be analyzed in the next chapter.

Durkheim's characterization of social pathology as a relative, normal, and functional reality was significant in shaping the way in which sociologists would, for generations, view social deviation. Social deviation was considered a representation of the natural conditions of social life, brought about by sociocultural "forces" that were themselves manifestations of the social system's attempt to keep itself in a state of balance. The rather simple definition of social pathology as a statistical departure from the average tendency in society made it quite practical for social scientists, as Durkheim had demonstrated in *Suicide,* to apply the methods of a positivistic sociology to the study of these social facts.[23] Sociology could ostensibly be a science like any other, for it had a subject matter that was (potentially, at least) mathematically measurable. As we will see in the chapters to come, the attempt to make sociology and, in particular, the sociology of social deviation into a positivist science has long been controversial.

Durkheim's admonition for sociologists to concern themselves with the rates of social deviation was not new (the early social statisticians Quetelet, Guerry, and von Oettingen, as well as positivists like Comte, had suggested the same).[24] But linked with Durkheim's basic theoretical model, this emphasis became a persuasive example of what sociologists could do with such data as official government statistics on crime or suicide and of why data sources like these were even advantageous. The problems of the interpretation and use of such data have become very serious issues for contemporary social scientists and have led many in search of very different types of data and methods of acquiring data.[25] However, the disciples of the Durkheimian perspective on and methodological approach to social deviation did not question the use of such statistics. The statistical rates of deviation, whether gathered by official agencies or by the sociological investigators themselves, became the empirical indicators of deviation. As Durkheim and other positivists had recommended, the analysis of the collective statistical representation of social facts became the basic task of sociological investigation. Not until the decades of the 1950s and 1960s did a serious challenge to these views develop within sociology; and at the forefront of this challenge were analysts in the study of deviation.

This chapter has focused primarily on the important departure that Durkheim's conception of social deviation took from previous understandings. It is also important, however, to point to the significant similarities between his and the other perspectives. Most significantly, Durkheim's perspective was ultimately meant to be a causal theory of deviation, as had most other important perspectives. Durkheim, as others before him, was primarily concerned with the predisposing social factors (forces and societal conditions like egoism, altruism, anomy, societal integration) that caused such pathologies as suicide and crime. Such theories are called *causal theories of predisposition.* Durkheim's theory differed from earlier ones, for it holds that the predisposing causal factor exists in the social and culture structures, and thus outside the deviant and the deviant act. Again, others had posited that the predisposing causal factor exists in the deviant's personality, in his biophysiological make-up, in his capacity for intelligence, as well as in many other individualistic sources.

As Chapter 1 has already indicated, causal theories of predisposition failed to deal with a number of significant behavioral factors; chief among these are two—the actualization of deviant behavior (the process by which deviant behavior is learned) and the actualization of deviance (the process through which the deviant is evaluated and labeled by society). Durkheim's structural–functional perspective was not concerned with such issues.

Although Durkheim strove to make sociology a unique and independent discipline, the positivistic model of science that he chose for it united it with other behavioral sciences, including psychology, that opted for the same model. Durkheim, as well as the psychologists, social psychologists, and social physiologists whom he criticized, were heirs to the Enlightenment and its leaning toward social positivism. The social philosophers of the Enlightenment (e.g., Montesquieu, Rousseau, Condorcet) were largely responsible for the belief that just as the Newtonian scientific method had been successful in its endeavor to study the natural-physical world and the search for its laws, so could scholars apply the methods of Newtonian natural science to the social world and search for the laws of social reality. This positivism united those behavioral sciences that wished to study social deviance, for it led to their concern with a causal analysis based on the mathematical measurement of the variables each considered significant. This emphasis led them away from the careful descriptive analyses that were needed to understand how individuals learn to become deviants and how they are treated by fellow members of society.

---

[1]Thomas S. Kuhn, *The Structure of Scientific Revolutions*. Chicago: University of Chicago Press, 1962, Ch. 12. "Paradigm shifts" refers to major changes in theoretical or conceptual frameworks that explain the subject matter of a discipline.

[2]H. Stuart Hughes, *Consciousness and Society: The Reorientation of European Social Thought 1890–1930*. New York: Knopf, 1958.

[3]Emile Durkheim, *The Rules of Sociological Method* (1895), trans. by Sarah A. Solovay and John H. Mueller; ed. by George E. G. Catlin. New York: The Free Press.

[4]George Simpson, *Emile Durkheim*. New York: Crowell, 1963, p. 4.

[5]Durkheim, *The Rules*, Ch. 3.

[6]Ibid., p. 56.

[7]Ibid., p. 70.

[8]William Graham Sumner, *Folkways*. Boston: Ginn and Company. This quotation is the title (Ch. 15, p. 521) of one of the most important chapters in this classic.

[9]Durkheim, *The Rules,* p. 45.

[10]Ibid., pp. 67, 66, 65, 72, 72.

[11]See, for example, Sumner's essay "The Absurd Effort to Make the World Over," in William Graham Sumner, *Social Darwinism: Selected Essays.* Englewood Cliffs, N.J.: Prentice-Hall, 1963, pp. 168–80.

[12]Durkheim, *The Rules.* pp. 70, 71, 72.

[13]Ibid., pp. 67–68.

[14]Emile Durkheim, *Suicide* (1897), trans. by John A. Spaulding and George Simpson; ed. by George Simpson. Glencoe, Ill.: The Free Press, 1951, pp. 362–63. Emphasis in original.

[15]Durkheim, *The Rules,* p. 71.

[16]See, for example, Jack D. Douglas, *The Social Meanings of Suicide.* Princeton, N.J.: Princeton University Press, 1967, Chs. 1 and 2, for a critical discussion of the theoretical significance of Durkheim's *Suicide.*

[17]Durkheim, *Suicide,* p. 81.

[18]Ibid., pp. 209, 210, 209.

[19] Ibid., pp. 226, 225.

[20]Ibid., Ch. 5, pp. 241–76. In a footnote to chapter 5 of book two of *Suicide,* Durkheim indicates that there is a fourth type of suicide—*fatalistic.* According to Durkheim, it is derived from "excessive regulation" imposed on individuals. He felt that it had little contemporary importance.

[21]Ibid., pp. 299–300. My emphasis.

[22]Ibid., p. 363.

[23]"Positivistic Sociology" had been made especially popular by Auguste Comte in several books.

[24]See for example, Adolphe Jacques Quetelet, *Treatise on Man.* Edinburgh: William and Robert Chambers, 1842, Ch. 3.

[25]See John I. Kitsuse and Aaron V. Cicourel "A Note on The Uses of Official Statistics," *Social Problems,* 12 (1963), pp. 131–39.

SELECTED READINGS

1895,
1964   Emile Durkheim, *The Rules of Sociological Method,* trans. by Sarah A. Solovay and John H. Mueller; ed. by George E. G. Catlin. New York: The Free Press. See especially Ch. 3, "Rules for Distinguishing between the Normal and the Pathological."

1897,
1951   Emile Durkheim, *Suicide,* trans. by John A. Spaulding and George Simpson; ed. by George Simpson, Glencoe, Ill.: Free Press.

1967   Jack D. Douglas, *The Social Meanings of Suicide,* Princeton, N.J.: Princeton University Press, Chs. 1 and 2.

CHAPTER 3

CAUSAL THEORIES OF PREDISPOSITION: Presociological Explanations

The most commonly asked question about social deviation is, what *causes* it? Scholars and laymen alike have always been concerned with the conditions or factors that can lead an individual to violate the rules of the group. Common sense seems to tell us that behaviors like drug use, prostitution, homosexuality, and suicide do not happen by themselves. Something or someone must be *responsible* for the deviant behavior in question. Imputing responsibility is not merely a consequence of viewing deviation in moral–ethical terms, but is more basically a result of a common-sense, cause-and-effect logic, which is also preliminary to the establishment of a science.

Causality, however, is a very troublesome concept. It is problematic mainly because it is very difficult to be certain we have discovered the cause of anything. Part of the problem seems to be anchored in what can be termed the "ultimate–proximate" schism and in what logicians call "the problem of infinite regress." When we say that poverty causes crime, do we mean that poverty is the ultimate, or major, cause of crime, that it is one of many factors that together cause crime; or, perhaps, that it is the closest, or most proximate, cause of crime?

There is great danger in calling anything an ultimate cause. "Ultimate causality" verges on a sort of mystical view of the world, whereby all is brought about by some supreme being or process. In any case, such a view falls prey to the problem of infinite regress. Poverty could not be the ultimate cause of crime, for we could point to factors that bring about poverty. Also, since many persons growing up in poverty do not become criminals, poverty is obviously not a sufficient cause of criminality. Most scientists are inclined to refer to "precipitating factors," or proximate causality, when making statements like "X causes Y" or "poverty causes stealing." They are suggesting that X is sufficiently related to Y so that when Y occurs, so does X, and X precedes the occurrence of Y. In social science it is often difficult to validate explanations of certain phenomena without recourse to causal statements.

Although we live in a "multicausal" or "multivariate" universe, in which no one factor acting alone produces another, our explanations for the occurrence of phenomena like social deviation have rarely been multivariate. Scholars have usually been content with singling out one factor or variable as most significantly related to the occurrence of a particular social deviation. By doing so, they have disregarded the observation that it is some incompletely specifiable *set* of factors that together bring about phenomena like crime. Scholars have usually maintained tunnel vision in explaining the cause of social deviation.

It is important to note the nature of the relationship between the causal factor and deviant behavior. In the theories and perspectives that will be analyzed in this chapter, the relationship is one of "predisposition." Some factor is said to predispose an individual either to commit a deviant act or to be a deviant. What is the nature of a relationship of predisposition?

A charge that has frequently been brought against theories of predisposition is that they deny the volition of the individual actor and thus seem to take responsibility for his actions away from him. Whatever factor is said to predispose one toward involvement in deviation, it seems to exist beyond the control of the individual. Its very presence somehow places limitations on the possible behavior of the individual or on what he can be or do. Just how these limitations are produced the theory does not specify. That alternative outcomes may be equally likely or probable is, in most cases, not seriously considered. A causal theory of predisposition usually stops short of explaining how a certain deviation actually comes about. It fails to explain, *given the presence of the predisposing factor,* the process by which the individual is constrained to act in the way he does.

The early versions of this perspective posited that the predisposing factor existed inside the deviant. Such explanations seemed to make the search for factors of motivation toward deviation rather unimportant. *Why* a person became a deviant was more a function of the predisposing factor than of conscious or unconscious motivation to engage in that behavior. The factor that was singled out established the conditions out of which emerged a "tendency" toward the behavior. Again, why this tendency influenced only some persons to engage in the behavior, and what produced a strong or weak tendency or predisposition toward actual involvement, were not always specified by proponents of these unicausal theories.

Although the analysis of predisposing factors is inextricably tied to causal investigation as practiced in the social sciences, it has not been without many problems. But we should realize that *these are considered problems primarily by other social scientists.* As common-sense explanations of deviant behavior, they usually have roots in the culture's folk wisdoms. Unicausal explanations for deviation predate any *systematic* attempt to explain deviation. We have usually seen the social world with tunnel vision, even though we have had suspicions that things were more complex than our speculations indicated. As we will see in Chapter 4, the explanatory logic of the sociology of the first half of this century has not significantly changed from that which existed in presociological explanations. The realization that other explanations are necessary to round out our understanding of the role of social deviation is a relatively recent one.

We turn now to the earliest varieties of causal theories of predisposition: those espoused by persons more concerned with controlling or eradicating deviant behavior than merely studying it. Their theories were most often rationales to justify their or others' actions against individuals whom they considered deviant.

DEMONOLOGICAL EXPLANATIONS

As we have seen in Chapter 2, Durkheim's formulation of the nature of social pathology was a significant departure from explanations that had posited the essence of deviation as residing in the *act* or in the *actor.* In answering questions of how an individual could come to engage in deviant behavior, reference was usually made to characteristics of the individual's constitution and to the inherently immoral characteristics of the act itself.

Before we look at the various factors within the individual that, through the ages, have been thought to predispose him toward deviation, we should examine the broader value base upon which many of these ideas rest. "Good" and "bad," as the early sociologist Sumner pointed out so well, are standards that reside in the folkways and mores of a people.[1] These folkways and mores, in turn, evolve from the fundamental needs and interests of a society. Organized religion, according to Sumner, develops out of the mores of one age and helps to develop those of another.[2]

In Western societies, the Church and Christian doctrine were responsibile for molding or shaping the a priori value base from which all deviations were measured. The Christian Church of the dark and middle ages took upon itself the task of establishing the criteria of what *ought* to be. It could do so because it had the social power and control necessary to sway both the masses and the secular elite. Its ability to crush dissent and silence critics of its doctrine and policies can only be paralleled in modern times by very powerful governmental regimes.

> The aim of the Church was to insure adherence to the Divine Law, keeping God in a "happy" and thus "loving" frame of mind toward his fallen creation, man. Hence, in the theological societies of the Age of Faith (middle ages), the Church was the dominant institution; the pope was God's representative on earth; kings ruled by divine right, cathedrals and religious icons and festivities were the leading social symbols; Latin was the official language; and sin, redemption, and salvation, Hell and Heaven, were the images and rhetoric that filled the popular imagination. To be truly human meant to worship God (Jesus), to be virtuous meant to be an undeviatingly faithful Christian (saint) and to be evil meant to be a heretic (witch).[3]

Behavior that the Church deemed aberrant or deviant was judged to be wicked, evil, and sinful. Goodness was equated with faithfulness and obedience to Church doctrine and practice. It is interesting to note that definitions of heresy were usually broad enough to include anyone who incurred the displeasure of Church officials for whatever violation of conventional behavior. Sumner quotes a twelfth-century definition of a heretic as any one who "in any way differed, in mode of life, from the faithful in general."[4] This catch-all definition of the heretic was understandably able to discover enormous numbers of transgressors of the law as ordained by God and interpreted by the Church. As Sumner points out:

> There could be no definition of a heretic but one who differed in life and conversation from the masses around him. This might mean strange language, dress, manners, or greater restraint in conduct. Pallor of countenance was a mark of a heretic from the fourth century to the twelfth."[5]

Those engaged in activity deemed evil by Church functionaries and the civilian powers they influenced were said to be morally and spiritually depraved. Moral depravity, however, meant the condition that the accused were said to manifest, not actually the explanation of the cause of their transgressions. The belief in moral depravity was not by itself sufficient to assess the *source* from which such behavior originated.

Theologians, in their attempt to discover the source of these transgressions, soon fixed their sites on demons—the culprits who, from time immemorial, had been blamed for bringing about sin and evil. No less a theologian than St. Thomas Aquinas recognized that much evil and corruption was due to Satan and his army of demons.[6]

The belief in the devil and demons certainly predates the Judaic and Christian eras. Scholars have traced the origin of organized belief in demons to the peoples of Mesopotamia and Persia.[7] Religions like Zoroastrianism were able to create complex hierarchies of demons, who influenced every area of men's lives. Out of the primitive dualism of the powers of good and bad, Zoroastrianism developed separate demons for arrogance, falsehoods, spoken lies, lust, meddlesomeness, and literally scores of similar and more severe evils. Beliefs such as these exerted great influence on Judaism and Christianity.[8]

The Old Testament shows the imprint of this Eastern dualism, in which the devil is presented as the causal agent of evil. The New Testament elaborates on the powers of Satan, and the Book of Revelation depicts the fate of the other fallen angels. Later theologians like St. Augustine systematized the understanding of the hierarchy of evil spirits that plagued men's lives. With such scholastic philosophers and theologians as Aquinas in the thirteenth century, the belief in demons became an integral part of Church doctrine.

> The demons were evil angels who had the ability to unite themselves to bodies and to communicate their knowledge and their commands to men. They were a hierarchically organized army in the service of Satan working for the perdition of the faithful. Satan and his hosts could tempt human beings into their service. . . .[9]

These beliefs culminated, in the fifteenth through the seventeenth centuries, in the Church's preoccupation with witches and witchcraft. Although we cannot go into any detail on the severe reactions against supposed witches, it is important to see the impact of these ideas on understandings of other forms of social deviation.

Many varieties of unconventional behavior were attributed to possession by demons or evil spirits. Since the days of the ancient Hebrews, Egyptians, and Greeks, madness had been attributed to demonic possession.[10] For the Greeks, the *Keres* (ghosts) of the spirits of the dead; the *nympholeptos,* or nymphs; the human deities, such as

Selene, Hecate, and Artemis; and other demonic and heavenly powers could take possession of a person and drive him to madness and the perpetration of other socially deviant behaviors.[11] Despite the prevalence of such beliefs from earliest times, however, there has also been an understanding of responsibility for one's own actions, an idea upon which most ancient legal doctrines rest.[12]

The distinction between behavior brought about by individual volition and that brought about by evil spirits or demonic possession was not easily established. Yet the belief in demons existed alongside the rationalistic understanding of human choice and volition. In the middle ages, scholars like Aquinas maintained that evil or harmful behavior can be due to both demons and free will:

> In this way the devil is not the cause of every sin: for all sins are commited at the devil's instigation, but some are due to the free-will and the corruption of the flesh. . . .[13]

This tension between the belief in causal factors of predisposition and the notion of behavior due to volition or free will remains in present-day versions of several theories of social deviation. As in our own society, the decision as to the presence or absence of responsibility was vital, for it often determined the societal reaction to the deviant. Plato tells us that a man possessed and in a state of madness would not be punished as a criminal in Athens. Murder committed by the sane was punishable by death, while murder committed by a madman or one possessed was punishable by exile from his native land. The determination of responsibility or intentionality was the task of the judge or judges, and it was upon their discretionary power that the offender's fate rested.[14]

In the middle ages, societal reactions to the possessed were varied: expulsion from the community, incarceration in prisons and former leper houses, and placement in monasteries, convents, and hospitals. The early forms of treatment for madmen were various forms of exorcisms and enforced pilgrimages to religious shrines.[15]

HOMOSEXUALITY AND DEMONIC POSSESSION

Homosexuality was widely practiced in the ancient societies that bordered the Mediterranean. It is well known that the Greeks accepted homosexuality and that their cultural values supported sexual practices that were later proscribed by Judeo-Christian doctrine. The Old and New Testament expressly forbade homosexuality: "You shall not lie with a male as with a woman; it is an abomination."[16] "If a man lies with a male as with a woman, both of them have commited an abomination; they shall be put to death, their blood is upon them."[17] Several authors have noted that the reaction to female homosexuality was far less severe than to male homosexuality.[18] Szasz attributes this to the less-than-human status ascribed to women in Western society. Kinsey and his associates, in a historical review of female homosexuality, indicated that there are few recorded cases in medieval European history of women being put to death for homosexuality, while numerous records exist of men being punished in this way.[19]

Although the proscriptions against homosexuality are clearly represented in the Bible and biblical commentary, not until the early middle ages do we see extended explanations for homosexuality. Robert Bell points out that

> with the rise of Christianity homosexuality became more and more tabooed. It is possible that the first theory of homosexuality came into existence during the medieval period when the homosexual was defined as a person in a supernatural state and being possessed of devils. As the years went on he was increasingly seen as the ultimate in depravity and excessive self-abuse.[20]

The Church opposed all sexual behavior that did not lead directly to procreation. All other sex was said to stem from carnal lust and desire, and therefore from moral depravity. The middle ages produced the understanding that this moral depravity could only have been caused by the influence of demons and evil spirits, which invaded the body of the homosexual. In fact, homosexuality, or sodomy, became equated with heresy.[21] Szasz states "for centuries, no penological distinction is made between religious unorthodoxy and sexual misbehavior, especially homosexuality."[22] Both were considered caused by demonological possession, and punishment for both was the same.

In Catholic Spain and Portugal, as well as in several Protestant countries of the North, the punishment for homosexuality was identical with that of heresy and witchcraft: burning alive and confiscation of property. The demons that caused women to engage in witchcraft could also invade men and cause them to engage in "unholy" sexual acts. To this day, the language used to proscribe homosexual behavior has maintained the heretical, and thus "unnatural," stamp of moral indignation:

> In English-speaking countries, the connection between heresy and homosexuality is expressed through the use of a single word to denote both concepts: buggery. The double meaning of this word persists to this day. Webster's *Unabridged Dictionary* (Third Edition) defines "buggery" as "heresy, sodomy";

and "bugger" as "heretic, sodomite." The word is derived from
the medieval Latin Bugarus and Bulgarus, literally Bulgarian,
"from the adherence of the Bulgarians to the Eastern Church
considered heretical.[23]

Homosexuality, like mental illness, was therefore explained by
medieval man as the outcome of demonic possession. Behavior so
divergent from acceptable behavior could only be caused by the powers of evil and darkness. The demons present within man *predisposed*
him toward these ungodly acts. It became important to identify those
who were said to be possessed and who were said to have engaged in
these behaviors. The "facts" of their transgressions could be confirmed by witnesses, and the accused was often faced with having to
endure various *ordeals,* or *trials.*

In many cases, these ordeals amounted to outright torture of the
accused. They included trial by drowning (throwing the accused,
bound, into a pool of water, holding that one possessed by demons
would float); trial by fire (asking the accused to hold white-hot irons
or coals for a specified period of time or place these on the tongue!);
trial by immersion in boiling oil, and numerous other equally grue-
some ordeals.[24] These methods have been used in many cultures
during many historical periods to discover evidence for demonic possession. The Hindu Code of Manu specified a number of such ordeals, and preliterate cultures in Borneo and Australia have had similar methods of discovering evidence for possession.[25]

The use of these ordeals seems to have reached an all-time high
in medieval Europe, as well as during the eras of witch mania both in
Europe and America. The medieval ordeals represented the most
primitive procedures for acquiring the evidence needed to deduce
the presence of some predisposing factor that led to social deviation.
Societies have developed many different procedures for obtaining
this type of information. Psychiatric diagnostic procedures are only
more recent procedures for gathering evidence for the presence or
absence of predisposing factors toward social deviation.

THE FOUR HUMORS

The belief in demons as causative agents of social deviation was
not far removed from the earliest biological or physiological explanations that have appeared in Western thought. The Greek physician
Galen, in his treatise *On the Natural Faculties,* indicated that the body
contained various humors: blood of various colorations, phlegm, and
yellow and black bile.[26] When these humors were out of balance—
when there were excesses or deficiencies of black or yellow bile—

certain primary pathologies or diseases, as well as "temperaments" and "modes of life," could result.[27]

From Galen's discussion it is clear that such ideas were also held by his predecessors, Hippocrates, Aristotle, Proxagoras, and Philotimus. They all believed that these bodily humors were governed by warm, cold, dry, and moist conditions that were said to influence all natural phenomena.[28] This belief in bad humors or in the unbalanced state of the humors became part of the folk wisdom and folk medicine of the middle ages. Similar beliefs had been advanced by the ancient Chinese physicians, who held that the balance of *Yin* and *Yang* forces in the body was the basis of all health. Mathison, commenting on the influence of these ideas on the beliefs and practices of the European middle ages, states:

> New and old ideas clashed in the centuries to come. The Greek doctrine of "four humors" won popular acceptance again. Man was a microcosm in a macrocosm. Blood was comparable to fire, phlegm to earth, black bile to water, and yellow bile to air. The stars guided man's destiny. Imbalance of the humors brought sickness, and the heavens caused the imbalance. There were recognizable types of men, and the imbalance could be treated by recognizing them. The physician could also peer into his urine flask and discern imbalance. As these humors were connected by tubes within the body, and intermingled, there was need to rid the body of excess humors. Blood-letting, guided by the astrologers, was a sure method. Pulse diagnosis, spring leeching, cupping and worm extraction all won recognition as time passed.[29]

These remedies were used not only for the conventional diseases of the body but also for the treatment of madness, homosexuality, and sexual promiscuity. The belief persisted that such maladies could only have their basis in the deviant's faulty biological constitution. This central belief has been maintained in many forms to this day.

It is surprising to see for how long a time the ideas of ancient scholars like Galen influenced the explanations of such deviant behavior as mental illness. Foucault, in his historical analysis of madness in the Age of Reason, says:

> For a long time—until the beginning of the seventeenth century—the discussion of melancholia remained fixed within the traditions of the four humors and their essential qualities: stable qualities actually inherent in a substance, which alone [the qualities] could be considered as their cause. . . .[30]

The treatment of individuals defined as mad often included such practices as branding with hot irons to set the humors back into balance; the use of purges and emetics; the use of leeches and other blood letting techniques; and the administration of hot and cold baths.[31] Similar techniques were used to treat various sexual deviations. Thus the concept of unbalanced bodily humors was substituted for the demons and evil spirits.

With the change from demonological theories of deviation to those of the unbalanced humors, we see the beginning of a very long history of biophysiological explanations for social deviation. From the middle ages to our own modern period, numerous theories have held that the predisposing factor toward deviation resided in the biological or physiological makeup of the deviant.

Perhaps the single most important reason these theories became so dominant was the rise to a position of power, prestige, and influence of the physician and the medical practice. The man of medicine and the "medical model," which was the ideological basis of his practice, became the major definers of social deviation. By the nineteenth century some of the major explanations for social deviation were being proposed by physicians, biologists, and physiologists.

THE MEDICAL MODEL

In his treatise on *The Manufacture of Madness,* Thomas Szasz traces the transformation of social deviation (specifically, mental illness and homosexuality) from moral and religious concerns to medical concerns; as he would call it: from heresy to illness.[32] The Enlightenment, or Age of Reason, has usually been characterized as significantly different from the earlier Age of Faith.

During the Enlightenment, great stress was placed on rationalism—the belief that virtually everything was subject to examination and that the natural and social worlds could be examined for their constitutive properties. It was an era in which the Newtonian model of scientific analysis seemed to offer limitless possibilities for understanding the laws of the natural order. The search for truth no longer ended in theological dogma. Men began a search for *verifiable* truths, which were sought through experience, observation, and experimentation using methods of Newtonian natural science. Medicine, physiology, and biology made major advances as the power of the Church declined. No longer was the Church able to effectively proscribe the study of the human body; anatomy and physiology were at the forefront of this scientific wave, and the understanding of physical pathology was fast developing.

During the same period, many leading physicians and pathologists were firmly convinced that bodily pathologies were the source of various forms of deviant behavior. Szasz has analyzed the ideas of

Benjamin Rush (1746-1813), the physician general of the Continental Army and the man who is considered the father of American psychiatry.[33] Szasz states:

> Rush is hailed as the founder of American psychiatry because he claimed that there is no difference between mental and bodily diseases, and because through his great personal influence as a successful physician and friend of the Founding Fathers, he was able to implement his ideas on mental illness. In short, he was the first American physician to urge the medicalization of social problems and their coercive control by means of "therapeutic" rather than "punitive" sanctions. . . .[34]

Szasz points out that "Rush was a master of the medical metaphor, recasting moral and social problems in medical terms."[35] For example, Rush very early tried to convince people that drinking alcohol was not a moral problem but really a medical one—very much like the contemporary view of alcoholism as a physical disease. Most significantly Rush was one of the first physicians to believe that deviant behavior was rooted in mental disorder. "Having started to move down the road of reinterpreting social deviance as mental illness, Rush was prepared to go all the way. Just how far he actually went will seem incredible, even to the contemporary reader accustomed to viewing all kinds of undesirable conduct as the manifestation of mental disorder."[36]

Rush claimed that suicide, crimes of every variety—lying, smoking, alcoholism—and similar social behaviors were all manifestations of mental disorder. Crimes like murder and theft were viewed as symptomatic of special mental illnesses, which he called "derangements of the will."[37] He was convinced that these mental disorders ultimately stemmed from bodily diseases. Medicine, he believed, could do more for the criminal than the prison; he could best be treated under medical supervision.

As Szasz points out, the significance of Rush's definition of social problems and deviation as medical problems was its justification of *medical control* over these behaviors. It also made the man of medicine the final judge of acceptable and unacceptable social behavior.[38] The physician was elevated to the top of the *hierarchy of credibility* regarding all matters of socially nonconforming behavior. The physician replaced the cleric at the highest rung of the ladder of credibility and moral entrepreneurship.[39]

With this belief that social deviation was ultimately a physical problem, many treatments and therapies were developed for those diagnosed as ill. Coercion and terror seem to have been general therapeutic strategies for Rush: he clearly considered various sorts of punishments as therapeutic.[40] Rush mentions "confinement by means of a strait waistcoat," "privation of their customary pleasant food," "pouring cold water under the coat sleeve," "blood letting," "solitude," and "darkness" as effective treatments. Another of Rush's favorite treatments was maintaining "an erect position of the body"— forcing the madman to stand erect for 24-hour periods.[41]

Although physicians like Rush were certainly motivated by intentions to heal, these techniques often fell little short of torture. Today many would applaud the removal of stigma from criminals, alcoholics, and sexual deviants by substituting a medical reaction. Yet Szasz holds that there are no differences between Rush's medical therapeutics and the contemporary therapeutics of institutional psychiatry.[42] His essential point is well taken. The substitution of medical definitions for theological and legal ones does not eliminate the *moral disapproval* of social deviance, which is at the basis of all these evaluations. Although moral indignation is often hidden in the language of scientific medicine, which is supposedly value free, it is at the basis of the medical view of social deviance. Szasz comments on a statement by the noted psychiatrist Karl Menninger that, as a psychiatrist, he cannot "condone" homosexuality and that homosexuality was a symptom of underlying pathology:

> If homosexuality is a "symptom," what is there to "condone" or not "condone"? Menninger would not speak of "condoning or not condoning" the fever of pneumonia or the jaundice of biliary obstruction, but he does speak of "not condoning" a psychiatric "symptom." His "therapeutic" recommendations for homosexuality bear out the suspicion that his medical role is but a cloak for that of the moralist and social engineer.[43]

While Rush was convincing his American public that illness was at the basis of social deviation, his physician colleagues in Europe were equally successful with their countrymen. Foucault has shown that the Enlightenment physicians in Europe at the end of the eighteenth century were convinced that the body was the source of such deviations as madness:

> The madman's body was regarded as the visible and solid presence of his disease: whence [come] those physical cures whose meaning was borrowed from a moral perception and a moral therapeutics of the body.[44]

These therapies were a strange mixture of medieval remedies and new-found drugs, semitortures, and purification rites. Vapors were inhaled, bleedings and purges were still prescribed, and unbelievable varieties of organic and inorganic matter were ingested— from parts of animals and insects to narcotic substances. Although the theories of the late eighteenth century were dressed in the vestments of science, the practices that grew out of them had changed little from the ancient and medieval periods.

The medical model of social deviation attracted advocates who, in turn, gave new variations to the basic explanatory theme. The nineteenth century saw the birth of the social sciences and the revival and modernization of biophysiological explanations for social deviation. With the growing industrialization and urbanization of European society and the awareness of urban problems, the physicians, physiologists, and new social scientists became increasingly interested in specific types of social deviation, such as crime. Like their eighteenth-century predecessors, they sought to discover those predisposing factors in the constitution of the individual that led to criminal behavior or made it more likely.

THE PHYSIOLOGISTS

Many factors led to the nineteenth-century concentration on biological and physiological characteristics in the analysis of crime and the etiology of deviation. The practice of relating physiognomy to human character and human types dates back to the fifteenth and sixteenth centuries; it included such mystical practices as divining or diagnosing deviation from the presence of moles on the body, lines on the forehead, and from other facial characteristics.[45] Medieval scholars, such as John of Indagine, Jaeger of Nuremberg, Bartolomew Cocle, and della Rocca of Bologna published books containing numerous drawings of persons that attempted to relate their physical features to deviation and personality characteristics.[46] One significant study was Cocle's *Compendium of Physiognomy,* published in Strassburg in 1533. Seligmann points out some of Cocle's beliefs:

> Men whose temples are covered by a dense growth of hair are simple, vain, credulous, stubborn, of mediocre intelligence and somewhat boorish in manners and language. Bearded fellows are brutal, vengeful, have poor memories, are unfortunate and covetous . . . those whose foreheads are short and covered with hair are quarrelsome and simple rather than refined. Others whose foreheads are too small in every way are simple, irascible, cruel, covetous. . . .[47]

Metoposcopy, another divining art, analyzed the lines on the forehead and related it to the character of the individual. Two scholars,

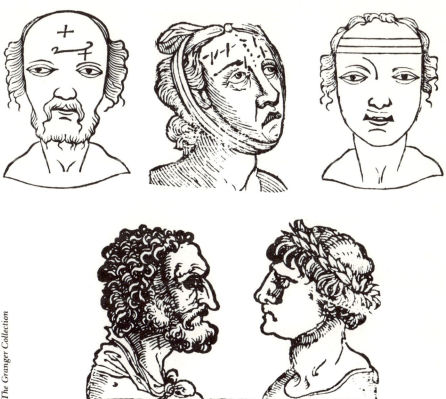

Geralomo Cardano in his *Metoposcopia* (Paris, 1658) and Phillip Phinella in his *De Metoposcopia* (Antwerp, 1648), were among the major advocates of this method.[48] In one of the drawings from Phinella's book, a woman is depicted with a bandage around the chin and head (see illustration), and on her forehead are numerous dots and lines. Seligmann says:

> Finally, Phinella's lady with the toothache is an ominously marked and ill-behaved person. In spite of her hypocritical piety and sad mien, she is a monster, libidinous and terrifying, a betrayer of her best friends, and the author of manifold ignominious deeds.[49]

In the late eighteenth century, a Swiss theologian, Johan Casper Lavater wrote a three-volume book entitled *Essays on Physiognomy* (London, 1789), which became very influential in the next century.[50] It was a comprehensive presentation and defense of physiognomic theory and practice. In it, Lavater studied the faces and skulls of the famous (e.g., Shakespeare, Johnson, Spalding, Attila, Judas, Dürer, and Socrates, as depicted in paintings or sketches of them), and of the infamous (criminals, the insane, etc.).

In Book II Lavater suggested that the shape of the human skull should tell us much about the character of the individual. He believed that the shape of the skull corresponded to certain predispositions toward power, friendliness, agitation, weakness, and so on. These potentialities constituted the individual's temperament and some of these were conducive to deviation. The shape of the forehead could distinguish the imbecile from the genius; the shape of the eyebrows could distinguish between the weak person and one of great strength.[51] Lavater made popular the discipline which became known as "phrenology." Phrenologists believed that the physiognomy of the head or skull could reveal individuals who were more apt to engage in antisocial or aggressive behavior.

CRIMINOLOGY AND PHYSIOLOGY: THE ITALIAN SCHOOL

The mid-nineteenth century also saw the development of one of the most significant scientific theories in the field of biology: the evolutionary development of animal and plant life. Darwin's theory of evolution had a profound influence on scholars interested in the analyses of social problems like crime. For many, the criminal or social deviant was an anomaly to socially and biologically evolved man. He was a throwback to a more primitive creature in previous stages of evolution. This theory of *atavism* posits the existence of individuals who are both physically and socially reversions to a less-evolved creature in the chain of evolution. When combined with the phrenological beliefs of scholars like Lavater and Gall and of an American, Charles Caldwell, we have the ingredients for one of the main schools of thought in criminology and social deviance during the nineteenth century.[53] The man most frequently identified with this amalgam of thought, Cesare Lombroso (1836-1909) founded the so-called "Italian School" or "Positive School" of criminology.

Lombroso, a physician by training, was a Darwinian evolutionist. In fact, he began his major work on crime, not by analyzing human crime, but by looking at crime in the plant and animal worlds! According to an account of the early twentieth century:

> The author [Lombroso] studies crime among the lower organisms, detecting it even in the vegetable world. Then he studies it among the animals, and finally in the human medium; in the infancy of the individual and of the species, in the child and the savage.[54]

Early in his writings, he was convinced that crime was caused by the physical, anthropological characteristics of the criminal.

For years Lombroso had studied the physiognomies of criminals in the Italian penitentiaries. He was impressed with the "savage-like" form of the body and particularly of the skulls of these inmates. Maurice Parmelee, in his introduction to the first English translations of Lombroso's *Crime: Its Causes and Remedies,* quotes from Lombroso's opening speech of the Sixth Congress of Criminal Anthropology at Turin in April 1906:

> In 1870 I was carrying on for several months researches in the prisons and asylums of Pavia upon cadavers and living persons in order to determine upon substantial differences between the insane and criminals, without succeeding very well. At last I found in the skull of a brigand a very long series of atavistic anomalies, above all an enormous middle occiptal fossa and a hypertrophy of the vermis analogous to those that are found in inferior vertebrates. At the sight of these strange anomalies the problem of the nature and of the origin of the criminal seemed to me resolved. The characteristics of primitive men and of inferior animals must be reproduced in our times. . . .[55]

Although Lombroso modified his views significantly to include numerous social and psychological factors, he maintained that the individual's physical heredity was the major predisposing variable toward criminality. To prove his thesis he instituted numerous statistical analyses of thousands upon thousands of criminals, mental patients, and juvenile delinquents—analyzing the size, weight, and morphology of their skulls and studying brains and general physiologies.

It is important to point out that Lombroso meant to explain not only crime but social deviation in general. In *Crime: Its Causes and Remedies* he discusses the application of his basic theory to alcoholics, sexual deviants, and the mental ill and shows that these individuals also display characteristic physical anomalies. He maintained that physical and moral degeneracy went hand in hand. Later in his career, he developed the thesis that there are different types of criminals: the occasional criminal, emotional criminal, born criminal, morally insane criminal, and the masked epileptic criminal. For the first two types in particular, psychological and social factors were very important as causative agents.

Despite the archaic nature of many of Lombroso's views on the causes of crime, his views on the administration of justice, punishment, and the general treatment of criminals are quite contemporary. He believed that children and very old persons ought not be punished like middle-aged adults; that occasional criminals ought not to be punished like career, or habitual criminals; and that some behaviors ought to be decriminalized and treated as civil offenses. He also believed that preventive and treatment institutions should replace penal institutions for those who were not "born criminals."[56] However, judging from Lombroso's views on the causes of crime and social deviation, and from the high rates of recidivism among prisoners then and now, not many would qualify for this status and thus for leniency and compassion.

The two other leaders of the Italian School who adhered to Lombroso's basic thesis on social deviation were Enrico Ferri (1856-1928) and Raffaele Garofalo (1852-1934). In their analyses of crime and the criminal, they built upon the theory of biological and physiological predisposition, adding nuances that made their formulations more compatible with other developing theories in the psychological and sociological communities.

Ferri was one of the first proponents of a multifactor theory of deviation. He stressed that crime was the result of *biological factors,* such as heredity and physiological constitution; *physical factors,* such as the relative lengths of day and night, climate, the seasons; and *social factors,* such as population density, emigration, public opinion, custom, religion, education, and so on.[57] Very much like Lombroso, he classified criminals under five basic types: criminal lunatics, the born incorrigibles, habitual criminals (those who have become criminals from acquired habit), occasional criminals, and emotional criminals.[58] Also like Lombroso, most of his attention was directed toward born criminals and "lunatic criminals," both of whom evidenced physiognomic and moral degeneracy. The other criminals, he believed, were influenced more by social and physical factors. Ferri was much more open to the influence of these social or environmental factors than Lombroso. However, Ferri adamantly asserted that for most habitual criminals—those who fit his habitual, born, and lunatic categories (most criminals)—free will was not an important factor. He wrote:

> No doubt the idea of a born criminal is a direct challenge to the traditional belief that the conduct of every man is the outcome of his free will, or at most of his lack of education rather than of his original physio-psychical constitution. But, . . . there are criminals who, without being mad, are still not as ordinary men; and the reporters call them "human tigers," "brutes," and the like.[59]

Again, like Lombroso, Ferri intended his theory of crime causation to be applicable more generally to other forms of social deviation:

> From the consideration that human actions, whether honest or dishonest, social or anti-social, are always the outcome of a

> man's physio-psychical organism, and of the physical and so-
> cial atmosphere which surrounds him, I have drawn attention
> to the *anthropological* or individual factors of crime, the physi-
> cal factors, and the social factors.[60]

In other words, all antisocial behavior, particularly when it was habitual for the individual, must have a basis in the deviant's organic
constitution.

Raffaelle Garofalo, the third member of this school, was a magis-
trate of great reputation, a national senator, professor of law, legal
scholar, and member of the Italian nobility (a baron, in fact). Like
Ferri, he was convinced that "evil inclinations" in the individual often
have a basis in his psychophysical makeup, not in his free will. In his
Criminology (1914, Part II, pp. 65–134) Garofalo first reviews the
ideas of his fellow Positive School members and concludes that habitual criminals, such as murderers, thieves, and sex offenders, have
"cranial anomalies," as well as other distinguishing physiognomic
characteristics.

Garofalo was influenced to a far greater extent than his colleagues by psychological motivations toward criminality. But for him
these psychological predispositions toward deviation could be part of
the person's heredity or be learned in early childhood. Garofalo referred to these psychological motivations as "moral anomalies":

> But in our opinion there is always present in the instincts of the
> true criminal, a specific element which is congenital or inher-
> ited, or else acquired in early infancy and becomes inseparable
> from his psychic organism.[61] . . . If we are right in supposing
> crime to be a want of that part of the moral sense which is the
> least refined, the least pure, the least delicate, the most akin to
> the organism, then the propensity or predisposition to crime
> must be hereditarily transmissible like all other phenomena of
> the same description. . . .[62]

In his review of other contemporary theories of crime and deviation, Garofalo was convinced that such economic and social structural variables as poverty, class conflict, lack of education, and various
cultural phenomena had little impact on crime and the habitual criminal. He, more than his colleagues already discussed, took up this
argument with economic and sociological theorists of crime and concluded that their explanations, while having some merit, could not
explain the major causes of antisocial behavior. He maintained that
the psychological and physiological causes of crime were paramount
and that all other factors were insignificant by comparison:

> All criminals possess a predisposition to crime, which is not
> the effect of external circumstances, but of something residing

> in the individual's moral organization, in his manner of feeling
> and thinking. . . . and if he is without a predisposition to crime,
> he will never commit it, whatever be the occasion. . . .[63]

It should be apparent to the reader how vastly different are Garofalo's views on crime from those of Durkheim, discussed in Chapter 2. In fact, it was Durkheim's opposition to the views of the Italian School theoreticians and their reliance on psychological and physiological explanation that prompted him to posit his radically *sociologistic* definition of social pathology.

Although the views of the "Italian School" and their predecessors may seem strange to us now, their explanatory logic remains with us. Biophysiological explanations of predisposition toward social deviation have many contemporary proponents.

SUCCESSORS TO BIOPHYSIOLOGICAL EXPLANATIONS: EARLY TWENTIETH-CENTURY CONCEPTIONS

Feeblemindedness and the Mental Testers

The period immediately preceding the outbreak of World War I and lasting roughly to the mid-1920s produced many new ideas about social deviation. Both in America and in Europe, scholars in the medical, biological, and behavioral sciences—seemingly fascinated with the relationship of physiology and psychology to social deviation, and imbued with the philosophy of "positivism"—began to discover factors that could predispose an individual toward deviation. One of the major developments of thought occurred in the area of psychology concerned with the measurement of mental capacity and ability. Around the turn of the century, the intelligence-measuring scale had been developed by the Frenchman Alfred Binet. Among the first to see the diagnostic potentials of this tool was the American psychologist Henry Herbert Goddard.

With the development of the intelligence-measuring scale, the pathology that had for centuries been referred to as "feeblemindedness" took on a scientific guise. Goddard was among the first to point out that feeblemindedness was a condition, now readily measurable (and thus "scientific"), that was surely related to other social problems. But what was the link between intelligence (or, really, the lack of it) and antisocial behavior? Goddard, in the beginning of his major treatise *Feeble-Mindedness: Its Causes and Consequences* (1914), hypothesizes that

> there are all grades of responsibility, from zero to the highest;
> or, there are all grades of intelligence from practically none up

> to that of the genius or most gifted. Responsibility varies according to the intelligence. . . .[64]

In other words the *less* intelligence the individual has, the *less* responsible he is for his actions, and the more probable is his participation in antisocial behavior. Since Goddard saw intelligence as based on the hereditary makeup of the individual, habitual deviation was ultimately a biophysiological reality. Although most scholars have referred to Goddard's attempt to link feeblemindedness to crime, he clearly saw a variety of social deviations as having a base in this condition.

The opening chapter to his major study includes not only his attempted linkage between this condition and crime, but also a discussion of the relationship between feeblemindedness and alcoholism, intemperance, and drunkenness; prostitution and other "immoral" sexual vices; poverty; truancy; and those whom Goddard calls "ne'er-do-wells"[65]:

> Every community has its quotá of people, who, because of their failure to act in harmony with those who are definitely working for the welfare of society, may perhaps be designated as undesirable citizens or ne'er-do-wells; while not paupers, they often have to receive assistance from others; while not criminal, prostitute or drunkard, are still shiftless, incompetent, unsatisfactory and undesirable members of the community. . . .
>
> In view of the proportions to which feeble-mindedness has grown, it certainly is not unwise to ask the question—may not some of these people be feeble-minded?[66]

Goddard of course answers in the affirmative. He felt that his research findings showed that many social deviants were, in fact, of low intelligence.

Goddard directed the research laboratory of the training school for feebleminded (retarded) children in Vineland, New Jersey. His research was based on the initial intelligence testing of the boys and girls in the school and the subsequent analysis of the genealogical table of the child's family to determine whether his ancestors might also have been feebleminded. To analyze these family trees, Goddard had fieldworkers interview relatives and observe family behavior to determine the extent of feeblemindedness. In some cases they would question children about their relatives three to six generations back. From these interviews they would construct a genealogical table of family retardation! Goddard's methodological techniques were absolutely absurd; yet his "research" drew numerous followers, who were equally impressed with the diagnostic potential of the intelligence scale.

Two years before the publication of *Feeble-Mindedness,* Goddard had published *The Kallikak Family: A Study in the Heredity of Feeble-Mindedness* (1912), the case study of a feebleminded family.[67] Goddard traced the family tree of Deborah Kallikak, a student in the Vineland Institute, back to her ancestors living during the Revolutionary War. In all, 480 descendants of these eighteenth-century Kallikaks were traced (a total of 1,146 relatives after marriages). Goddard concluded that of the 480 original descendants,

> thirty-six have been illegitimate. There have been thirty-three sexually immoral persons, mostly prostitutes. There have been twenty-four confirmed alcoholics. There have been three epileptics. Eighty-two died in infancy. Three were criminal, eight kept houses of ill fame. . . .[68]

He also points out that many of these people married into families that evidenced both feeblemindedness and "rampant immorality." In all, his accounts of the social deviation manifested by this family are staggering. Goddard's diagnosis of the deviation of one Kallikak family of the early 1800s included various types of criminals, alcoholics, sexual immorality of various sorts, mongoloids, epileptics, mental illness, and, of course, the feeblemindedness of the majority. With research that was incredibly inadequate and rather bizarre, Goddard tried to convince his readers of the "irrefutable" link between feeblemindededness and social deviation. Goddard's thesis was accepted by many other psychologists in America and Europe in the 1920s and 1930s.

Goddard's thesis is no longer seriously accepted by contemporary analysts of social deviation. Substantial evidence exists that there is no significant relationship between intelligence and social deviation. Studies have also demonstrated that deviants of various types have intelligence scores that differ very little from those of the nondeviant population.[69] A major problem with the early studies that attempted to assess this relationship was that the researchers based their studies on populations of "kept" deviants—those in prisons, mental hospitals, reformatories, or similar institutions. In general, these institutions contained inmates from the lower socioeconomic classes who thus had far less education than the average population upon which the intelligence scales were based. In addition, the early intelligence tests were biased in favor of the well educated. Furthermore it is very doubtful whether the tests that were used actually measured the innate intelligence of the subjects. As Clinard points out:

No one knows the actual components of innate intelligence because the effect of social experience on the latter is such that it appears to be impossible to measure. It is now generally agreed that the so-called intelligence test measures only "test intelligence" and not innate intelligence. Moreover, there is increasing evidence that the IQ can be somewhat modified by experience. On logical grounds, moreover, there is nothing in the nature of subnormal intelligence that implies a relationship with either attitudes or personality traits. The idea that persons with low intelligence are likely to engage in deviant behavior must be regarded simply as an assumption, since one might also argue that low intelligence could lead to rigid compliance with traditional ways of acting and higher intelligence could be associated with deviant behavior when traditional values are violated. Although studies have not been made, the great proportion of persons with low intelligence scores undoubtedly are non-deviants, whereas there are large number of persons with above normal intelligence who are.[70]

"Somatotype" Explanations

The decades of the 1920s and the 1930s also witnessed the emergence of somatotype explanations of deviation, which are based on the initial premise of the Positive School. As demonstrated by the support it still receives from contemporary scholars, it has endured. Somatotype explanations also see a correlation between social deviation and the morphology, or form, of the human body. In this case there are said to be body types and associated personality features or temperaments that predispose an individual toward participation in antisocial behavior. Four names stand out as twentieth-century advocates of a revitalized and somewhat more sophisticated Lombrosian theory: Kretschmer, Hooton, Sheldon (and colleagues), and, more recently, Sheldon and Eleanor Glueck. Their ideas have also produced advocates of this position in the 1970s.

In 1925, Ernst Kretschmer, professor of psychiatry and neurology at the University of Marburg in Germany, published *Physique and Character: An Investigation of the Nature of Constitution and of the Theory of Temperament.* In it he postulated the existence of three body types: (1) the "asthenic" type (thin, lean, and narrowly built; with thin muscles, sharp rib cage, flat chest, thin stomach, delicate hands), (2) the "athletic type" (strong skeleton and musculature, wide shoulders, "a superb chest," "magnificent legs," above-average height, tapering body trunk), and (3) the "pyknic" type (middle height, rounded figure, broad face, rounded shoulders, short and thick neck, a tendency toward a covering of fat).[71] These three types were in various ways related to schizophrenia and manic-depressive psychoses. Kretschmer further held that the Pyknic type had an "affinity" with manic-depressive conditions, while asthenics and athletics had a "clear biological affinity" with schizophrenia.[72]

Schizophrenics and manic-depressives also had peculiar "temperaments" that caused them to behave in distinct ways. For example, Kretschmer held that the schizophrenic temperament lent itself to sexual impulses of an uncontrollable nature, hence asthenics and athletics had a clear tendency toward sexual deviations. Manic-depressives, on the other hand, had temperaments that were not conducive to such deviations. The advanced schizophrenic temperament was generally conducive to social deviation[73]:

> The congenitally anti-social, weak-minded individual of the schizoid genre may, in later life on account of some Katatonic jolt, betray his obvious membership in the schizophrenic group. All these severely disintegrated, defective conditions, whether they are inborn or acquired, whether they are tinged with the colour of criminal hostility to society, or sulky eccentricity, or dull-wittedness or heboid foolishness, invariably bear the typical stamp of schizophrenic psychology.[74]

This small sample of Kretschmer's ideas should suffice to indicate the relationship between physiology, psychological temperament, and social deviation that he wished to posit. His theories and typologies are highly confusing, and the explanatory logic is often highly questionable. Many of the biological, physiological, psychological, and medical "facts" he drew upon would today be considered false or inaccurate.

The American Version

The somatotype theory of social deviation took on a more contemporary and significantly more complex guise in the formulation of the American psychologist, physical anthropologist, and physician William H. Sheldon. In his *Varieties of Delinquent Youth* (1949) Sheldon built upon Kretschmer's and his own earlier formulations of the relationships between somatotype temperament and social deviation. Like Kretschmer, he posited the existence of three ideal body types, which he labeled (1) *endomorphic* (soft, round, and rather pudgy), (2) *mesomorphic* (muscular, large bone structure, very strong), and (3) *ectomorphic* (thin, more fragile bone and muscle structure, tall).[75] Sheldon's typology differs fundamentally from Kretschmer's, for an individual is evaluated on the extent to which he shares characteristics of *each* of these three body types. He constructed a seven-point scale for each set of somatotype characteristics; thus, for example, an individual with a 4–3–2 somatotype configuration was 4 parts endomorphic, 3 parts mesomorphic, and 2 parts ectomorphic. In this instance, the upper torso of the body might be somatotypically endomorphic, the arms and legs might be mesomorphic, and the individual might have slight ectomorphic features in others parts of his body.[76] Sheldon also hypothesized that each somatotype corresponded to one of three basic temperament types, which he labeled as follows:

1. *viscerotonia* –endomorphic (love of eating, complacent, indiscriminate amiability, relaxed under influence of alcohol, greed for affection, love of physical comfort, etc.)

2. *somatotonia*–mesomorphic (energetic, love of domination and power, love of risk and chance, competitive aggressivness, ruthlessness, aggressive under influence of alcohol, etc.).

3. *cerebrotonia*–ectomorphic (overly fast reactions, inhibited, unpredictability of attitude, apprehensive, hypersensitivity to pain, resistance to alcohol, chronic fatigue, etc.).[77]

With his somatotype and temperament scales Sheldon analyzed the physiologies and biographies of 200 males who had been inmates of the Hayden Goodwill Inn in Boston, a rehabilitation home for delinquent boys. All 200 biographical sketches are included in *Varieties of Delinquent Youth,* and despite Sheldon's attempt to be objective by using his measurement scales, these sketches contain abundant subjective evaluations of the personality characteristics of each individual.

Sheldon concluded that there was indeed a strong relationship between somatotype and temperament, on the one hand, and the social deviation of both the boy and his family, on the other. In general, the most markedly antisocial or deviant cases were endomorphic mesomorphs or mesomorphic endomorphs with matching somatotonic temperaments. All the "advanced criminals" in the study (cases 185–200) displayed these characteristics; and those with "mental insufficiency" also tended toward endomorphic mesomorphy.[78] When the entire sample was compared with a control population of male college students, it was apparent from Sheldon's charts that the 200 delinquents tended toward mesomorphy and somatotonia, while the "normal" control group seemed to be randomly distributed throughout the somatotype categories.[79] However, Sheldon does not compare his control group with his "experimental" group on the basis of temperament—one of many questionable methodological procedures. In short, Sheldon concluded that there was indeed a relationship be-

tween somatotype, temperament, and social deviation; and that therefore more attention should therefore be given to the hereditary and
psychological bases of social deviation.

Sheldon's somatotype theory has been used more recently by
Sheldon and Eleanor Glueck in a series of books on delinquency. The
Gluecks, however, take a decidedly "multifactor" approach to causes
of delinquency. They see body type as one of many factors that together can lead to delinquent behavior:

> Consequently it is not bodily structure, or strong instinctual
> impulse, or an hereditary aggressive tendency, or a weak inhi-
> bitory mechanism, or low intelligence, or excessive emotional
> lability, or marked suggestibility, or residence in a poverty-
> stricken "delinquency area" or in a region with a tradition of
> delinquency, or broken homes, or "differential association"
> with those already criminal or any other biological or sociol-
> cultural factor that either exclusively or inevitably conduces to
> delinquent behavior. Any of these factors alone or in various
> combinations may or may not bring about delinquency de-
> pending on the balance of energy-and-inhibitory tendencies of
> the particular individual at the particular time.[80]

Despite the disclaimer, the Gluecks indicate that the body types
they used (slightly different from those of Sheldon) were correlated
with the psychological temperaments and dispositions conducive to
delinquency. Therefore, say the authors,

> suggestions regarding the management of delinquency should
> take account of bodily morphology with special reference to
> those traits found in the present work to yield a varied delin-
> quency *potential* to each of the physique types, those traits and
> sociocultural factors demonstrated to exert an *excessive* cri-
> minogenic impact on one or another of the body types....[81]

They add that each body type is influenced by different environmental and situational factors, which together bring about delinquency. Thus, the principal task for the analyst of antisocial behavior
should be the clear delineation of the interplay of all these factors.
The Gluecks firmly believe that one's body type, along with such
psychological traits as the tendency to act out frustrations and feelings
of aggression, thirst for adventure, and acquisitive impulses—all of
which are linked to certain body types—predisposes one to delinquency. In other words, they basically agree with Sheldon's findings.[82]

In the decade of the 1970s the views of Kretschmer, Sheldon,
and the Gluecks have had their contemporary following. For example, Cortes and Gatti (1972) in a very provocative book, present us

with an updated multifactor theory of delinquency, based on the linkages that they, too, feel exist between physique, temperament, and delinquency.[83] The authors base their ideas on a study that compared 100 delinquent boys, 100 nondelinquent boys, and 20 criminals on body type characteristics and *self-descriptions* of temperament. The latter approach to understanding psychological temperament differs from approaches previously used by somatotype researchers. The authors concluded:

> Different types of physique or body build *predispose* more than others [mesomorphic in particular] to certain temperamental traits. We are not saying that physique causes or determines some common traits. This would be a generalization unwarranted by our findings. Yet it seems reasonable to assume that through the organs of the body, glandular secretions, and the particular chemotype, physique limits the range of temperamental traits in individuals and, together with other variables, predisposes toward some traits more than toward others. It appears that boys with stronger physiques will be more active and energetic than boys with frail or fat physiques. Only a biased approach toward constitutional psychology will flatly reject such an interpretation."[84]

The authors further conclude that delinquents have characteristics of body type and temperament significantly different from those of nondelinquents; thus, they believe that their study allows them to conclude:

> Nature and nurture always work together and in the field of temperament, the role of biological and constitutional factors appears to have a slight margin of preponderance.[85]

Discussing social deviation, the authors also feel that their facts point in the direction of "nature" as having a slightly more significant role than "nurture." Cortes and Gatti, after a lengthy examination of their own and others' research, state:

> We would advance that the factors or conditions that appear to be closest to the cause of delinquency are FAMILY DISRUPTION, PARTICULARLY WHEN THE CHILDREN ARE MESOMORPHIC.[86]

The literature criticizing the somatotype perspective is quite vast.[87] Clinard has pointed out that the leaps from body type to temperament to deviation have not really been demonstrated by adherents to somatotype theory.[88] They do not clearly demonstrate how body types correspond to the temperaments that they posit. In fact, there is no necessary relationship between these major variables. Sheldon and other somatotype analysts fail to give cultural factors a major role in the determination of deviation. They do not sufficiently emphasize that delinquency and criminal behavior are learned; that labeling deviance and crime involves numerous evaluations and value judgments; and that it is therefore difficult to relate them to so stable a factor as body type, particularly "mesomorphy."

They also fail to demonstrate that temperament is necessarily related to tendencies toward deviation, and to see that what they call temperaments are often based on cultural conventions of behavior, not on the "constitutional structure" of the individual. Delinquents are often "aggressive," because such behavior is supported by their subculture. What the analyst defines as "ruthlessness" in the individual's temperament has more to do with the analyst's standards of evaluation than with the psychological or physiological constitution of the alleged deviant. The same is true for temperament traits like amiability, competitiveness, unpredictability, and greed. Although some deviants probably fit the models these analysts have developed, most do not.

Another major problem with somatotype studies is that too often institutionalized populations of deviants are used; these are hardly representative of the population at large or of all deviants. Most individuals who perfectly match the high-delinquency groups on body type and temperament are not labeled deviant and do not engage in any significant deviant behavior, whereas many who are deviant do not evidence these characteristics of body type and temperament.[89] Had Sheldon compared his group of 200 young men with a random sample of 200 men engaged in intramural or collegiate sports, rather than with the 4,000 he finally studied, he might have found many more nondeviant endomorphic mesomorphs than he reported. Although it would be foolish to say that no linkage of body type and temperament to deviance can ever be made, the analyses of its proponents do not warrant their claims for such a relationship. Advocates of these ideas must demonstrate under what conditions and for what types of deviance these traits have any influence, the relationship between learning, and the predisposing roles these traits are said to have.[90]

OTHER BIOPHYSIOLOGICAL EXPLANATIONS

In recent years we have witnessed the formulaton of other biophysiological theories of predisposition, which share many of the problems of the perspectives we have just discussed. One of the most widely known came to the attention of the American public with such cases as that of Richard Speck, the convicted murderer of eight Chicago nurses in April of 1968. In that case, Speck's attorney said that they would appeal the conviction because it had been discovered that Speck possessed what was called the "XYY chromosome syndrome." Genetic researchers in France, Scotland, Australia, as well as in America, had discovered in the mid-1960s that some of the prisoners and mental patients whom they had examined ("Karyotyped") had XYY chromosome genotypes, or configurations. Normal male cells have one X and one Y chromosome, and female cells contain two X chromosomes. However, there are atypical chromosome configurations, such as XXYY, XXY, and XYY.[91] These researchers believed that there might be a causal relationship between the XYY syndrome and antisocial or deviant behavior.[92]

Amir and Berman, in a review of this literature and the research findings, believe that a strong case can be made that, in some instances, deviants are 60 times as likely to possess the extra Y chromosome as members of the general population.[93] They cite a study by W. H. Price and associates in *Lancet* (1966), which concluded that men who possessed the extra Y chromosome (or gonosome, as it is sometime called) were more likely to evidence "aggressive and disturbed behavior" and had characteristics that simulated "the classic picture of psychopathy."[94] Amir and Berman, while cautioning against too quick an acceptance of chromosomal abnormalities as explanations for crime and social deviation, state:

> Even if we do not know the way in which the extra Y gonosome influences criminal behavior, the possibility of such an influence cannot be discounted; perhaps, intermediary factors are involved. Secondly, it can be assumed that as with other biological factors, the extra Y gonosome exerts its influence on personality, and to the extent that criminal behavior is a resultant of personality development or immediate situations encouraging specific types of behavior, a relationship, although as yet unclear, can be assumed to exist between the specific genetic load of the extra Y gonosome and other specific biological factors on the one hand, and on the other hand, behavior which is defined as criminal.[95]

In contrast to the conclusions of Amir and Berman, other reviewers of this literature are not so convinced about the supposed relationship. Sarbin and Miller, in their critical article "Demonism Revisited: The XYY Chromosomal Anomaly," indicate that the conclusions of these studies are overdrawn.[96] In most cases when normal control groups are used, there are no statistically significant relationships between the presence of a Y gonosome and deviation. Where studies have shown some relationship, advocates too quickly jump to a causal explanation. Too many of these studies are conducted among relatively small institutional populations, and not among normal or "at-large" populations. On the other hand, some studies show that the majority of recognized cases with the Y gonosome never become involved in any deviant behavior.[97] Shah and Roth (1971) point out that "some of the investigators whose earlier studies and reports led to some of the premature speculations about the XYY anomoly in recent years have urged more cautious conclusions. . . ."[98]

If most persons who have the extra Y gonosome do not become deviant and if the vast majority of those labeled deviant do not have the Y gonosome, such explanations can hardly become convincing arguments for the causal role of genetic or biophysiological factors in determining social deviation. Such explanations suffer from many of the problems of the other biophysiological perspectives. We need more convincing research to indicate the precise relationship that biological factors have to one's *actually becoming a deviant.* As is true for all the causal theories of predisposition we have examined, not enough emphasis is given to factors that bring about the "actualization" of deviation for particular individuals or groups of individuals.[99]

In recent years, theories of hormonal imbalance, brain disease, and brain-function impairment, among others, have sought to explain participation in deviant behavior.[100] They are subject to the same comments and reservations that have already been made. Although such factors might be related to a small number of cases of deviant behavior, it seems clear to contemporary analysts of deviation that most persons defined as deviant are biophysiologically quite "normal." In any case, much more research and scholarly debate are necessary before we even fully understand what role these factors have as *predisposing variables,* let alone what relationship they have to the actualization of deviant behavior.

SUMMARY

This chapter has reviewed the historical development of causal explanations for social deviation that have posited the predisposing factor toward deviation as residing "within" the individual. Beginning with the demonic-possession explanations we have charted the transition to biophysiological and medical-model explanations. From the early theories of bad humors, to the physiognomic phrenological, somatotypic and feeblemindedness theories, to the newer chromosome theories, scholars have maintained that a causal link exists between atypical or deviant behavior and atypical or deviant body constitution and related individual characteristics.

These understandings of social deviation have developed alongside of, and very often *because of,* the advances in the physical and life sciences. These sciences offered scholars explanatory models that had withstood the tests of observation and scrutiny in areas of their original discovery and were now deemed applicable to social behavior: after all, goes the common-sense reasoning, an anomaly in one area ought to be related to anomalies in other areas. Because of such explanatory models, deviation in our own society seems to be correlated with aberrant emotional states and personalities. As scholars like Szasz and Foucault have so well indicated, the medical–psychiatric model of deviation is the historical end product of equating nonconformist behavior with the "evils" as they were defined by the popular sentiments of a given historical period. In the Age of Faith, deviance was equated with heresy; in the Age of Reason, with antirationalism or madness; in the age of biological, medical, and natural science, with biological, physiological, and medical causes.

The explanatory frameworks that we have reviewed have each focused on one or a very few factors that were said to bring about social deviation. They each, however, were more concerned with predisposition than with "actualization." After all, these were prebehavioral-science explanations of deviation; most of these early analysts did not seriously consider the later "nature or nurture" debate. There was as yet no well-developed behavioral science that could engage in debate with the already well-established biological, medical, and physical sciences over these issues.

With the development of the social sciences, a set of alternative explanations came to challenge those that had enjoyed dominance for so long. These, like their predecessors, were causal theories of predisposition. But as a result of efforts by theoreticians like Durkheim, the predisposing factors were now located in the social environment, not in an individual's biophysical or psychological constitution.

---

[1]William Graham Sumner, *Folkways: A Study of the Sociological Importance of Usages, Manners, Customs, Mores, and Morals.* Boston: Ginn & Company, 1906, p. 58.

[2]Ibid., p. 221.

[3]Thomas Szasz, *The Age of Madness.* Garden City, N.Y.: Anchor Press, Doubleday, 1973, p. 1.

[4]Sumner, *Folkways,* p. 242.

[5]Ibid., p. 243.

[6]The "Summa Theologica" of St. Thomas Aquinas literally translated by Fathers of the English Dominican Province, Third Number (CXIV), London, 1912, pp. 496–505.

[7]Kurt Seligmann, *Magic, Supernaturalism and Religion*. New York: Pantheon, 1971, pp. 1–21. Original edition published in 1948.

[8]Ibid., p. 15.

[9]Alan C. Kors and Edward Peters, eds., *Witchcraft In Europe 1100–1700*. Philadelphia: University of Pennsylvania Press, 1972, p. 8

[10]Montague Summers, *The History of Witchcraft and Demonology*. New York: University Books, 1956, p. 200.

[11]George Rosen, *Madness in Society*. New York: Harper Torchbooks, 1968, pp. 75, 80–81.

[12]Edward Norbeck, *Religion in Primitive Society*. New York: Harper & Brothers, 1961, p. 215.

[13]Kors and Peters, *Witchcraft*, p. 68.

[14]Plato, *Laws*, 926A, Jowlett Translation, Vol. II, p. 665.

[15]Rosen, *Madness*, p. 142.

[16]Leviticus 18:22.

[17]Leviticus 20:13.

[18]A.C. Kinsey, W.B. Pomeroy, C.E. Martin, and Paul Gebhard, *Sexual Behavior in the Human Female*. Philadelphia: Saunders, 1953, p. 484.

[19]Ibid., p. 484.

[20]Robert R. Bell, *Social Deviance*. Homewood, Ill.: The Dorsey Press, 1971, p. 248.

[21]Thomas S. Szasz, *The Manufacture of Madness*. New York: Harper & Row, 1970, Ch. 10.

[22]Ibid., p. 164.

[23]Ibid., p. 165.

[24]*Encycolopedia Brittanica*, Vol. 16, p. 853.

[25]Ibid., p. 853.

[26]Galen, *On The Natural Faculties*, trans. by Arthur John Brock. London: William Heinemann, 1916, Book 2, Ch. 8, pp. 165–95.

[27]Ibid., p. 191.

[28]Ibid., Book 2, Ch. 9, pp. 195–219.

[29]Richard R. Mathison, *The Eternal Search*. New York: Putnam's, 1958, p. 36.

[30]Michel Foucault, *Madness and Civilization*. New York: Pantheon, 1965, p. 119.

[31]See Mathison, *The Eternal Search* for a historical analysis of various techniques used to remedy these physical and social maladies.

[32]Szasz, *The Manufacture*.

[33]Ibid., p. 160. pp. 138–39.

[34]Ibid.

[35]Ibid., 140.

[36]Ibid., 141.

[37]Ibid., 142.

[38]Ibid., p. 143.

[39]See Howard S. Becker, "Whose Side Are We On?" *Social Problems*, 14, pp. 239–47, for a description of "the hierarchy of credibility"; and Becker's *Outsiders*, Chs. 7 and 8, for a description of the "moral entrepreneur."

[40]Szasz, *The Manufacture*, pp. 147–48.

[41]Ibid., pp. 148–49.

[42]As we will see in our discussion of the societal reaction to deviation, Szasz's ideas are still considered radical by most of his colleagues in psychiatry and psychology and perhaps by the educated lay public who have heard of his views.

[43]Szasz, *The Manufacture*, p. 171.

[44]Foucault, *Madness*, p. 159.

[45]Seligmann, *Magic*, p. 261.

[46]Ibid., pp. 263–64.

[47]Ibid., p. 264.

[48]Ibid., p. 257.

[49]Ibid., pp. 259–60.

[50]Johan Caspar Lavater, *Essays on Physiognomy*, trans. by Thomas Holcraft. London: G.G. J.&J. Robinson, 1789.

[51]Ibid., pp. 165–70, Book 3.

[52]Franz Joseph Gall, *Craniologie, ou Decouvertes Nouvelles, Concernant le cerveau, Le Crane et les Organes*. Paris: Nicolla, 1807.

[53]See Arthur E. Fink, *Causes of Crime: Biological Theories in the United States 1800–1915*. Philadelphia: University of Pennsylvania Press, 1938, Ch. 1, for a discussion of Caldwell's contributions.

[54]C. Bernaldo De Quiros, *Modern Theories of Criminality*. Boston: Little, Brown, 1912, p. 12.

[55]Cesare Lombroso, *Crime: Its Causes and Remedies*, trans. by Henry P. Horton. Boston: Little, Brown, 1918. See p. xiv of the introduction to the English Version by Maurice Parmalee.

[56]Ibid., pp. 406–28.

[57]de Quiros, *Modern Theories*, p. 20.

[58]Enrico Ferri, *Criminal Sociology*. New York: D. Appleton, 1897, pp. 20–21. In fact by Ferri's own account, Lombroso's typology followed Ferri's formulation.

[59]Ibid., p. 29.

[60]Ibid., pp. 52–53.

[61]Baron Raffaele Garofalo, *Criminology*, trans. by Robert Wyness Millar. Boston: Little, Brown, 1914, p. 95.

[62]Ibid., p. 94.

[63]Ibid., pp. 132–33.

[64]Henry Herbert Goddard, *Feeble-Mindedness, Its Causes and Consequences*. New York: Macmillan, 1914, p. 2.

[65]Ibid., pp. 10–20.

[66]Ibid., p. 18.

[67]Henry Herbert Goddard, *The Kallikak Family: A Study in The Heredity of Feeble-Mindedness*. New York: Macmillan, 1912.

[68]Ibid., p. 18.

[69]For a discussion and list of research that bears on this supposed relationship, see Marshall Clinard, *Sociology of Deviant Behavior*. New York: Rinehart, pp. 116–19.

[70]Ibid., pp. 118–19.

[71]Ernst Kretschmer, *Physique and Character*. New York: Humanities Press, 1951, pp. 22, 25, 30, 30–31. Originally published in 1925.

[72]Ibid., p. 37.

[73]Ibid., pp. 91–92.

[74]Ibid., p. 154.

[75]William H. Sheldon, *Varieties of Delinquent Youth*. New York: Harper & Brothers, 1949.

[76]Ibid., pp. 14–15.

[77]Ibid., pp. 26–27.

[78]Ibid., pp. 728–46.

[79]Ibid., pp. 728–29.

[80]Sheldon Glueck and Eleanor Glueck, *Physique and Delinquency*. New York: Harper & Brothers, 1956, p. 268.

[81]Ibid., p. 251.

[82]Ibid., p. 271.

[83]Juan B. Cortes with Florence M. Gatti, *Delinquency and Crime: A Biopsychosocial Approach*. New York: Seminar Press, 1972.

[84]Ibid., p. 70.

[85]Ibid., p. 71.

[86]Ibid., p. 210. Emphasis in original.

[87]See, for example, Edwin H. Sutherland, "A Critique of Sheldon's *Varieties of Delinquent Behavior*," *American Sociological Review*, Vol. 16 (February 1951), pp. 10–13; Clinard, *Sociology*, pp. 122–25; and Richard M. Snodgrasse, "Crime and the Constitution Human: A Survey" *Journal of Criminal Law, Criminology and Police Science*, Vol. 42 (May–June 1951), pp. 18–52.

[88]Clinard, *Sociology* pp. 122–24.

[89]Ibid.

[90]The hope is to arrive at some understanding of how deviance might be "actualized" and not simply "predisposed" by these factors, if it can be proved that they do in fact predispose toward deviance.

[91]Nicholas N. Kittrie, "Will the XYY Syndrome Abolish Guilt?" *Federal Probation*, Vol. 35 (June 1971), pp. 26–31.

[92]Menachem Amir and Yitzchak Berman, "Chromosomal Deviation and Crime," *Federal Probation* (June 1970), pp. 55–62.

[93]Amir and Berman cite W. H. Price et al., "Criminal Patients with XYY Sex Chromosome Complement," *Lancet*, Vol. 1 (1966), and Richard G. Fox, "The XYY Offender: Modern Myth?" *Journal of Criminal Law, Criminology and Police Science* (March 1971),

[94]Amir and Berman, "Chromosomal Deviation," p. 58.

[95]Ibid., p. 60.

[96]Theodore R. Sarbin and Jeffrey E. Miller, "Demonism Revisited: The XYY Chromosomal Anomaly," *Issues in Criminology*, Vol. 5 (Summer 1970), pp. 195–207.

[97]Saleem A. Shah and Loren H. Roth, "Biological and Psychophysiological Factors in Criminality," in Daniel Glaser, ed., *Handbook of Criminology*. Chicago: Rand McNally, 1974, pp. 101–73.

[98]Ibid., pp. 136–37.

[99]See the explanation of "actualization" in Chapter 1.

[100]See Shah and Roth, "Biological . . . Factors."

SELECTED READINGS

1970   Thomas S. Szasz, *The Manufacture of Madness*. New York: Harper & Row.

1971   Kurt Seligmann, *Magic, Supernaturalism and Religion*. New York: Pantheon.

1918   Cesare Lombroso, *Crime: Its Causes and Remedies,* trans. by Henry P. Horton. Boston: Little, Brown.

1914   Henry Herbert Goddard, *Feeble-Mindedness, Its Causes and Consequences*. New York: Macmillan.

1949   William H. Sheldon, *Varieties of Delinquent Youth*. New York: Harper & Brothers.

1972   Juan B. Cortes with Florence M. Gatti, *Delinquency and Crime: A Biopsychosocial Approach*. New York: Seminar Press.

1971   Nicholas N. Kittrie, "Will the XYY Syndrome Abolish Guilt?" *Federal Probation,* Vol. 35 (June 1971), pp. 26–31.

1970   Theodore R. Sarbin and Jeffrey E. Miller "Demonism Revisited: The XYY Chromosomal Anomaly," *Issues in Criminology,* Vol. 5 (Summer 1970), pp. 195–207.

SELECTED APPLICATIONS

The following articles illustrate the more contemporary explanations for deviant behavior that posit an underlying biophysiological cause. Two selections discuss the XYY chromosome anomaly, one (Graham) taking a more positive position toward the scientific findings, the other (from Time) a more cautionary tone. The third selection is a newspaper article that reports the research findings linking hereditary factors to functional mental illness. The reader should note that in each article an underlying issue is the attribution of responsibility for the behavior in question.

CHROMOSOMES AND CRIME
J. A. Maxtone Graham

For many years, sociologists have believed that crime and delinquency are the result of environment. Now, according to a pair of Scottish doctors, it seems likely that a sizable proportion of hardened criminals have actually inherited their unfortunate characteristics.

According to Dr. William Price and Dr. Peter Whatmore, it is a matter of chromosomes. Chromosomes are vital to the transmission of hereditary characteristics; most of us have got 48 of them; according to their make-up, we are blue-eyed or red-haired, tall or southpaw, male or female.

It is the sex-determining chromosomes that Price and Whatmore have been examining. A child's mother always passes on a female (X) chromosome; the father can add either another X, making the child a girl, or a Y, which produces a boy. In biological shorthand, therefore, females are XX and males XY. The trouble comes when, by some inexplicable freak, a person inherits an *extra* sex chromosome. For instance, boys —perhaps one in every 1500—can inherit an extra X (female) chromosome, making them XXY's. These—"eunuchoid" males—have a tendency to breast development and infertility.

Recently, Price and Whatmore have been studying XYY's. These are those males—fewer than 1 in 2000—who have inherited an extra male (Y) chromosome. Dr. Whatmore works at Carstairs Hospital, Lanarkshire, Scotland, whose patients need special security on account of their dangerous or criminal propensities. The 342 inmates are mainly sexual deviants, alcoholics, firebugs, aggressive or inadequate psychopaths.

Blood tests showed that nine of them are XYY's—"double-males". A random control group of 18 normal XY's was taken from the rest of the hospital; for nearly three years the doctors then collected every possible detail about the past history of all 27 people—schooling, parentage, upbringing, social status and incidence of crime among relatives.

The results were startling. Among the 18 normal XY's, it was perfectly easy to account for their criminal past. There was a convincing history of crime among their 99 immediate relatives: in fact, families of seven of the XY patients shared as many as 139 convictions.

By contrast, among the XYY's, there was hardly a family crime pattern at all. There was no insanity or lawbreaking among the parents of these doubles-males, and only one of the three siblings had had a clash with the law—over the theft of $14 from an employer. They came from model families, modern homes and good schools. How, then, could these nine men have become committed so early to a life of crime, including assault, sexual offences against children and murder? (Their first conviction was at the average age of 13.1 years: among the XY's it was about 18.)

Genetic Irregularity   The Scots doctors are fairly sure that chromosome irregularity is the cause. They compare it with the Mongoloid condition in children which is also caused by unusual chromosome make-up. "The parents of Mongoloid children are perfectly normal," says Whatmore, "but when a Mongoloid baby is born it is possible to predict quite precisely the course of its development." So with the XYY's: unstable, irresponsible, unaffectionate, intolerant of frustration, with only a few utterly unrealistic plans for the future. They were persistent, recidivist criminals, working with little skill, and showing little financial gain. "The link with criminal violence is not firmly established yet," Dr. Whatmore continues, "but our experiments indicate a strong probability that can only be confirmed or denied by further studies." He would be glad to hear of parallel investigations being started in other countries.

If the studies do confirm such a link between unusual chromosomes and inexplicable crime, penologists will be able to screen recurrent lawbreakers from those whose environment sent them wrong and those who were born like that and couldn't help it. The former, presumably, could be cured; the latter, not. A cheap and simple blood test can quickly determine the pattern of a person's chromosomes. By passing a hollow needle through the wall of a pregnant woman's uterus, and withdrawing some amniotic fluid, it is even possible—although with some risk—to test the chromosome make-up of an unborn baby.

It might make strong ammunition for the eugenists, who could claim that violent criminals are thus detectable before birth. Other social and legal problems may arise: for example, will chromosome patterns be quoted by criminal "double-males" in court, to prove partial or complete lack of responsibility?

In the meantime, parents of XYY's can take comfort in only two things: the child can't help it, and it was no fault of either parent. The situation is the result of a tragically unfortunate draw in the biological lottery.

GENETICS:
Time Magazine

Of Chromosomes and Crime   A microscopic piece of genetic material known as the Y chromosomes made headlines last week. It is nothing new or rare; every man has one in practically every cell, or he would not be a man. But a few men have two. Richard Speck is said to be one such; his attorneys are now preparing an appeal against his death sentence for the 1966 slaying of eight nurses in Chicago. Another is Daniel Hugon, awaiting trial in Paris on a charge of having murdered a prostitute. His lawyers contend that he is mentally unfit to stand trial because of his chromosomal abnormality, and the Paris court has appointed a panel of experts, including both a psychiatrist and one of the world's most brilliant geneticists, Dr. Jérome Lejeune, to advise it.

The theory that a genetic abnormality may predispose a man to antisocial behavior, including crimes of violence , is deceptively and attractively simple, but will be difficult to prove. The argument in its favor rests upon the fact that in a few prisons sampled in the U.S., Britain and Australia, the proportion of inmates with an extra Y chromosome has been found to be higher than in the general population. The objections to the

Reprinted by permission from *Time,* The Weekly Newsmagazine. © *Time,* Inc., 1968.

theory are that no one knows the true incidence of the extra-Y abnormality, and that even when it is shown to exist, no one knows how the second Y can influence personality, let alone criminality.

Supermale?   Nature intended every man and woman to have 46 chromosomes per cell: 22 pairs of autosomes, which determine countless characteristics other than sex, and two gonosomes or sex chromosomes. In the female, these are a pair of Xs; in the male, an X and a Y. When a sperm fertilizes an ovum, each supplies half the 46 chromosomes for the combination of cells that will grow into a baby. If the sperm contains an X chromosome, the baby gets that X plus one from the mother, and will be an XX girl. If the sperm contains a Y chromosome, the baby gets that plus an X from the mother; the potent male Y overpowers the single X, and it's a boy—normally, XY.

But sometimes, when the first cells are dividing and both lines of chromosomes are supposed to make duplicates of themselves, nature slips up. Instead of splitting them into two neat rows of 23 each, it leaves an extra X or Y in one row. If the supernumerary is an X, the baby has an XXY pattern and will grow into a sterile, asthenic "male," usually with some breast enlargement and mental retardation—a condition that physicians call Klinefelter's syndrome. This has been recognized since 1959. Despite the factor of low intelligence, it has not been linked with criminality.

If the extra chromosome is a Y, the baby gets an XYY pattern and is unquestionably male. Or, as evidence gathered by an all-woman team of researchers in Scotland now suggests, he may be a supermale, overaggressive and potentially criminal. Dr. Patricia A. Jacobs and her colleagues working at Western General Hospital in Edinburgh knew that a number of mentally defective men with a double dose of both sex chromosomes, or XXYY, had been found in Swedish and English institutions as criminals or hard-to-manage inmates.[1] This made the researchers wonder whether it was the extra Y that predisposed the men to aggression. They decided to check on simpler, XYY cases, previously seldom reported.

Among 197 inmates at Carstairs State Hospital, they found no fewer than seven XYY men, or 3.5% (as well as one XXYY). This, they estimated, was 50 to 60 times the normal incidence. To check this estimate, the Edinburgh investigators examined 266 newborn boys and 209 adult men without finding a single XYY. In a random collection of 1,500 karyotypes, they found only one XYY.

The XYY inmates averaged 6 ft. 1 in. tall, whereas the average for other Carstairs inmates was 5 ft. 7 in. In Melbourne, Dr. Saul Wiener found that the same was true of four Australians, all XYY, who were doing time for murder, attempted murder or larceny. Dr. Mary A. Telfer of Pennsylvania's Elwyn Institute found five XYY abnormalities among 129 inmates of Pennsylvania prisons and penal hospitals selected for study because of their height.

Property Offenses.   The consensus so far among the few investigators who have studied the problem is that an extra Y chromosome seems to be associated with below-average intellignece, tall stature and severe acne—traits that might result from the hormone-stimulating effects of the duplicated chromosome. But little more is known about the Y chromosome's effects. Dr. William Price, who works with the research group in Edinburgh, doubts that the XYY pattern can be linked with crimes of violence or sex. Among the XYY men studied at Carstairs, he points out, the proportion whose offenses were against property—such as petty theft and house-breaking—was greater than that among convicts generally.

The XYY males, according to Price, do not suffer from brain damage, epilepsy, or any recognized psychosis such as schizophrenia. They are psychopaths, also called sociopaths—"unstable and immature, without feeling or remorse, unable to construct adequate personal relationships, showing a tendency to abscond from institutions and committing apparently motiveless crimes, mostly against property."

Scotland's XYY convicts tended to get into trouble earlier (around age 13) than the average (about 18). But among their siblings there was an unusually low incidence of criminality. And in the only case so far reported of an XYY with several children, the abnormality was not transmitted: an Oregon XYY has had six sons, but all have a normal XY, pattern.

---

[1]Chromosome patterns or "karyotypes" are usually made by taking white blood cells, growing them in the laboratory and dousing them with a weak salt solution. This explodes the cells, separating the chromosomes. These are stained, spread on a slide and photographed. From an enlargement, pairs of chromosomes are laboriously cut out, paper-doll fashion, lined up by size and shape in seven groups, and numbered from one to 22 (the "Denver classification"). X and Y are usually placed at the end.

SCHIZOPHRENIA IS INHERITED, RESEARCHER SAYS
Chicago Sun-Times

A psychiatrist who just finished a study of the inheritance factor says schizophrenia is hereditary and not produced by environment.

"Just as tall parents have tall children, schizophrenic parents prod·ice schizophrenic children," Dr. Paul Wender said.

Wender, professor of psychiatry at the University of Utah College of Medicine, said his study of adopted children in Denmark deals a

---

From the Chicago Sun-Times, August 18,1974. Reprinted by permission of United Press International.

serious blow to the idea that schizophrenia—one of the most common mental illnesses—is caused by environmental factors.

"This study may get psychiatrists and social workers off the backs of parents with mentally ill children," Wender said. "For years they have been blaming parents for destroying the mental health of their children."

"This attitude is incorrect, cruel and hurts the chances of the children for getting treatment."

Wender and four other doctors begun the study in 1963 using former mental patients in Denmark as test subjects. Denmark keeps detailed records of persons hospitalized for mental disorders, and the team chose 79 parents who showed symptoms of schizophrenic disorders.

The research team located, interviewed and tested these patients' children, who had been placed for adoption as infants. The study found definite evidence of schizophrenia among these children—even if they had been reared by normal parents.

The study then looked at 30 children who had normal natural parents but who had been reared by schizophrenic adoptive parents. The results showed that these children were no more psychologically ill than children whose natural and adoptive parents were psychologically healthy.

And, he said, the results remained the same when the team studied adults, both schizophrenic and normal, who had been adopted as children.

Wender defined the chronic schizophrenic as "the typical state hospital psychotic" who has a history of social maladjustment, exhibits periods of confusion and often suffers from delusions and hallucinations.

He said severe cases usually can be treated, "but they seldom get back into the mainstream of society." However, he said, studying the schizophrenic may help identify the "borderline" schizophrenic.

"This could be of considerable importance because so-called borderline schizophrenia affects between 5 and 10 per cent of the population," he said.

He said the borderline schizophrenic often is considered eccentric, has trouble relating to others and suffers from chronic mild depression. "But if we can identify these people through the study of records and relatives, we may be able to help them before they become really schizophrenic," he said.

Wender said the same techniques—studying parents and then looking at the behavior of children adopted into a different environment—may be used to study other human problems. "Other researchers have taken the idea we began with and are now studying alcoholism and even criminality to see if there is a genetic correlation," he said.

CHAPTER 4

SOCIOLOGICAL THEORIES OF PREDISPOSITION

In the period immediately following World War I, social scientists in Europe and America initiated an extensive examination of the relationship of numerous social factors to social deviation. Many were influenced by perspectives of scholars like Emile Durkheim, which deemphasized the importance of biophysiological, medical, and psychological explanations. Others were influenced by theoretical developments in such areas as urban sociology and demography.[1] Still others became interested in the role of class and culture conflict in the genesis of deviant behavior, some taking a decidedly Marxist approach to "social problems" in general. Although they more often disagreed about particulars, their common goal became the theoretical and empirical exploration of the "social environment" to ascertain what factors within it could predispose an individual to engage in antisocial or deviant behavior. The primary question of their analyses was what causes deviation from social norms? The answers, they were convinced, could best be sought *outside* of the individual and the act of deviation itself. This general mode of analysis became predominant in the sociology of deviation in the decades following 1920.

Three sets of explanatory variables came to dominate the attention of social scientists during this period: (1) ecological and demographic factors; (2) social-structural and social-systems factors; and (3) culture-value and value-conflict factors of predisposition. These are not entirely mutually exclusive sets of factors, but there are rather distinct traditions of scholarship that emphasized one set over the others. Each orientation included many suborientations, with their own nuances of perspective and the different types of deviant behavior that they meant to explain. We will now examine the theoretical perspectives that continue to play a major role in the sociology of deviant behavior.

ECOLOGICAL AND DEMOGRAPHIC THEORIES: THE CHICAGO SCHOOL TRADITION

In 1925 Robert E. Park, Ernest W. Burgess, and Roderick D. McKenzie published one of the earliest and most influential texts on urban sociology, *The City*. This book contained essays dealing with the ecological perspective on the urban community and a variety of urban issues. "Ecology," a term borrowed from the biological sciences, is the study of the relationship of living organisms to their physical environment. The authors of *The City* were convinced that the physical environment of the city was interwoven with the sociocultural patterns of the urban population and urban life. The physical organization of the city was both a reflection and product of human nature. That physical organization, in turn, had a profound influence on the sociocultural patterns of urban life. The "Chicago School" urbanologists, as they came to be known, shared an interest in the relationship of the city's physical structure to the moral order that was influenced by it. In particular, they were interested in the relationships between urbanism, "natural areas," and social disorganization.[2]

Ernest W. Burgess described the city as composed of natural areas, which were not randomly distributed but developed in an orderly, predictable fashion. These natural areas were represented as concentric zones that served to schematize the growth of the metropolis. With Chicago as his laboratory, Burgess proposed his general theory of urban growth,[3] as shown in Figure 4-1.

Robert E. Park stressed the importance of studying what he called the "moral regions" of a city.[4] These are urban regions in which, Park believed, the inhibitions and suppressions of natural impulses and instincts are relaxed and deviation is more likely. These areas gave licence to nonconforming behavior. Park posed the following questions as a general design for research on these "moral regions."

Investigations of the problems involved might well begin by a

Figure 4–1   Natural Areas and Urban Zones

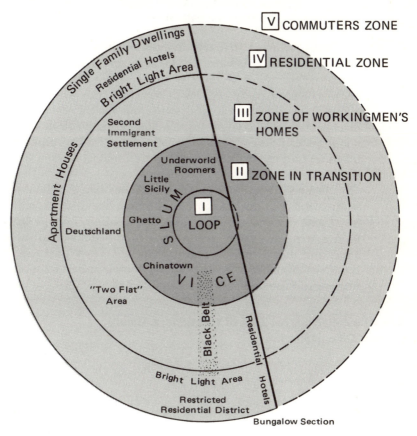

Adapted with permission from *The City* by Robert E. Park, Ernest W. Burgess, and Roderick D. McKenzie (Chicago: The University of Chicago Press, 1925), p. 55

study and comparison of the characteristic types of social organization which exist in the regions referred to.

What are the external facts in regard to the life in Bohemia, the half world, the red-light district, and other "moral regions" less pronounced in character?

What is the nature of the vocations which connect themselves with the ordinary life of these regions? What are the characteristic mental types which are attracted by the freedom which they offer?

How do individuals find their way into these regions? How do they escape from them?

To what extent are the regions referred to the product of the licence; to what extent are they due to the restrictions imposed by city life on the natural man?[5]

Park believed that the analysis of these "moral regions," and thus of deviant behavior, would help reveal the impact of social–spatial organization of the city upon its inhabitants. These "moral regions" were natural regions of the city. They were not necessarily abnormal in the pathological sense, but rather regions "in which a divergent moral code prevails."[6] Since these regions demonstrated one significant side of man's human nature, Park recommended them to students of the urban community as a vital laboratory for sociological analysis.

From 1915 to 1940 students of these Chicago School sociologists studied the relationship of rates of crime, delinquency, suicide, mental illness, divorce and desertion, prostitution, homosexuality, alcoholism, drug addiction, and other deviant behavior to these natural areas and moral regions within the city.[7] Their goal was to understand the influence of ecological and demographic factors on community organization and disorganization.

Social Deviation and the Zone of Transition: A Theory of Social Disorganization

There are numerous similarities in the research reports and findings of Chicago School sociologists who studied deviant behavior. Most reports contain maps of the city of Chicago upon which are presented the rates of deviant behavior (in the 1920s and 1930s) obtained from various municipal agencies and departments. These can be admission rates to mental hospitals, rates of delinquency or crime obtained from the courts or police department, or rates of divorce obtained from the courts. No matter what the deviation, the indicators used for it, or the source of the statistics, almost invariably the highest rates of deviant behavior are to be found in the midsection of the city, in the area referred to as the Zone of Transition. In most cases, moral regions were found here. The fascination that this finding had for these social scientists was due to its theoretical relevance. No matter what ethnic, racial, or religious groups inhabited the Zone of Transition, the rates of deviation that these investigators used as indicators remained high. Because the rates did not vary markedly with changes in the composition of the population, something about the natural area itself must predispose individuals to engage in deviant behavior.

One of the most popular studies in this series of publications was Robert E. L. Faris and H. Warren Dunham's *Mental Disorders in*

Urban Areas: An Ecological Study of Schizophrenia and Other Psychoses (1939). It claimed to be the first study to show that urban areas characterized by high rates of social disorganization also evidence high rates of mental disorganization. The authors claimed that functional mental impairments like schizophrenia are distributed in a nonrandom spatial pattern throughout the city. Using admission statistics for state mental hospitals, they demonstrated that the highest rates are found in the Zone of Transition, in the area just outside the central core. In addition, this research report showed that rates of alcoholic psychoses and drug addiction were also highest in this zone and became less pronounced in the outlying zones.[8] What was there about the Zone of Transition that led to these high rates of deviant behavior?

In analyzing the high rates of schizophrenia in this zone, the authors indicate that "seclusiveness" and "isolation" seem to underly this clinical condition. This isolation is produced, in turn, by some interference with normal social contacts. A major characteristic of the Zone of Transition is that the mobility of its population—the in- and out-migration of persons—makes it very difficult to form social relationships. Where the population is transient, social contacts are superficial and lack those attributes that Cooley felt belong to "primary relations"—intimacy, face-to-face association, and cooperation.[9] The Zone of Transition is characterized by secondary relations, in which impersonalism, distrust, suspicion, and social distance and lack of social contact predominate. Alienation becomes a distinct possibility, and disorders like schizophrenia become more likely. Other Chicago School scholars such as Cavan (1928), Anderson (1923), Wirth (1926), and Zorbaugh (1927), attributed the same role to these characteristics in the genesis of suicide, hoboism, delinquency, and criminal behavior.

Migration and cultural succession were not the only characteristics of the Zone of Transition that were related to high rates of social deviation. Population instability, when combined with population density, low family income, deteriorated housing conditions, and low levels of educational attainment, were considered major predisposing factors toward community disorganization and individual deviation. E. Franklin Frazier, in *The Negro Community in Chicago* (1932), another publication in the Chicago School tradition, indicated that behavior characteristics usually attributed to blacks, such as crime, delinquency, vice, illegitimacy, and desertion, are more a function of geography and ecological patterning than of race. The "black belt" in Chicago in the 1920s and 1930s was the southern half of the Zone of Transition, and Frazier maintained that the social disorganization of the black community was a direct result of the problem-producing characteristics generally present in the zone.[10]

Juvenile Delinquency

Of the many specific types of social deviation analyzed by scholars in the Chicago School tradition, juvenile delinquency was probably the most intensively studied. Frederic M. Thrasher, Clifford R. Shaw, and Henry McKay were Chicago School sociologists who were primarily interested in the ecological basis of juvenile delinquency.[11] Thrasher's classic study *The Gang* (1927) was the first of a long series of publications that related juvenile delinquency to the general social disorganization of the Zone of Transition. Thrasher studied 1,313 gangs in what he called the "socially interstitial" area in this city.

> In nature foreign matter tends to collect and cake in every crack, crevice, and cranny—interstices. There are also fissures and breaks in the structure of social organization. The gang may be regarded as an interstitial element in the framework of society and gangland as an interstitial region in the layout of the city.[12]

The very first chapter of this book, in fact, is not on gangs per se, but on "gangland," the geographic regions in which gangs are found. As Thrasher pointed out, "Gangland is a phenomenon of human ecology."[13] The gang is a response to the sociocultural disorganization present within the Zone of Transition:

> The gang functions with reference to these conditions in two ways: It offers a substitute for what society fails to give, and it provides a relief from suppression and distasteful behavior. It fills a gap and affords an escape. Here again we may conceive of it as an interstitial group providing interstitial activities for its members. Thus the gang, itself a natural and spontaneous type of organization arising through conflict, is a symptom of disorganization in the larger social framework.[14]

The disorganization of the Zone of Transition was, as Thrasher put it, the soil that favored the growth of delinquency, vice, and ganging. In *The Gang,* Thrasher gave students of juvenile delinquency one of the earliest and most extensive detailed accounts of how these factors of community disorganization influence the lives of gang members.

In the 1930s and 1940s Clifford Shaw and Henry McKay continued the exploration of the ecological base of juvenile delinquency. The Chicago Area Project, created in the early 1930s, was designed to carry out basic research on the causes, treatment, and prevention of juvenile delinquency. The project was comprehensive and enlisted the participation of researchers, correction-department workers, students, neighborhood residents, and the delinquent boys themselves. Shaw and Meyer (1929) and Shaw and McKay (1931) indicated that juvenile delinquency had a definite geographical distribution throughout the city. Initially studying about 60,000 males who had been dealt with by various agencies as alleged truants, delinquents, or criminals, the authors were able to demonstrate clearly that the Zone of Transition contained the highest concentration of juvenile delinquents. Other areas with high rates of delinquency were also "interstitial" areas that shared the same sociolcultural conditions as the Zone of Transition. Shaw and McKay (1939) confirmed Thrasher's thesis that physical deterioration of housing, sharply decreasing population rates, low economic status, presence of foreign-born and black populations, and cultural succession (rapid in- and out-migrations of ethnic and racial groups) were related to delinquency and other forms of social deviation.[15]

Shaw and McKay believed that delinquency was related to the process of city growth. The invasion of industry and commerce and the succession of populations bring about low rent and deteriorating housing. This brings in families with the lowest economic status. These communities were characterized by an "absence of concerted collective action toward the solution of common problems."[16] The authors state:

> Underlying the present study of juvenile delinquency is the basic assumption that stable habits and attitudes in the child develop under the influence of a relatively stable and consistent set of social standards. Where the routine of social life is broken up by any form of rapid change and the child is subjected to the influence of a great variety of divergent and conflicting standards of conduct, the problem of developing a stable life organization is extremely difficult. As we have already suggested, the social life in the deteriorated and disorganized areas of Chicago fails to provide a sufficiently consistent set of conventional values for the development of stable and socially approved forms of behavior among children. In the natural process of city growth the conventional traditions and neighborhood organization tend to disintegrate in these areas. This process of social disorganization and the consequent breakdown of neighborhood control is accentuated by the influx of large foreign and racial groups with varied cultural backgrounds. . . .
>
> In this chaotic and confused situation it is not surprising that many of the children fail to acquire an attitude of respect for the law and the traditions of conventional society.[17]

Deviation, in short, was the product of a series of ecosocial forces and processes. Invasion and succession led to the physical disorganization of the community. These conditions, in turn, brought about social disorganization and inadequate normative controls. This series of forces and processes outlined, if not the direction of "cause," then at least the direction of influence in the genesis of deviation. The authors were understandably cautious in attributing a causal role to specific ecological variables. It is clear from the context of their analysis, however, that "cause" is in fact what they meant when the play of these factors on deviation was considered as a whole. These basic findings were again corroborated by the authors in 1942 and by McKay in 1969.[18]

Some Problems with the Ecological Perspective

Other urban ecologists have taken notable exception to the nature of this relationship between ecological area, social disorganization, and deviance. Ronald Freedman (1950), in a study of migration to Chicago, questioned the finding that indices of social disorganization decrease with distance from the center of the city and that population succession, mobility, and migration are closely related to patterns of specific types of social disorganization. Freedman found that when black-population statistics are eliminated from the analysis and we only look at "white" areas and population statistics, there is no statistically significant relationship between intracity migration and rates of juvenile delinquency. He also states, that "the correlation of juvenile delinquency rates with the inter-city migrant rate is not significantly different from zero. . . .[19] This is true even when black population statistics are included. In other words, population succession does not have a clearcut relationship to rates of juvenile delinquency.

Freedman also questioned the findings of Faris and Dunham that rates of schizophrenic psychoses are positively related to ecological areas with high rates of population succession. Although he did not invalidate the hypotheses that schizophrenic disorders are related to the social isolation produced by excessive mobility, he indicated that his data showed no necessary relationship between schizophrenia and inter- or intracity residential mobility. These are the indicators that have traditionally been used to measure population succession.[20]

Sociologists of a nonecological persuasion have also questioned the basic theoretical tenets of the Chicago School. For example, some have argued that high rates of delinquency in the center city and high rates of admission to mental hospitals for Zone of Transition residents result from societal reaction policies and the social-class characteristics of those labeled as deviant. Juveniles of *all* social classes and in all areas commit delinquent acts, but only some are caught and get their names placed in juvenile-court records. The mentally ill who come from high income areas seek private facilities and care and are not likely to show up in the admission records of public mental-health facilities (the source for mental illness statistics in the Faris and Dunham study). In other words, the high rates of deviation in the Zone of Transition can be explained by variables other than those central to ecological theory. Even if we grant that there is a rather distinct ecological patterning to types of social deviation, the explanations for these ecological distributions (population succession, invasion of industry, deterioration of housing, social isolation, inadequacy of traditional values as reference models for behavior) can be questioned. What we need are studies that more clearly demonstrate how these factors relate to the actualization of specific types of social deviation.

A general problem with these ecological interpretations is their reliance on indicators that depend on official statistics and thus on recognized deviation. Contemporary analysts have indicated the problems of using official rates.[21] For some varieties of deviation—homosexuality and alcoholism, for example—there are no reliable statistics for the incidence or prevalence of these behaviors in the community. These are, after all, examples of secretive behavior. Even if these behaviors were less secretive, there is considerable evidence that the explanations proffered by Chicago School analysts do not apply. This is not to say that there is no ecological or demographic patterning of social deviation—as, for example, homosexuality. Research evidence shows that there are neighborhoods in our larger cities where homosexuals tend to congregate and in which they have higher concentrations.[22] The traditional explanations for social disorganization do not, however, readily apply to homosexuality and other forms of behavior judged to be deviant.

A distinction has to be made between the ecological and demographic patternings of deviation and the social-disorganization theory used by Chicago School analysts to explain deviation. Again, much more research is needed before the claims of the social-disorganization theory for specific kinds of behavior can be validated. In fairness to the Chicago School analysts of juvenile delinquency, the studies of the social conditions in which gang formation takes place has become the basis of most contemporary discussions of delinqeuncy and gang behavior. The social-disoganization theories of the Chicago School are most directly applicable to gang formation.

Population Density

In recent years, ecological analysts have focused on other eco-demographic variables as possible causes of deviation. The original group of Chicago School scholars emphasized the decrease or increase of population size in a given area as the factor leading to social disorganization and deviance. Shaw and McKay, in their analyses of delinquency in Chicago, indicated that delinquency areas were marked by decreasing populations, which they attributed to the invasion of industry and the deterioration of housing.[23] Little attention was given to the influence of population density itself. The Chicago School scholars were more interested in the effect that the *rate of change* in population size had on social disorganization than the influence that *high concentrations of population* had on the genesis of deviant behavior.

The research of contemporary ecological analysts on animal as well as human populations has pointed to *population density* itself as a causal factor in social disorganization. Using such measures as the number of persons per room, the number of rooms per housing unit, the number of housing units per structure, and the number of structures per acre, they have reported a positive relationship between density or overcrowding and rates of juvenile delinquency and admissions to mental hospitals. Galle, Gove, and McPherson (1972) point out that persons per room is one of the best predictors of "social pathology" (juvenile delinquency and mental illness). They point out that

> as the number of persons in a dwelling increases, so will the number of social obligations, as well as the need to inhibit individual desires. This escalation of both social demands and the need to inhibit desires would become particularly problematic when people are crowded together in a dwelling with a high ratio of persons per room. Second, crowding will bring with it a marked increase in stimuli that are difficult to ignore. Third, if human beings, like many animals, have a need for territory or privacy, then overcrowding may, in fact, conflict with a basic (biological?) characteristic of man.[24]

The authors add that irritability, meanness, and withdrawal are just a few of the possible reactions to these conditions of overcrowding and that these and other psychosocial factors can lead to social pathology. Based on their own research findings, they indicate that juvenile delinquency, in particular, is influenced by population density.

The relationship between population density, emotional strain, and family disorganization (important intervening variables in the relationship between density and deviation, according to proponents of this perspective) has been questioned by Mitchell (1971) in his study of high-density housing in Hong Kong. Mitchell indicates that high density has little effect on individuals and families, although he points out that there is some loss of parental control over children.[25]

It is possible that Mitchell's findings reflect a difference in the spatial requirements or the social meaning of space to cultural and ethnic groups. Cultural factors may be only one of many sets of intervening variables that mediate the influence or lack of influence of eco-demographic variables like population density. We still require studies that carefully examine the interaction effects that exist or do not exist between ecodemographic variables and those of social structure, culture, interaction, and learning. How all these variables influence each other and, in turn, relate to deviation has still to be studied by sociologists.

SOCIAL DISORGANIZATION AND DEVIATION: A REVIEW

Let us step back at this point and review the social-disorganization theory, which is central to the explanatory framework of the Chicago School studies. Natural, interstitial, and moral areas in the city—most notably, the Zone of Transition—are characterized by the presence of specific ecodemographic processes: invasion of industry, high levels of population succession or migration rates, deterioration of housing, and high population density. These ecodemographic factors help to bring about several social and social-psychological "conditions." Somehow the ecological and demographic instability of the area causes a disruption in the functional ability of community institutions, including the family, to control the behavior of residents. The traditional values of ethnic culture no longer have the same force of persuasion, and children in particular are forced into a position of marginality. They lack the group identifications and allegiances that are conducive to behavior the conventional society finds "acceptable." In some cases, neighborhood play groups or peer groups fill the void that has been created and offer solutions to this marginal existence— solutions that lead to delinquent behavior. In situations in which no group is present to act as a reference point for behavior, continuing isolation and seclusiveness can lead to schizophrenic psychoses, alcoholism, drug use (Faris and Dunham), or suicide (Cavan). There is some opposition between these claims and the explanations given for the same deviant behaviors by proponents of population density. An increase in population density results in social obligations and demands, overstimulation, and lack of privacy. Thus ecodemographic analysts of deviation and social disorganization seem to be saying that either extreme understimulation (social isolation) or extreme overstimulation (such as the violation of personal-space requirements) can bring about mental illness, suicide, and alcoholism.

An extensive literature in the sociology of deviation and in related fields indicates that the ecodemographic theory of social disorganization and deviation is very plausible. As a theory of predisposition it ranks as one of the most clearly conceived and extensively researched explanations of deviant behavior. However, it shares the same major shortcomings with other theories of predisposition. (1) It fails to demonstrate the *necessary* relationship between these explaining variables and deviation. (2) It does not tell us why only some of the many who are subject to the same disorganizing conditions become deviant. Therefore it lacks the ultimate quality of "sufficiency." (3) It fails to adequately explain why those who are not subject to these conditions become deviant. (4) It does not account for the influence of intervening factors, such as the selection bias of the societal reaction to deviation and the consequence of using suspicious statistical rates of deviation on which to base the supposed ecodemographic patterning. (5) Most significantly, such explanations remain incomplete, for they fail to bridge the gap between predisposition and actualization—they do not tell us how deviant behavior actually comes about.

AMERICAN STRUCTURAL-FUNCTIONALISM: ANOTHER APPROACH TO SOCIAL DISORGANIZATION

The 1930s and 1940s were marked by the appearance of a structural–functional perspective on social disorganization. Its American proponents, in many ways the disciples of Durkheim, formulated an elaborate model of the functioning of social systems that took a decidedly macroscopic and "sociologistic" view of the genesis of social deviation. Deviation was considered the by-product of a social system out of kilter; a system forced into a state of imbalance. Functionalist theory incorporated a model of society and of social relationships that emphasized the structural bases of social disorganization.

The functionalist perspective, like the ecological, depended heavily on biological analogy for its underlying assumptions. Unlike the ecological framework, which emphasized a processual analysis of change in the socioecological order (development, growth, succession, invasion, decay, and deterioration), the functionalist model borrowed a structural and functional analog from biology. Essentially social systems, like biological organisms, were said to be composed of many interdependent parts or structures. For the heart, brain, and lungs the functionalists substituted various types of groups, institutions, and subsystems. Each of these parts had its unique functions, but they shared an ultimate purpose: to maintain the social system. System maintenance (preservation of the social order) was a major feature of the *organismic analogy*. Societies were seen as "naturally" in a state of order and organization until the malfunctioning of the substructures upset the system's precarious balance, or "homeostasis."[26]

The functionalist model thus emphasized the significance of conformity to the prevailing normative order. It assumed that allegiance to institutional structures contributed to the fulfillment of social-system requisites. The values and norms of a society were seen as the bonds that held together the social structure. This theoretical framework was thus, in a literal sense, "conservative"; its central assumption was the *necessity* of conserving the structural basis of society. A major question for functional theorists was what system factors or forces could cause an imbalance in this natural equilibrium. They were also concerned with explaining the linkages between the more general conditions of disorganization and the behavior of deviants. Finally, as Durkheim himself had suggested, the discovery of the latent or underlying functions of deviation in its "normal" representations became a popular theme and many explanations went well beyond the function of boundary maintenance.

Representative Structural-Functionalist Analysis

The structural–functional perspective on social disorganization has its foundations in the writings of Durkheim. In *Suicide,* Durkheim stressed the significance of "social integration" as the major social explanation of social disorganization and suicide rates. Social integration refers to the "inter-connectedness" of social-system parts. At the individual level of behavior, it refers to the extent to which the actor feels a part of relationships and associations in the social order.

American structural–functionalists also became interested in the role of "social integration" in the genesis of individual and group deviation. Like Durkheim, they assumed that individuals who were sufficiently integrated into group and community life, who were "properly" socialized to accept the dominant or traditional values of their society would be its norm-abiding members. Deviants were thus assumed to be inadequately socialized and to be alienated from the institutionalized norms and values of a society.

Like Durkheim, these sociologists were primarily concerned with rates or collective representations of deviant behavior. However, American structural–functionalists were also concerned with bridging the theoretical gap between disorganization, disequilibrium, and individual deviation—that is, between social structure and individual behavior. The general structural–functional model formulated by the American sociologist Talcott Parsons was not, by itself, able to explain these theoretical linkages.[27] The general theory could not explain where the critical disorganization or disequilibrium lay, nor was it able to specify how these directly influenced the behavior of drug users, mental patients, delinquents, and criminals. What was needed was a more focused theory—a theory of the "middle range"—that explained individual deviation based on the assumptions of the structural–functional perspective.[28] Into this theoretical void stepped a student of Parsons, Robert K. Merton.

Social Structure and Anomie

Merton, in his classic essay "Social Structure and Anomie" (1938), characterized deviation as the individual adaptation to pressures that emanate from the social structure.[29] But what were these pressures exerted by the social structure? Merton initially postulated the existence of a *cultural structure* and a *social structure*. The cultural structure offered members the legitimate objectives, goals, and values of that society: in our own culture these would include financial success, prestige in the eyes of others, and living the "good life"—that is, the extreme emphasis upon achievement. The social structure supplies members with legitimate means for achieving these goals and objectives. Merton writes:

> It is, indeed, my central hypothesis that aberrant behavior may be regarded sociologically as a symptom of dissociation between culturally prescribed aspirations and socially structured avenues for realizing these aspirations.[30]

The underlying assumption of this perspective is that most members of the society share these cultural objectives and values. The most significant differential is individual access to the socially prescribed and structured means to attain these culturally designated goals. The perspective further holds that individuals who are blocked from these legitimate means will turn to alternative and illegitimate means. Thus, the basis of social disorganization is the differential opportunity structure. Therefore, social disorganization is lodged in the disjunction between the success values of a society and the institutional structures that control access to these opportunity channels. Social-class position and attendant social-stratification factors become the major independent variables.

However, the problem of *individual* deviant behavior remained. How is the individual influenced by this disequilibrium between the structural components of society? Merton indicated that the individual's acceptance or rejection of these cultural goals and institutionalized means would reveal their behavioral patterning or adaptation to this disequilibrium. Five modes of adaptation were logically possible:[31]

Figure 4-2   Modes of Individual Adaptation

	Culture Goals	Institutionalized Means
1. Conformity	+	+
2. Innovation	+	−
3. Ritualism	−	+
4. Retreatism	−	−
5. Rebellion	±	±

KEY:

+ = acceptance
− = rejection
± = reject old and substitute new

Innovation   The most common variety of deviation is the "innovation" response or adaptation. Many juvenile delinquents and adult criminals, according to Merton, have internalized the culture's success goals but have not internalized the norms that designate the acceptable means for attaining those goals.[32] Their delinquency or criminality functions as an alternative means to attain the goals of financial success and prestige. For lower-class delinquents and criminals, blockage of the means to educational and occupational opportunities produces anomic conditions, which are resolved by the rejection of these institutionalized means. Merton points out that middle- and upper-class crime also evidences an innovation mode of adaptation. At these levels, access to the opportunity structure through educational and occupational attainment is not so much at issue as the inability of legitimate structures to offer even greater opportunities for financial gain, prestige, and power. Innovation, however, is more significantly related to the sociocultural conditions of the lower classes. According to Merton:

> Whatever the differential rates of deviant behavior in the several social strata, and we know from many sources that the official crime statistics uniformly showing higher rates in the lower strata are far from complete or reliable, it appears from our analysis that the greatest pressures toward deviation are exerted upon the lower strata.[33]

Merton adds that the status of the unemployed and unskilled or low-skilled laborer and their low income "cannot readily compete in terms of *established standards of worth* with the promises of power and high income from organized vice, rackets and crime."[34]

Ritualism   The individual adaptation that Merton termed "ritualism" is not clearly related to the deviant behaviors usually studied by the sociologist. When the individual rejects the culturally prescribed goals, but maintains or accepts the institutionalized means to obtain them, we can speak only of an overconformity that might seem odd to some. This adaptation, though one of the logical behavior patterns in Merton's typology, does very little to explain the relationship between social structure and deviation.

Retreatism   "Retreatism," however, has a more direct relation to the deviant behaviors that members of society consider significant. The retreatist abandons both the prescribed cultural goals and the institutionalized means for attaining them. In effect, this is the "drop-out" adaptation. The individual withdraws from the social game, so to speak. As Merton points out:

> People who adapt (or maladapt) in this fashion are, strictly speaking, *in* the society but not *of* it.[35]

This category includes outcasts, hobos, vagrants, drug addicts, chronic alcoholics, some suicides, "psychotics," and "autists." This person must contend with anomic forces that produce defeatism and resignation and that lead to "escapist" solutions. Escape seems possible with the renunciation of both means and goals. The hobo or skid-row derelict has been depicted in both popular and sociological literature as one who, after repeated failures to attain cultural goals, resigns himself to his inability to succeed and "shucks it all." He gives up the "rat race" for the street culture of the "bottle gang" and perhaps the compatriotism of fellow "drop-outs."[36] According to Merton this mode of adaptation is, however, a "privatized" rather than a collective mode of adaptation.[37] Isolation is the more usual social condition of this behavioral pattern; perhaps the typical representative of this category is the lower-class heroin addict.

Rebellion   "Rebellion" leads those who reject the society's goals and means to create new goals and values and a new opportunity structure that will permit their realization. In this day of urban guerillas, liberation fronts, and terrorists, it is surprising that sociologists have not adequately studied this behavioral pattern. Of all the major types of deviant behavior in Merton's typology, this has been most neglected.

Rebellion, according to Merton's analysis, should not be viewed only as a revolutionary reaction to the state by organized political extremists. He also includes certain types of gang delinquency in this category. However, he clearly indicates that rebellion should not be confused with what others have termed "resentment"—a sour-grapes hostility toward the establishment because one feels unable to live up to the culture's values.[38] Rebellion is a genuine substitution of new goals, values, and the institutionalized means of attaining them. Not all gangs, guerilla groups, or revolutionaries want to change both the means and the ends. In rebellion, anomie arises from the frustrations encountered not only in the opportunity structure of society, but also —and more basically—in the rejection of the values and goals to which that opportunity structure is oriented.

Merton's individual-adaptation model of social deviation assumes that the competitive economic system, with its differential-opportunity structure, produces a strain toward anomie. Although Merton mentions other cultural values like intellectual achievement, artistic creativity, and success as alternative goals, he assumes that monetary success is the primary value orientation of our culture. Like Durkheim before him, Merton was convinced that a proportion of the deviation produced by these pressures and strains was normal, and that therefore the individual adaptations to them were equally normal. Merton, like Durkheim, also fails to distinguish adequately between normal and pathological collective representations of these individual adaptations to anomie. When does the *rate* of deviation indicate that social-structural pressures have become symptomatic of genuine social pathology? Again, structural–functional formulations fail to tell us.

As a theory of predisposition, Merton's perspective singles out the class structure of society (the individual's position within it), poverty, and economically based oppression as the major predisposing variables. In this respect, it has some limited affinity with Marxist explanations of deviant behavior. Wilhelm Bonger, the Dutch criminologist and a contemporary of Durkheim, had also indicated that social-class and economic oppression were at the source of criminal and deviant behavior.[39]

Merton's perspective differs fundamentally from Marxist explanations, for it sees the class-based social structure as functional for the maintenance of society. Although Merton and his followers observe the problems inherent in a class system that is theoretically open, but in reality evidences obstacles to mobility, they view the class system as inevitable. The differential-opportunity structure is considered a positively functioning stimulus for societal maintenance.

Some Problems with the Anomie Theory

Merton's theory places an extreme emphasis on lower-class deviation and on deviation that has an obvious origin in alienation from a success-oriented society. It fails to give an adequate explanation for the criminal activities of the middle class and elite, as well as for such forms of deviant behavior as homosexuality that have a more homogeneous distribution.

A major problem with Merton's perspective is that it was initially based on the "facts" of deviation normally found in official statistics on crime and delinquency. These statistics and official rates of deviation are weighted in favor of just those activities that are found in the lower strata of the society. The Crime Index of the FBI and of local law-enforcement agencies, in fact, include none of the white-collar crimes that one would find among the middle and upper classes.[40] As the next section of this chapter will show, the same problems are found in studies that have attempted to relate social class to other varieties of deviant behavior. The reliance on official rates has a biasing effect on the formulation of theory and empirical investigation.[41]

The major theoretical problem with Merton's structural–functional model is its implication of a structural determinism in the genesis of deviant behavior. This is very questionable. The implicit notions of socialization in this perspective give the actor the appearance of a nonparticipating, acted-upon object whose fate is a function of his position in the social structure. This model leaves little room for *true* individual adaptation based upon subjective interpretations of situations in which deviation is likely. It thus fails to account for a series of possible intervening variables that adequately portray deviation as the interactive, interpersonal, socially meaningful phenomenon it seems to be. Merton's individual adaptations are merely the logical outcomes of determinants already deemed significant.

Merton's model does not tell us how and why these individual adaptations are actualized by particular individuals. Why do some who are subject to these same structural conditions and anomic forces not succumb to deviant adaptations, and why do some of those who are not subject to them become deviant? Is social deviation necessarily related to anomic forces? Again, as we have found for other theories of predisposition, these essential questions remain virtually unanswered. Merton fails to give an adequate portrayal of the socialization process whereby the goals, values, and modes of adaptation are assimilated and deviant behavior is actualized. Without this there can be no adequate understanding of the relationship between social structure, anomie, and individual deviation.[42]

Functionalist Interpretations

In addition to Merton's extension of the Durkheimian structural-functional perspective on social deviation, other sociologists also contributed to aspects of the original model. Durkheim had insisted that all normal social facts were by definition functional or useful for the maintenance of some part of the social order. Social deviation, as a normal collective representation, maintained the boundaries between acceptable and nonacceptable behavior. This perspective stressed the significance of the *underlying* function of social practices, behaviors, and structural entities. Merton labeled such functions *latent functions* and distinguished these from *manifest functions,* which are more direct and recognized consequences of these phenomena.[43]

Kingsley Davis outlined the latent functions of prostitution.[44] He claimed that prostitution was an institution whose function had been little understood by its moral critics. Davis noted that prostitution, as a sexual institution, shared much in common with other, more "respected" sexual institutions, such as engagement and marriage.

Davis claimed that all sexual institutions (on a continuum from marriage to prostitution) provide sexual gratification but that they differ in the way they relate to specific social functions. The social functions of marriage and the family are more obvious: they organize the procreative and socialization requirements of society so that clear-cut and exclusive responsibility, as well as behavioral restrictions, are assigned to family members. Davis points out that

> commercial prostitution stands at the lowest extreme; it shares with other sexual institutions a basic feature, namely the employment of sex for an ulterior end in a system of differential advantages, but it differs from them in being mercenary, promiscuous and emotionally indifferent. From both these facts, however, it derives its remarkable vitality.[45]

Davis adds that prostitution, while satisfying needs for sexual gratification, also has a latent function vital to maintaining balance in the social system—it helps maintain the institution of the family. A major function of the family institution is to limit sexual access and contact. Prostitution offers alternative forms of sexual gratification by providing for "the craving for variety, for perverse gratification, for mysterious and provocative surroundings, for intercourse free from entangling cares and civilized pretense."[46] In other words, it provides for those functions that the most esteemed sexual institution, the family, cannot provide. Thus by offering this outlet for sexual gratification, prostitution helps preserve the family institution in its structural organization and its functionality. Davis, echoing the functionalist interpretation of deviation as a normal reality, concludes that

> we can imagine a social system in which the motive for prostitution would be completely absent, but we cannot imagine that the system will ever come to pass. . . . Not only will there always be a system of social dominance that gives a motive for selling

> sexual favors, and a scale of attractiveness that creates the need for buying them, but this form of prostitution is, in the last analysis, economical...."[47]

In light of Davis's functional analysis of prostitution, it is interesting to note his analysis of the social role of homosexuality. Davis concludes that it arises from an individual's inability to cope with "normal adjustments in life."[48] He sees it as a failure to handle normal life obligations and, therefore, as reflecting a personal inadequacy.

> One way for a man to escape the dominance struggle among men is to give up and assume a feminine role: he retreats into being a woman and yet has few of the obligations that an actual woman has. A dominant male homosexual has no need to assume the obligations that relations with women require....[49]

Davis adds that homosexuality presents a myriad of problems for the community: homosexual prostitution, the spread of venereal disease, and the seduction of the young by adult male homosexuals.[50] Davis concludes that homosexuality is truly pathological and that homosexuals have significant psychosocial problems.

Coming from a functional theorist this analysis is indeed strange. Although Davis admits that homosexuality (like prostitution) has been known to exist in most societies and thus has its own normal collective representations, he denies its latent functionality. Interestingly, Davis uses every stereotypic characterization of homosexuals that we now consider very questionable. Homosexuals are not refugees from typical male dominance struggles; most do not consider themselves females, nor do they hate females; they are not principally responsible for the spread of venereal disease; most do not seduce young children; and they are not necessarily psychologically abnormal. Contemporary studies on homosexuality have found these characterizations to be inaccurate.[51] It is very difficult to see how Davis can conclude that the sexual institution of prostitution is more functional than that of homosexuality.

Davis failed to see that homosexuality might also be on the continuum of sexual institutions and may, by his own criteria, have its corresponding latent functions. On theoretical grounds, it is difficult to see why homosexuality should necessarily be dysfunctional, and thereby hangs a major problem for functional analysis. Howard S. Becker has indicated the basic problem of functionalism as it relates to social deviation:

> It is harder in practice than it appears to be in theory to specify

what is functional and what dysfunctional for society or social group. The question of what the purpose or goal (function) of a group [or sexual institution] is and, consequently, what things will help or hinder the achievement of that purpose, is very often a political question. Factions within the group [or sociological experts in society] disagree and maneuver to have their own definition of the group's function accepted. The function of the group or organization, then, is decided in political conflict, not given in the nature of the organization. If this is true, then it is likewise true that the questions of what rules are to be enforced, what behavior regarded as deviant, and which people labelled as outsiders must be regarded as political. The functional view of deviance, by ignoring the political aspect of the phenomenon, limits our understanding.[52]

In other words, it is very difficult to determine the objective value or functionality of a behavioral practice or institutional order, for "usefulness" and "purposefulness" are judgments, subject to much disagreement. In fact, they are often direct equivalents of judgments of good and evil and have frequently been bootlegged into sociology through such terms as "function" and "dysfunction." What the sociologist often sees as "useful" is seen by the moralist as anathema to the human condition and a threat to societal stability. The fact that the lay observer cannot see the value of behavior and institutions that the theoretician defines as functional also indicates the degree to which the latency function is "forced" by the functionalists. It is forced by their need to account for societal stability and maintenance.

This particular form of functionalist analysis has not had an extensive following, but it indicates a direct continuity of thought with Durkheim's characterization of the normalcy and functionality of social deviation. Although functionalists have also analyzed the latent functionality of other forms of deviant behavior (such as Merton's rebellion adaptation), this mode of analysis has received criticism from both functionalists and nonfunctionalists.[53] It assumes that the very existence or persistence of a normal behavioral form means that it performs positive functions for maintaining some structural units. Davis's characterization of homosexuality reveals inconsistencies in the application of these theoretical assumptions to particular types of deviation and bears out Becker's criticism.

Merton's social-structure and anomie model of deviation and the corresponding emphasis on the relation of social class to deviant behavior have been extremely influential for theory and research. Two forms of behavior have received the special attention of adherents to this theoretical framework: juvenile delinquency and mental illness.

Anomie, Social Class, and the Genesis of Deviation

Merton's model of individual adaptation to problems stemming from one's position in the differential-opportunity structure of society contributed to an examination of the role of social class and anomie in the genesis of deviation. Numerous studies attempted to draw the causal link: position in social structure → differential access to opportunity structure → anomie → individual deviance. Only a few of the more prominent studies can be cited here.

Mental Illness   The research of Faris and Dunham on the ecological distribution of mental disorders in Chicago had already indicated a relationship between social class and mental illness.[54] Patients hospitalized for schizophrenia came from the Zone of Transition and other areas close to the central city, and had low socioeconomic status. The methodology used to obtain these findings was inadequate. Yet this study, along with Merton's theoretical framework, was extremely influential in stimulating research on the relationship between social class and mental illness.

A major flaw in the methodology of the Faris and Dunham study was that hospital records alone were used to establish rates of mental illness; no attempt was made to measure the prevalence or incidence of mental disorder in the larger population. Hollingshead and Redlich (1959), in a study of treated mental illness in New Haven, attempted to eliminate this methodological bias by including information from private psychiatrists, private out-patient clinics, and private hospitals. Holding sex, age, race, religion, and marital status constant, they found that social class has a statistically significant relationship to *treated* mental illness:

> Stated in different terms, a distinct inverse relationship does exist between social class and mental illness. . . . Class V [the lowest class], almost invariably, contributes many more patients than its proportion of the population warrants. Among the higher classes there is a more proportionate relationship between the number of psychiatric patients and the number of individuals in the population.[55]

Initially (1953), the authors were very careful to indicate that they did not fully understand why these social-class differences prevailed. Later, in their full presentation of their research (1958), they believed, along with the psychoanalysts, that psychosocial factors accounted for personality characteristics, including mental illness. Using Henry A. Murray's concepts of "press" (pressure or force exerted by the environment on the individual's personality) and "stress" (internal or individual fears, guilts, and conflicts), the authors claimed that lower-class patients tended to be influenced by the former and higher-class patients by the latter. Hollingshead and Redlich indicate that

> throughout the mature years, the external problems of lower class individuals, as well as threats to their economic, social, and physical security, are much stronger than to members of the higher classes. Sensitivity to internal threats, fears, guilts, and conflicts however appear to be greater in Class II & III [the lower- upper and middle classes] than in the other strata.[56]

These "presses" amounted to what other structuralists have called social disorganization. Hollingshead and Redlich did not sufficiently analyze how these presses and stresses operated. This task was left to Jerome K. Myers and Bertram H. Roberts, who wrote *Family and Class Dynamics in Mental Illness* (1959), the second part of the research study on mental illness in New Haven.

Myers and Roberts argued that two major presses—economic insecurity and isolation from and hostility toward community institutions—were particularly strong in Class V, the lowest class; and this led to strong internal stresses: suspicion, hostility, alienation, and frustration.[57] In turn, these factors were directly related to advanced functional disorders like schizophrenia. In lower-class families, parental control was said to be minimal. There was little love, affection, protection, and stability; patients were said to have had "defensive" relationships with their parents and to fear them.[58] Lower-class patients felt neglected and rejected most of their lives;[59] they experienced economic insecurity and, as the authors point out,

> they felt exploited and "beaten down" by life. . . . the parent's inability to provide either economic or emotional security for the patients led to a sense of "not belonging" or of being "lost."[60]

In other words, these presses, or factors of social disorganization, brought about anomic forces that helped produce functional mental illness.

The authors also found a significant amount of serious mental illness in Class III, the middle-class portion of their sample. The presses operative here were different. For middle-class patients, the presses due to social mobility were the most significant. Middle-class patients manifested a discrepancy between their aspirations and their achievements. Although their mobility efforts were said to be successful, the mobility strivings of Class III patients were frustrated for various reasons.[61] According to the authors, adolescent aspirations had to be abandoned, thus creating a significant amount of internal stress. The major stresses of "tension, frustration, isolation, shame and guilt"[62] were brought about by specific presses, all related to hampered social mobility and middle-class values: (1) parent pressure to be respectable; (2) shame and guilt about their parents' social status; (3) social isolation due to patients' drifting away from friends; (4) lack of continuity in their identification with parental figures; (5) the necessity to learn new behavior patterns as they (initially) moved socially upward; and (6) the parents' financial inability to provide patients with the higher education they desired.[63] In short, the severe functional impairments of middle-class patients were also due to anomic forces. These forces, in turn, became operative as a result of the patients' inability to find access to institutionalized opportunity channels. In this sense, middle-class mental illness more purely conforms to the social-disorganization theory of social structure and anomie. Lower-class mental illness conforms to the social-disorganization theory inherent in the ecological model, in which family and community instability are emphasized over differential access to the opportunity structure and feelings of relative deprivation.

Myers and Roberts, like Hollingshead and Redlich before them, were reluctant to say clearly that these "presses" and "stresses" *caused* functional mental impairment; but it is quite clear from their respective analyses that they considered these the prime predisposing factors that led to it.

Since neither part of this large-scale study of mental illness employed "control groups" or actually measured the true incidence or prevalence of mental illness in the community, major problems exist in interpreting these findings. The argument may be made that with forms of deviation like mental illness we need not concern ourselves with the process of "actualization"—how mental illness is learned or evaluated by others. There are factors of actualization that are equally significant in the New Haven studies.

A major intervening variable between factors of "press" and "stress" and mental illness is the nature of the societal reaction to mental illness. These studies assume very little variation in the means by which patients are selected by the different mental-health treatment settings, the application of diagnostic theories and procedures, and organizational contingencies that affect the daily reactions of patients as they experience various treatment modes and facilities. Considerable research indicates that these factors must be taken into account before the predispositional relationship between social class press and stress, and mental illness, can be fully understood.[64] Intervening variables and alternative explanations must be evaluated. In particular, there is a strong need for analysis of the rate-producing process:[65] the entire process of reaction, diagnosis, and labeling and treatment at both the official and, initially, the informal level (family, friends, associates), to understand why persons come to be designated as mentally ill. We also need to know why some are designated as in need of professional help, and the consequences of being or not being helped.[66]

Juvenile Delinquency   Merton's model of individual adaptation to structural stresses has had its greatest impact on the study of juvenile delinquency. A number of sociologists in the 1950s and 1960s attempted to test this model of deviation by applying it to the formation of delinquent subcultures among juveniles. Merton's model of ostensibly individual adaptations to anomic forces was extended to collective adaptations to problems emanating from differential access to society's opportunity structure. Gang membership and participation in delinquent behavior offer boys alternative means to satisfy their status and achievement needs.

   Cloward (1959) and Cloward and Ohlin (1960) have argued that the delinquent subculture offers the functional equivalent of the larger society's opportunity system. Lower-class youth, accordingly, aspire to the same success goals maintained by conventional society. Yet their relative low status vis-à-vis the opportunity structure thwarts any attempts to close the large gap between aspirations and what is realistically available to them.[67] This discrepancy causes like-situated, alienated lower-class youth to join in a collective effort to establish an illegitimate but functionally alternative opportunity system. Cloward and Ohlin, however, add a new twist to the basic Mertonian formulation: just as there is differential access to the legitimate-opportunity structure of the dominant society, there is also differential access to the illegitimate opportunity structure. The behavioral character of the delinquent subculture (and supposedly of the gang members themselves) is determined by the differential availability of three illegitimate means, which are hierarchically arranged in the opportunity structure to which delinquents tacitly give allegiance.

   At the top of the hierarchy are *criminal means* and thus *criminal subcultures*. According to Cloward and Ohlin, those deprived of access to the legitimate-opportunity structure and the primary goal of financial success might reach the top of the illegitimate-opportunity structure, where alternative means to financial success are available. This is possible primarily through criminal means. Criminal subcultures are found in relatively stable lower-class neighborhoods, which are "characterized by close bonds between different age-levels of offenders and between criminal and conventional elements."[68] In these neighborhoods the young delinquents are subject to the control of older criminals, but their participation in criminal lifestyles offers sufficient rewards to compensate for the constraints exercised over them.

For lower-class youth who are blocked from the legitimate-opportunity structure and who, in addition, do not have access to criminal means, the possibilities for achieving success goals are significantly narrowed. For them, there exists a second illegitimate-opportunity route. Cloward and Ohlin maintain that such youth tend to live in urban areas that are unstable and evidence a great deal of social disorganization. There is not only a loss of social control exercised by legitimate community institutions, but also a lack of control exercised by illegitimate control agents and groups. The youth in such lower-class neighborhoods are

> deprived not only of conventional opportunity but also of criminal routes to the "big money." In other words, precisely when frustrations are maximized, social controls are weakened. Social controls and channels to success-goals are generally related; where opportunities exist, patterns of control will be found; where opportunities are absent, patterns of control are likely to be absent too. . . ."[69]

What remains for such youths is participation in subcultures in which *violence* is the characterizing activity of its members.

Thus, criminal activity directed toward financial gain is replaced by violence as the stepladder toward status, esteem, power, and related goals offered by this second opportunity structure.

Finally, for those who neither qualify for entrance to the channels of legitimate opportunity nor have access to the illegitimate opportunities afforded by the criminal and conflict subcultures, there remains the *retreatist subculture.* Cloward (1959) orginally called this retreatist adaptation the "double failure."[70] Unlike Merton's retreatist adaptation, which rejected the legitimate cultural goals and institutionalized means, Cloward and Ohlin's retreatist fails at both the legitimate and illegitimate means. Such youths supposedly form dropout subcultures, in which alcoholism, drug use, and other retreatist activities become the characteristic forms of delinquent participation. In discussing pressures that lead to retreatist subcultures, the authors state that

> retreatism is often conceived as an isolated adaptation, characterized by a breakdown in relationships with other persons. Indeed this is frequently true, as in the case of psychotics. The drug-user, however, must become affiliated with others, if only to secure access to a steady supply of drugs. . . . Because of these restrictions on the availability of drugs, new users must become affiliated with old users. They must learn the core of drug use, the skills required in making appropriate "connections," the controls which govern the purchase of drugs. . . .[71]

In other words, members of retreatist subcultures join together for the purpose of solving the common problems associated with their unique deviant activities. However, the concept of a retreatist delinquent subculture is problematic. Few examples of delinquent subcultures displaying this retreatist pattern of drug-using behavior can be found. Users of hard drugs are not likely to form the interpersonal bonds necessary to sustain a subcultural milieu. Many researchers have shown that hard drug-using behavior among such youth is a far more individualistic phenomenon than Cloward and Ohlin's characterization indicates.[72] Evidence also indicates that not all drug users are failures in the illegitimate-opportunity structure. Many users who are able to support their habits through legitimate or illegitimate means maintain positive self-images, and receive the esteem and respect of others within the community.[73]

Deviance, Social Class, and Anomie: A Summary Evaluation

The sociology of deviant behavior in the 1950s and early 1960s was dominated by attempts to relate social class and anomie to the genesis of individual and collective forms of deviation. Several basic problems with these perspectives have already been mentioned. By reviewing the central assumptions that these perspectives have in common, we can best evaluate both their advantages and shortcomings in the study of social deviation.

The key assumption of the social-class, status-deprivation, and anomie theories is that an individual's position in the lower strata of the status hierarchy was a significant predisposition to deviant behavior. At face value, this is a satisfying explanation, for it corroborates commonsensical understanding of what motivates or forces people to become criminals, "crazy," and "losers" in society. Poverty is commonsensibly correlated with most social ills, and the concept of "status deprivation," or "unequal access to the opportunity structure," intuitively establishes the theoretical linkages between social-structural constraints, anomic forces, and individual adaptations to them. Whether we lean in the direction of Marxist structuralism or Durkheimian and Mertonian structural–functionalism, these commonsensical notions are borne out: people become criminals, alcoholics, delinquents, prostitutes, and drug addicts because they simply have not had the opportunities that the rest of us have had. There are severe limitations, however, to these theoretical relationships.

The principal problem with this perspective is that it ignores the fact that deviation knows no class boundaries. Whether we refer to mental illness, criminal behavior, alcoholism, drug use, or homosexuality, research findings indicate that many individuals with middle- and upper-class status characteristics also participate in such activities.

Thus, although this perspective seems to be a viable causal explanation for lower-class involvement, it cannot adequately explain the participation of those who, theoretically at least, are not disadvantaged and are thus not subject to these anomic forces. Thio (1973), in a critique of the leading sociological perspectives on deviation, has indicated that they share a common class bias, associating deviation with lower-class status. In his description of such supposedly value-free perspectives as Merton's, he stated that because

> the official statistics, which show the criminals and delinquents as predominantly from the lower classes, are clearly biased against these classes, Merton's basically class-biased "anomie theory" (that deviance is the greatest among lower-class people) can be considered as only speciously supported . . . In some ways, Merton's reliance on the seriously class-biased data resembles the early psychologist's reliance on the seriously race-biased I.Q. tests which were widely used during the First World War. . . .[74]

The inability of sociologists to transcend the established biases of official rates and statistics and, thus, the *rate-producing process* itself has seriously biased both their findings and their theoretical assumptions.

Even if we assume that differential access to the legitimate- or illegitimate-opportunity structure is a significant predisposition to social deviation, it would seem that some varieties of deviant behavior, more than others, are subject to such influences. Status deprivation does not seem to be a necessary or sufficient factor in one's becoming a homosexual, a hallucinogenic-drug user, an unwed mother, a shoplifter, an alcoholic, a student radical, or draft resister.[75] Status deprivation as an explanation of predisposition would seem to lend itself to more pecuniary forms of deviation or to those types of behaviors that are clearly seen as approved adaptations to status deprivation by some deviant subculture. In any case, it seems applicable to only a limited variety of deviation. This does not mean that social class is unrelated to certain other forms of deviation, but simply that the predicted relationship is not demonstrably influential in their genesis.

The relationship between differential access to opportunity structures and anomie is also problematic. Anomie theory, in its various guises, has generally neglected the role of the actor in interpreting the meaningfulness of the constraints, pressures, and deprivations to which he is subject. These social forces or conditions acting on the individual have been viewed as objective determinants of or predispositions toward engagement in deviant behavior. However, whether people will feel frustrated, anxious, alienated, disturbed, or threatened depends upon what *meaning* they assign to their differential access to opportunity structures. Status deprivation ultimately depends on the actors' subjective interpretation of their own and others' status situations. It is apparent that objective constraints can have different consequences for behavior if there are different threshold levels for frustration, or if the meanings given to deprivating circumstances are significantly different. In other words, anomie theory fails to bridge the rather substantial theoretical gap between structural variables and their *differential* impact on actors in the social system. Merton's model of individual adaptation to anomic forces fails to consider the individual factors that mediate that very adaptation. Individual adaptation is not an automatic response to objective stimuli; yet this theory assumes that adaptation is a *process* in which a person evaluates, interprets, or defines the situation in such a way that deviant behavior is or is not likely. These definitions may be influenced by feelings of status deprivations, but they are also subject to a myriad of other definitions of the situation, such as mind expansion, desire for new experiences, comradeship, sexual fulfillment, and excitement. In any case, individual adaptations result from situations in which actors, in interaction with others, impart meaning to their social circumstances and behave accordingly. Merton was certainly correct in assuming that a sociological theory of deviant behavior must explain individual adaptation; but he too narrowly defines the sources of those adaptations and failed to come to theoretical terms with the very nature of those adaptations.

Merton's framework must be commended, however, for the insights it has allowed for particular forms of deviant behavior, most notably juvenile delinquency. With the additions and clarifications made by Cloward and Ohlin, anomie (or differential-opportunity) theory has become a significant cornerstone of the sociological understanding of juvenile delinquency. It has been one of the four most influential theories in the sociology of deviant and criminal behavior in the past 50 years.[76] We turn now to a few of the structural perspectives on deviant behavior that have taken exception to various characteristics of the Merton's and Cloward and Ohlin's explanation of deviant behavior and, specifically, of juvenile delinquency.

SUBCULTURES, VALUE CONFLICT, AND DEVIANT BEHAVIOR

An offshoot of the sociological analysis of juvenile delinquency has been a concern with the formation of deviant subcultures and their role in the maintenance of deviant careers and lifestyles. If many forms of social deviation evidence subcultural characteristics (i.e., a group of individuals with unique values, beliefs, knowledge, language, habits, and lifestyles), the explanation for subcultural formation and maintenance would help explain the genesis of deviant behavior itself. Sociologists who have focused on deviant subcultures for their answers to the development of deviant behavior began by isolating the components of subcultural life that they deemed significant.

Albert K. Cohen (1955), in his study of the culture of delinquent gangs, began by specifying the subculture's "content." He described it as *non-utilitarian, malicious,* and *negativistic.*[77] Most delinquency, he claimed, is not clearly a means to some rationally conceived goal, such as financial success. Delinquency also evidences a significant amount of *malice,* "an enjoyment in the discomfiture of others, a delight in the defiance of taboos itself."[78] Delinquency is also characterized by a "flouting" of conventional rules and norms and by a generalized "orneriness"—a negative reaction to "respectable" society. As Cohen says, "the delinquent sub-culture takes its norms from the larger culture but turns them upside down."[79]

What produces this? Cohen maintains that delinquency is predominantly a lower-class phenomenon and that delinquents have "status problems"; namely, "problems of achieving respect in the eyes of one's fellows."[80] Delinquent gangs are composed of individuals with similar status problems, which originate when lower-class youth are evaluated by middle-class standards. This occurs characteristically in the contacts they have with teachers, social workers, ministers, and church workers, as well as with other adult representatives of the establishment and its middle-class standards and values. In school, for example, the lower-class youth is evaluated by the following standards and values:

1. ambition or a high level of aspiration, with "an orientation to long-run goals and long-deferred rewards"[81]

2. individual responsibility, self-reliance, and resourcefulness

3. academic achievement

4. rationality, planning, the budgeting of time, and a tendency to distrust the workings of chance

5. polished manners, neatness, and sociability—the ability to get along with people and make friends

6. the control of aggression and hostility, and a fostering of competition based on intellectual and social skills

7. leisure time used for "wholesome" and "constructive" purposes, such as the pursuit of a hobby

8. respect for the property of others.[82]

Cohen maintains that the lower-class cultural setting does not stress these values in the socialization of its youth. Middle-class parents are better able to enforce conformity to these values because of the greater control they exercise over the child's daily life.[83] The middle-class child, in turn, is more motivated to conform to parental expectations because of his greater dependence on parental approval.

The lower-class child's socialization is more "easy-going," according to Cohen.[84] He is more dependent on his peer group for the satisfaction of various emotional needs; thus, peer-group values become predominant as reference points for behavior. The youth's leanings toward delinquency are further influenced by his inability to live up to the middle-class standards by which he is evaluated. As a result, he experiences status deprivation. To counter this, the youth engages in what psychologists call a "reaction formation," repudiating these same crucial standards. This repudiation manifests itself in an intense "over-reaction."[85] Cohen summarizes this overreaction by stating that

> we would expect the delinquent boy who, after all, has been socialized in a society dominated by a middle-class morality and who can never quite escape the blandishments of middle-class society, to seek to maintain his safeguards against seduction. Reaction-formation, in his case, should take the form of an "irrational," "malicious," "unaccountable" hostility to the enemy within the gates as well as without: the norms of the respectable middle-class society.[86]

The delinquent subculture, then, has its basis both in status deprivation and in this repudiation of middle-class values and standards. Thus, a conflict of values lies at the source of this variety of social deviance. Cohen, like Merton, stresses the ultimate significance of the differential-opportunity structure in creating this mode of adaptation to blocked channels of status attainment. However, Cohen emphasizes class and cultural value conflict and the attendant "reaction-formation" as the more specific nature and consequence of the status deprivation produced by the differential-opportunity structure.

Cohen's value-conflict model has elicited both a substantial following and many critical challenges. Walter B. Miller has been a leading challenger of the key assumptions of Cohen's perspective. Miller (1958) maintains that no cultural pattern like gang delinquency can persist if it is based upon value conflict or motives of negation and rejection. Gang delinquency can only be explained by factors of *conformity* to the central or focal concerns of the general lower-class culture.[87] These focal concerns, according to Miller, show a patterning in the lower class that differs significantly from that of the middle class.[88] They include concerns for toughness, smartness, excitement, being lucky, having freedom from authority, and a concern over "trouble" —getting into it, as well as staying out of it.[89] Gang delinquents merely display the focal concerns of their predominantly lower-class culture; they are not rebelling against or rejecting middle-class values, as Cohen maintains. Lower-class youth, according to Miller, have many needs that are met by the one-sex peer group: it may be the most stable primary group they will experience, and it offers more consistent support than the family unit.[90] Their needs for belonging and status are more adequately met in this group. In short, Miller believes that *positive* forces lead individuals into careers of deviation.

Cohen's value-conflict explanation of the genesis of delinquent behavior has not been the only one to emphasize these negative and rejective forces. Students of deviation, delinquency, and crime who do not take a markedly structural approach have also focused on culture-value conflict. Sellin (1938), in a review of the early culture-conflict perspectives, points out that Chicago School students of deviation (such as Wirth, Shaw, and Burgess) believed that the value conflicts between different cultures are internalized as mental conflicts.[91] These mental conflicts, in turn, lead to participation in delinquent activities. Burgess, in the "Discussion" of Shaw's classic book on juvenile delinquency, *The Jack-Roller,* states that:

> the experiences of any individual person reflect group opinion; . . . habit in the individual is an expression of custom in society; and . . . *mental conflict in the person may always be explained in terms of the conflict of divergent cultures.*[92]

The culture-conflict perspective of the Chicago School influenced the theoretical formulations of one of the most outstanding sociological criminologists, Edwin H. Sutherland.

Sutherland, in the first edition of his *Principles of Criminology* (1934), stated that

> the conflict of cultures is therefore the fundamental principle in the explanation of crime. . . . the more the culture patterns conflict, the most unpredictable is the behavior of a particular individual.[93]

Sutherland believed (as had the case-study analysts of delinquency from the Chicago School before him) that such factors as social mobility, immigrant status, and various types of cultural marginality potentially lead to delinquent and criminal behavior.[94] He believed that this culture conflict is part of the content of the differential associations through which delinquent or criminal behavior is learned.[95] The definitions that deviants learn concerning their deviant activities are grounded in conventional society's projection of law and of rule-abiding behavior. The delinquent cannot remain completely neutral to the law-abiding definitions of conventional society, for they threaten his self-esteem and are generally discordant with the rationalizations proffered by his immediate culture. The rejection of definitions unfavorable to law violation intensifies the acceptance of definitions favorable to this and other such nonconforming behavior. Culture conflict is thus significant in shaping the attitudinal or meaningful framework from which deviants came to view themselves and define their activities. In this regard, Sutherland's views are quite similar to Cohen's later formulations of the role of value conflicts in the genesis of delinquent behavior and subcultures.

As David Matza has so well indicated, Sutherland's earlier formulations of how individuals become delinquent or criminal, though beset with problems, were substantially different from those of his predecessors in the Chicago School.[96] While maintaining a concern with factors of social disorganization and the impact of culture conflict on the genesis of deviation, he departed radically from the concern with predisposing factors that had preoccupied the structural theorists. With Sutherland and sociologists like Tannenbaum, the analysis of deviation enters a decidedly new phase. In Matza's words

> Sutherland had gone far enough. He had brought the subject to the brink of humanity by providing a setting for his conversion consisting of definitions of the situation, beliefs, reasons, justifications, techniques, or, in summary, *meaning.* Though it was possible to conceive these as "forces" or "factors," their ordinary human character was in full display. Behind the blown-up physicalist rhetoric were little people talking, perhaps cajoling or intimidating. . . .[97]

The theoretical assumptions with which Sutherland began his explanation of delinquency and crime profoundly influenced the sociology of deviation for decades to come.

Culture Conflict and Deviant Behavior: A Summary Evaluation

The belief that culture conflict undergirds social disorganization and individual deviation has deep roots in sociology. A general Marxist tradition, for example, relates social disorganization to the conflict between the class interests and values of the owners of the means of production and those of the working class. Another culture-conflict perspective has its intellectual ancestry in the sociology of Georg Simmel, one of the principal theoreticians on the roles of conflict in society.[98] Simmel realized that conflict between groups often functions to pull group members together. External conflict often strengthens the bonds that exist between like-situated individuals, who are forced to cooperate to counter the perceived threats. This view is essentially the same one that supports Cohen's argument for the formation of delinquent subcultures.[99] These classic theoreticians, however, did not fully confront the nature of the relationship between culture-value conflict and deviation.

The American sociologists of the 1920s and 1930s were very much influenced by the prevailing conditions of American society. Our large cities contained sizeable populations of recently arrived immigrants, whose lifestyles and values were noticeably different. Sellin, for example, was primarily concerned with the conflict between the cultures of various foreign-born immigrants (and their first- and second-generation progeny) and the culture of the dominant society.[100] The nation's economic instability intensified the realization of class and cultural differences between segments of the American population. The melting pot that America was said to be had not yet been warmed sufficiently.[101] In these class and cultural differences, sociologists began to see explanations for deviation, delinquency, and crime. These phenomena could be explained by the rejection of one set of values and the intensified adherence to value systems opposed to the dominant system.

This framework shares some of the basic problems of the other theories discussed in this chapter. First it assumes that cultural diversity will of itself lead to conflict. It also assumes that deviation inherently involves the rejection of one value system in favor of another. As contemporary students of deviation point out, deviant behavior is very often a "normal" response to the exigencies of a certain cultural lifestyle, normative system, and pattern of socialization, rather than an active rebellion against other value systems.

Value-conflict theories also contain a significant class bias, for they assume that those who are the disadvantaged in the conflict between cultural values and those of the cultural *minority* are the ones who will turn to deviation. The culture-conflict model does not give us an adequate explanation of deviation among those who are members of the cultural majority, or establishment.

Value conflict, as a predisposition toward deviant behavior, suffers many of the same problems as other theories of predisposition; yet a few adherents to this perspective, most notably Sutherland, moved beyond the explanatory framework of predisposition. Again sociologists like Sutherland were able to discover the theoretical gap between causes of deviation and explanations for how people learn to become deviant. By attempting to connect predisposing variables like culture conflict with patterns of interaction, shared definitions of the situation, constructions of social meaning, and the socialization processes in which these are found, Sutherland and sociologists of similar and related theoretical persuasion were able, for the first time, to see beyond the explanatory frameworks that had preoccupied students of deviation for centuries. We turn now to an analysis of various attempts to move beyond theories of predisposition.

---

[1]Demography is the study of human populations. It is primarily concerned with the size, distribution, and development of populations and the influence of population variables on society and social behavior. Demographers have been interested in the impact of such factors as population movement (migration) and the density of population upon social deviation.

[2] *Urbanism* refers to the nature and development of city life and lifestyles. *Natural Areas* were geographical areas within the city that had distinct physical and cultural characteristics. Social disorganization is the breakdown of structural arrangements of a group, society, or social system.

[3]Cities developed around an urban core (e.g., the Loop in Chicago), which became the main business district of the city. This was Zone I. Outside of the main business core of the city was Zone II, the zone of transition—an industrial zone that included residential buildings in an advanced stage of deterioration because of the encroachment of industry. Here, rents were low and the neighborhoods were inhabited by factory workers, unskilled workers, and their families. Zone III was the area of workingmen's homes. This was a more stable area than Zone II, and included numerous single-family residences, as well as two- and three-flat structures. Zones IV and V were the middle-class, apartment-house, and single-family residence districts; these experienced little social disorganization. (See Figure 4-1.) Chicago School sociologists believed that the rate and growth of natural areas was related to the rates of social disorganization in those same areas. Because Zones II and III were the most unstable in terms of mobility patterns and population growth, they were subjected to higher rates of deviant behavior.

[4]Robert E. Park and Ernest W. Burgess, *The City*. Chicago: University of Chicago Press, 1925, p. 43.

[5]Ibid., p. 44.

[6]Ibid., p. 45.

[7]The list of publications is very extensive. Among the better studies are Thrasher, *The Gang;* Shaw and McKay, *Social Factors in Juvenile Delinquency;* Zorbough, *The Gold Coast and the Slum;* Frazier, *The Negro Family in Chicago;* Anderson, *The Hobo;* Cavan, *Suicide—A Study of Personal Disorganization;* Faris and Dunham, *Mental Disorders in Urban Areas;* Wirth, *The Ghetto*. See Bibliography for complete listings and citations.

[8]Robert E. L. Faris and H. Warren Dunham, *Mental Disorders in Urban Areas: An Ecological Study of Schizophrenia and Other Psychoses*. Chicago: University of Chicago Press, 1949, p. 110.

[9]Charles Horton Cooley, *Social Organization*. New York: Scribner's, 1909; Schocken, 1962.

[10]E. Franklin Frazier, *The Negro Family in Chicago*. Chicago: University of Chicago Press, 1932. See especially Chs. 6 and 7.

[11]See Clifford R. Shaw and Henry McKay, *Juvenile Delinquency and Urban Areas*, rev. ed. Chicago: University of Chicago Press, 1972 and Shaw and McKay, "Social Factors in Delinquency." See also Frederic M. Thrasher, *The Gang*, abridged ed. Chicago: University of Chicago Press, 1927, 1967, p. 20.

[12]Thrasher, *The Gang*, p. 20.

[13]Ibid., pp. 20-21.

[14]Ibid., p. 33.

[15]Shaw and McKay, "Factors in Juvenile Delinquency," 1931, p. 69.

[16]Ibid., p. 387.

[17]Ibid., pp. 114–15.

[18]McKay's 1969 edition of *Juvenile Delinquency and Urban Areas.*

[19]The rate was (− .03± .12). Ronald Freedman, *Recent Migration To Chicago.* Chicago: University of Chicago Press, 1950, p. 184.

[20]Ibid., p. 188.

[21]See, for example, John I. Kitsuse and Aaron V. Cicourel, "A Note on the Uses of Official Statistics," *Social Problems*, Vol. 2, no. 2 (Fall 1963), pp. 131–39 and Marvin Wolfgang, "Uniform Crime Reports: A Critical Appraisal," *University of Pennsylvania Law Review*, Vol. III (April 1963), pp. 708–13, 725–36.

[22]See, for example, Evelyn Hooker "The Homosexual Community," in John H. Gagnon and William Simon, eds., *Sexual Deviance*. New York: Harper & Row, 1967. See also Laud Humphreys, *Out of the Closets: The Sociology of Homosexual Liberation*. Englewood Cliffs, N.J.: Prentice Hall, 1972, pp. 80–82.

[23]Shaw and McKay (1942) pp. 27–31, 137–39, 198–202, 235–36, 251–53, 272–74.

[24]Omer R. Galle, Walter R. Gove, and J. Miller McPherson, "Population Density and Pathology: What Are the Relations for Man?" *Science*, Vol. 176 (April 1972), pp. 23–30, 28.

[25]Robert Edward Mitchell, "Some Social Implications of High Density Housing," *American Sociological Review*, Vol. 36 (1971), pp. 18–29.

[26]*Homeostasis*, like so many other concepts in both the ecological and functional perspectives, is borrowed from the physical and biological sciences.

[27]See, for example, Tolcott Parsons, *The Structure of Social Action*. New York: McGraw-Hill, 1949.

[28]Merton defines "middle-range" theories as those "that lie between the minor but necessary working hypotheses that evolve in abundance during day-to-day research and the all-inclusive systematic efforts to develop a unified theory that will explain all the observed uniformities of social behavior, social organization and social change." From Robert K. Merton, "On Sociological Theories of the Middle Range," in Merton, *On Theoretical Sociology*. New York: Free Press, 1967, p. 39.

[29]Robert K. Merton, "Social Structure and Anomie," *American Sociological Review*, Vol. 3 (October 1938) pp. 672–82.

[30]Robert K. Merton, "Social Structure and Anomie," in *Social Theory and Social Structure*, enlarged ed. New York: Free Press, 1968, p. 188.

[31]Merton, "Social Structure," p. 676.

[32]Merton, *Social Theory*, p. 195.

[33]Ibid., p. 198. ,

[34]Ibid., p. 199.

[35]Ibid., p. 207. Emphasis in original.

[36]For a description of "bottle gangs"—groups of individuals engaged in street drinking—see Earl Rubington, "Variations in Bottle-Gang Controls," in Rubington and Weinberg, *Deviance: The Interactionist Perspective.*

[37]Merton, *Social Theory*, p. 209.

[38]Ibid., pp. 209–10.

[39]Wilhelm Bonger, *Criminality and Economic Conditions.* Bloomington: Indiana University Press, 1969.

[40]The FBI publishes an annual report, *Uniform Crime Reports for the United States,* which is used by the press and social scientists to measure the extent of crime and to give us information on the background characteristics of crime and criminals. This method of measuring crime is beset with many problems. See footnote 21.

[41]A more complete examination of these biases will be made in Chapter 7.

[42]A more detailed critique will be given in the next section of the chapter, in which research and theoretical formulations based on Merton's model are reviewed.

[43]See Robert K. Merton, "Manifest and Latent Functions," in Merton, *Social Theory,* pp. 73–138. The underlying, or "not readily apparent," function of a social phenomenon was, according to structural–functionalists, often important for its potential for producing social solidarity.

[44]Kingsley Davis, "The Sociology of Prostitution," *American Sociological Review,* Vol. 2 (1937), pp. 744–55.

[45]Ibid., p. 749.

[46]Ibid., p. 753.

[47]Kingsley Davis, "Sexual Behavior," in Robert K. Merton and Robert A. Nisbet, eds., *Contemporary Social Problems,* 2nd ed. New York: Harcourt, Brace & World, 1966, p. 370, 372.

[48]Ibid., p. 345.

[49]Ibid.

[50]Ibid., p. 346.

[51]See, for example, Carol A. Warren, *Identity and Community in the Gay World.* New York: Wiley, 1974 and George H. Weinberg, *Society and the Healthy Homosexual.* New York: St. Martin's Press, 1972.

[52]Howard S. Becker, *Outsiders.* New York: Free Press, 1963, p. 7.

[53]See Robert K. Merton, "Social Problems and Sociological Theory," in Merton and Nisbet, eds. *Contemporary Social Problems,* p. 844.

[54]See, for example, Faris and Dunham, *Mental Disorders,* p. 79.

[55]August B. Hollingshead and Frederick C. Redlich, *Social Class and Mental Illness: A Community Study.* New York: Wiley, 1958, p. 217.

[56]Ibid., p. 365.

[57]Jerome K. Myers and Bertram H. Roberts, *Family and Class Dynamics in Mental Illness.* New York: Wiley, 1959, p. 197.

[58]Ibid., p. 254.

[59]Ibid., p. 255.

[60]Ibid.

[61]Ibid., pp. 151–52.

[62]Ibid., p. 152.

[63]Ibid.

[64]This will be discussed in Chapter 6.

[65]See Aaron V. Cicourel and John I. Kitsuse *The Educational Decision-Makers.* Indianapolis: Bobbs-Merrill, 1963, pp. 8–12. See also Jack D. Douglas, *The Social Meaning of Suicide.* Princeton, N.J.: Princeton University Press, 1967, esp. Ch. 12, "The Nature and Use of the Official Statistics on Suicide."

[66]See Ch. 6.

[67]Richard A. Cloward and Lloyd E. Ohlin, *Delinquency and Opportunity: A Theory of Delinquent Gangs.* New York: Free Press, 1960, p. 86.

[68]Ibid., p. 171.

[69]Ibid., pp. 174–75.

[70]Ibid., p. 175.

[71]Ibid., pp. 178–79.

[72]See, for example, James F. Short and Fred L. Strodtbeck, *Group Process and Gang Delinquency.* Chicago: University of Chicago Press, 1965, p. 209. See also Lindesmith & Gagnon, "Anomie & Drug Addiction," in Marshall Clinard, ed., *Anomie and Deviant Behavior.* New York: Free Press, 1964, pp. 158–88.

[73]See, for example, Marshall Clinard, ed., *The Sociology of Deviant Behavior.* New York: Holt, Rinehart and Winston, 1974, p. 117.

[74]Alex Thio, "Class Bias in the Sociology of Deviance," *The American Sociologist,* Vol. 8, no. 1 (February 1973), pp. 1–12, 4. The author also criticizes other perspectives on deviation for the same class bias.

[75]See, for example, Mary Owen Cameron, *The Booster and the Snitch.* New York: Free Press, 1964, for a description of how this relates to shoplifting. The motivation for such behavior does not seem to derive from status deprivation.

[76]In this author's opinion, the most influential perspectives have been (1) ecological theory, (2) social structure and anomie, (3) differential association, and (4) labeling perspective.

[77]Albert K. Cohen, *Delinquent Boys: The Culture of the Gang.* New York: Free Press, 1955, p. 25.

[78]Ibid., p. 27.

[79]Ibid., p. 28.

[80]Ibid., p. 65.

[81]Ibid., pp. 88–91.

[82]Cohen originally lists nine points, but his fourth point is contained in the very first: "worldly asceticism and the ability to delay gratification."

[83]Ibid., pp. 97–99.

[84]Ibid., p. 99.

[85]Ibid., p. 133.

[86]Ibid.

[87]Walter B. Miller, "Lower Class Culture as a Generating Milieu of Gang Delinquency," *Journal of Social Issues,* Vol. 14 (Summer 1958), pp. 5–19, 19.

[88]Ibid., pp. 6–7.

[89]Ibid., p. 7.

[90]Ibid., p. 14.

[91]Thorsten Sellin, *Culture Conflict and Crime.* New York: Social Science Research Council. Bulletin 41 (1938), p. 67.

[92]Ernest Burgess in Clifford Shaw, *The Jack-Roller.* Chicago: University of Chicago Press, 1930, 1938, p. 186. My emphasis.

[93]Edward H. Sutherland, *Principles of Criminology.* Philadelphia: Lippincott, 1934, p. 52.

[94]The same view was held by such sociologists as Shaw, Thomas and Znaniecki, and Wirth.

[95]Sutherland, *Principles,* pp. 77–80.

[96]David Matza, *Becoming Deviant.* Englewood Cliffs, N.J.: Prentice-Hall, Inc., 1969, pp. 106–8.

[97]Ibid., pp. 107–8.

[98]Simmel was also influenced by the Marxist view on conflict. See also Rolf Dahrendorf, "Toward a Theory of Social Conflict," *Journal of Conflict Resolution,* Vol. 2 (June 1958), pp. 170–83.

[99]See Georg Simmel, *Conflict and The Web of Group Affiliations,* trans. by Kurt H. Wolff and Reinhard Bendix. New York: Free Press, 1955, pp. 91–93, 96, 17–20.

[100]See Sellin, *Culture Conflict,* pp. 57–116. (Ch. 4, "The Conflict of Conduct Norms").

[101]It is, in fact, doubtful how accurate their "melting pot" idea was for many ethnic groups.

SELECTED READINGS

See footnote 7 for a list of the Chicago School studies of deviation. These works are also cited in the Bibliography.

1938   Robert K. Merton, "Social Structure and Anomie," *American Sociological Review,* Vol. 3 (October 1938), pp. 672–82.

1960   Richard A. Cloward and Lloyd E. Ohlin, *Delinquency and Opportunity: A Theory of Delinquent Gangs.* New York: Free Press.

1973   Alex Thio, "Class Bias in the Sociology of Deviance," *The American Sociologist,* Vol. 8, no. 1 (February 1973), pp. 1–12.

1955   Albert K. Cohen, *Delinquent Boys: The Culture of the Gang.* New York: Free Press.

1938   Thorsten Sellin, *Culture Conflict and Crime.* New York: Social Science Research Council, Bulletin 41.

SELECTED APPLICATIONS

The story of Mace Brown illustrates a very common explanation for the careers of many criminals: the structural/environmental forces that lead an individual away from law-abiding behavior. The boast "I'm either going to die rich or die young" is represented as the motivational force that leads to Brown's criminal involvement. Underlying the author's explanation is a commonsensical understanding of what structuralists would call the "differential-opportunity" factors that predispose persons toward criminal behavior.

PORTRAIT OF A KILLER
Kenneth Y. Tomlinson

On October 14, 1970, Mace Brown drove a rented green Javelin up the entrance ramp of the Charter House Motel in Washington, D.C. Carrying an attaché case which identified him as a salesman for a Harlem-based fashion company, he took a $17-a-day room where he slept for six nights. But the samples of African clothes were never removed from the attaché case, because Brown was not really a salesman. He was a professional killer.

Early on October 21, Brown parked in the 2300 block of Lincoln Road, near the crest of the hill, from where he could best view this quiet, shrub-lined street. In six days he had come to know the block well. At 7:10 a.m. Charles (Popeye) Hailes—a onetime narcotics chieftain, expected to testify for the prosecution in a major trial of heroin distributors—would emerge from an apartment building to drive his wife to work.

Hailes was on time. Brown slipped from his car, stepped up behind him, placed a .32-caliber pistol with silencer at his victim's head and pulled the trigger. There was a nearly inaudible "pop," and Hailes fell dead. Hysterical, his wife screamed for help.

Sixty feet away, a policeman walking to work in civilian clothes heard the cry. He wheeled and shouted, "Stop, police!" Brown fired at him, then leaped into his car and sped away. Within minutes a description of the green Javelin was radioed to every scout car in the city. Twenty minutes later, Mace Brown was captured.

The killing sent a chill through law enforcers. For informants reported that Brown had been hired to kill not only Hailes but two others: the prosecutor and presiding judge in the same trial.

In the weeks that followed, Brown refused to answer any questions about who his employers were. Although the case against him appeared to be airtight, he was confident he would go free. He was found guilty of murder and, on March 24, 1971, sentenced to death in the electric chair, but even this did not faze him. Then, last October, in a carefully organized jailbreak, Brown escaped. He went on the FBI's "Ten Most Wanted" list.

To lawmen, Brown's escape was a symbol of organized crime's ability to frustrate their earnest efforts. To impressionable young hoodlums, he was a folk hero, representative of a new generation of urban criminal, a real-life "Super Fly" too cunning for justice to contain. And herein, perhaps, lies the major significance of Mace Brown.

Dead Serious Born in 1943, Mace Brown grew up in Newark, N.J., not in a ghetto but in a lower-middle-class Italian neighborhood that was slowly undergoing racial change. His father had a steady job as a presser in a tailor

shop; his mother was a department-store salesclerk, and later a reception-
ist for the Newark Housing Authority.

As a child, Brown was often at odds with his father, his mother
taking her son's side. As he grew older, the youngster took more and more
to the streets. Inside the butcher shops and candy stores in his section of
Newark were bookmakers, loan sharks and numbers runners. Mob figures
wearing tailor-made suits, driving custom-styled Cadillacs, moved freely
about—symbols of an exciting, drudgery-free life.

Mace stood out from the gang he began to run with as an early
teenager—he was the smallest in stature, the only black, and the one who
could drive the stick-shift cars they stole for joyrides. In street battles he
fought with a dead seriousness that scared everyone. "You don't hit hard
enough," he chided his friends. "You gotta hit to *kill*."

In 1956, Brown, then just 13, was arrested while driving a stolen car. Three weeks later he was picked up for stabbing another youngster with an ice pick. In the next three years he was convicted of 11 break-
ins. Court-ordered stays with relatives in other cities did little good. At 16
he was sentenced to the state home for juvenile offenders in Annandale.
Others there at the time recall his talk of being a big-time gangster, having
a big car and sharp clothes, living off a stable of prostitutes.

"Die Rich" During a subsequent stay at Annandale, Brown began mainlining
smuggled-in heroin, and by his 19th birthday—out on the street again—he
was a junkie, supporting his habit with holdups and burglaries. Next stop
was the Bordentown state penitentiary. Here a psychiatric examination
showed him to be "high average" in intelligence but plagued by "hostility
toward the father figure and disrespect for authority."

Released from Bordentown in December 1966, he had kicked
heroin and renewed his resolve to gain money and prominence. "I'm either going to die rich or die young," he boasted. To satisfy his parole
officer, Brown took a job as a construction worker—but it lasted only a few
weeks. For a while he hijacked trucks for a group of Jersey City thugs.
Then he moved to armed robberies, and later into narcotics, selling heroin
and cocaine to street dealers in Newark.

Brushes with police were frequent, but Brown had learned to
use bail and court delays to his advantage. In early 1968, caught at the
wheel of a burgundy Cadillac, he was charged with possession of currency
stolen in a $3000 robbery. Posting $1000 bail, he skipped town, moving
across the Hudson River to New York.

A string of young women contributed to his support through
prostitution or the sale of narcotics. Friends say Brown maintained strict
discipline. Once, when he found heroin needle marks on the arm of one
girl, he was enraged. "Don't you know cops are picking up people with
tracks?" he shouted, then burned away the marks with a straightening
comb, leaving lifelong scars.

Life-Style Living in New York, Brown used the roll of bills in his pocket as the key
to glory. He wore the finest fabrics, the newest fashions; his shoes were

alligator, custom-made. From smoking marijuana he moved on to cocaine at $500 an ounce, and on a day of pleasure would go through hundreds of dollars of "coke" with his friends, listening to albums of the Impressions or the Supremes, his favorites. When he treated a girl to a night on the town it was first-class: a fine restaurant, a nightclub show.

Yet when he had underlings out selling narcotics, Brown often went days without sleep, working to ensure his profit was collected. "Nothing comes to a sleeper but a dream," he was fond of saying.

But New York, too, became uncomfortable for Brown, with two arrests which he beat by giving an alias, posting bail, and then disappearing. In the spring of 1969, he transferred his operation to the Jersey shore, settling for a while in Asbury Park. Sitting in a bar, he would sip champagne on the rocks while three or four of his women sold heroin at cut-rate prices on the streets. Soon he had organized his own local dealers, cutting out previous suppliers. "There ain't but one gorilla in this town, and I'm it," Brown told objectors.

On May 8, four ski-masked men walked into the Keystone Savings and Loan in Asbury Park. While their leader, believed to have been Brown, covered employees with a sawed-off .30-caliber rifle, his underlings gathered up nearly $30,000 in cash. A rash of similar bank jobs followed in central New Jersey.

By late 1969 Brown was back in the New York area, apparently as an enforcer for big-time narcotics dealers. He had the kind of reputation useful in ensuring collections. "When Mace fought, he'd hurt people bad," a friend says. "Like he was setting an example for people to see." Others recall an incident in Newark in early 1968 when a narcotics pusher crossed him. Brown shot the man in both knees.

Little is known about Brown's criminal activities during this period, though in November 1969, near a Harlem nightclub, he was shot in the stomach. No complaint was ever filed. Informants say that while trying to collect from a pusher Brown drew a pistol, but it jammed. The pusher's didn't.

Over the Fence   In October 1970, District of Columbia authorities were going to trial against 55 members of a multimillion-dollar New York-to-Washington heroin operation, the largest such prosecution in D.C. history. Included in the group were Lawrence (Slippery) Jackson, regarded as Washington's major drug dealer, and Enrico Tantillo and Carmine Paladino, identified by federal authorities as members of a New York Mafia family. Charles Hailes, an original defendant in the case, was expected to turn government witness.

Early that month Brown traveled to Washington under an assumed name. While there he taxied to a suburban apartment development in Maryland. Which apartment he visited has never been determined but he emerged with a shoebox. "I've got money now," he chortled to a companion.

Back in New York he got the brother of a girl friend to rent the green Javelin. He used it to return to Washington, this time registering in a motel under his real name. Seven days later Hailes was dead, and Brown was in jail.

Although reports linked Hailes' killing to his reputed cooperation with the government, no one is sure what the real motive was. Did Brown also have a contract to kill the prosecutor and judge? Only Brown and those who hired him know the answers.

When Brown came to trial, he was represented by two of Washington's most expensive law firms. Who paid the tab? His family paid for one—in cash. "I don't know who retained me," a lawyer from the second firm told the court.

The legal objections they raised could not refute the evidence against Brown and he was sentenced to death. Yet in the months that followed, he remained cool and defiant.

Last October 2, the regular cellblock head count in the D.C. jail was moved back one hour to 8:30 p.m. to allow inmates—and guards—to watch the Monday-night pro-football game without interruption. Covered by the noise of television, Mace Brown and seven other inmates sawed through bars in the prison's maximum-security section. As they made their way onto the prison roof, two cars drew up outside the jail. The prisoners used a fire hose to reach the ground, then scaled two 12-foot fences to the cars, where accomplices waited with heavy weapons and at least one machine gun, in case of trouble. There was none. Mace Brown had reason for his confidence after all.

But even for a man with his connections and luck, time was running out. For several months he disappeared. Then it happened. On the morning of April 18, with two accomplices, he attempted to rob a branch of the Chase Manhattan Bank in New York City. The police were alerted, and in the ensuing gun battle Brown was shot and killed.

Mace Brown, dead at 30. But there is much to be learned from his short, violent life. He symbolized a new generation of urban criminal whose hunger for illicit wealth represents a major threat to all Americans. If we fail to cope effectively with the Mace Browns of our society, what sort of society will we leave to our children?

Chapter 5

THEORIES OF ACTUALIZATION

The behavioral sciences have contributed many fundamental ideas to the understanding of the individual and society. Theoreticians and philosophers would certainly differ over which ideas they consider most important to a general social-science perspective. High on most contemporary lists, however, would be the observation that human behavior is, to a great extent, *learned.* This rather simple and currently taken-for-granted notion was nevertheless the focal point of much spirited debate between spokesmen for the emerging behavioral science and the entrenched natural sciences. Is human behavior essentially *determined* or *ascribed* by the innate or "natural" characteristics of indivduals? Or are we the sum total of the experiences, knowledge, and meaningful associations that we *acquire* as members of society? In its more popular guise, the debate has been referred to as the "nature or nuture" controversy; and the reader might not find it difficult to conjure up images of the quasi-social experiments in "Pygmalion" or "My Fair Lady," designed to determine whether someone could actually be *taught* respectability! Social scientists, along with George Bernard Shaw, have opted for the nurture, or learning, hypothesis and have decided that one learns to be both respectable and (in others' eyes) nonrespectable.

The behavioral sciences not only opted for the learning hypothesis but also made *learning* a principal subject of their analyses. In sociology, the process through which individuals learn to become members of a society—*socialization*—became a cornerstone in the foundation of the discipline. In psychology, the acquisition of individual patterns of behavior, the organization and functioning of human perception, the formation of personality, and the learned response to schedules of stimuli reinforcement became early, major areas of concentration and eventually formed the very foundation of that discipline. Cultural anthropology not only focused on the organization and functioning of cultural patterns and practices but also (like its sister disciplines) studied the *transmission* of culture from one generation to the next, and thus the acquisition of the norms that characterize the social core of the culture.

Scholars have attempted to characterize the early fascination of behavioral scientists with this fundamental theme and have sought to establish the common concerns of the founders of the various disciplines. H. Stuart Hughes (1958), in his analysis of European social thought from 1890 to 1930, has emphasized the significance of the dual concepts of *consciousness* and *conscience* as unifying categories for the "classical" behavioral scientists.

Intellectuals like William James, Sigmund Freud, Max Weber, and Emile Durkheim were commonly interested in the *development, acquisition,* and *functioning* of individual and group consciousness.[2] Consciousness, however, is always consciousness of something or someone—it is inherently phenomenal. These scholars were concerned with the objects of consciousness. For James, an early student of socialization, and for other rather philosophical social psychologists (e.g., Dewey, Cooley, and G.H. Mead), the learning of *self*-consciousness or *self*-identity became a principal concern. The early sociologists Weber and Durkheim were interested in the acquisition and ramifications of collective or group consciousness and of the moral-value structure that supported and augmented it. Freud concentrated more on the submerged side of consciousness and on the internalized moral-value structure, in the form of individual conscience or super-ego. For him the *unconscious,* but nevertheless learned and acquired, elements of individual personality, took center stage. Human behavior then, was not to be viewed as a fixed reality, but as a changing, developing, and dynamic process. Most importantly, the behavioral sciences had to account for this process.

PREDISPOSITION, ACTUALIZATION, AND DEVIANT BEHAVIOR

Noting this concern with accounting for the acquisition of human social behavior, we can be somewhat puzzled that, in the study of deviant behavior, the analysis of its *learning* should have been delayed for as long as it had. In fact, a frontal assault on the issue of learning deviant behavior was not initiated in sociology until the mid-1920s; and it did not become established as a proper concern in the sociology of deviant behavior among American sociologists until the post–World War II period.[3] Our previous discussion of the historical development of deviation analysis gives a partial explanation for the retarded growth of this type of investigation.

The early students of deviant behavior were primarily interested in its causes and in the factors of predisposition that established the necessary context for the genesis of such behavior. The sociologists among these students concentrated on the social-structural determinants, or correlates, of deviant behavior. Social class, differential-opportunity structures, status deprivation, anomie, ecological area, culture-value conflict, and other theories were variously seen as significant in this genesis. The principal sociologists in the field shared a very similar intellectual heritage—positivism, structural analysis, and an *objectivist* view of human behavior and society.[4] It is worthwhile to digress from the more specific discussion of deviant behavior and briefly review the more important assumptions of these intellectual traditions. It will also be necessary to explore *reactions to* these traditions, which were later to have a significant impact on the analysis of deviant behavior.

BACKGROUND ASSUMPTIONS

Positivism and *objectivism* were the most significant intellectual traditions uniting the early analysts of deviant behavior. In the sociology of Emile Durkheim, these traditions were dramatically and effectively united with structuralism and, more significantly, with functionalist analysis. All these traditions combined to cast the mold of sociological investigation for decades to come. The nonconcern with individualistic patterns of behavior and, thus, with *individual* learning served as substantial barriers to a sociological and social-psychological investigation of the *actualization* of human behavior in general.[5]

The belief that a sociological analysis of objective behavior could achieve a causal understanding of that behavior independent of inter-

vening subjective processes is questioned even by sociological proponents of causal analysis. R.M. MacIver (1942, 1964), in an excellent
book on causal analysis, points out that

> the primary contrast between social causation and the causa-
> tion revealed in physical and in biological phenomena is that
> the former involves the sociopsychological nexus. . . .The
> realm of conscious experience is also the realm of society, and
> thus in its actual operation the psychological nexus practically
> always manifests itself in a socio-psychological form.[6]

In other words, the understanding of human social behavior cannot
stop at a structural, objectivist explanation of predisposition, without
at least considering *shared* subjective understandings of that behavior.
Although this author does not completely agree with MacIver's position on the role of causal analysis in social science, MacIver's insistence on the social-psychological bases of social explanations can only
be interpreted as a radical and useful departure from sociological
explanations modeled after explanations in the biological and physical sciences: namely, a positivistic model of sociology.

This radical departure from sociologistic, objectivist, and positivist explanations has an important intellectual history of its own,
which can be dated at least as far back as the mid-nineteenth century
and thus at the very period in which sociology claims its modern-day
conception.

DEPARTURE FROM THE POSITIVIST MODEL: TOWARD A
SOCIOLOGY OF SUBJECTIVE UNDERSTANDING[7]

Sociology, like most of the other behavioral sciences, is substantially a child of the Enlightenment. The Enlightenment,[8] as we have
already mentioned, was characterized by *rationalism*—the belief nothing is so sacred that it can not be questioned and known—and by
positivism—the quest for verifiable truths obtainable through natural-
science methods of observation, experimentation, and mathematical
manipulation of the natural order with a design toward predicting the
aspects of that order. Enlightenment scholars like Montesquieu, Condorcet, and Rousseau were presociological analysts who were greatly
impressed with the potential applications of positivist methods to the
analysis of social institutions and human relations. The progenitors of
sociology, Saint-Simon, Comte, and (later) Durkheim, were very
much imbued with the spirit of the Enlightenment and its implicit
design for the study of society. In this respect, modern sociology is a

child of the post–French Revolutionary period.[9] To a large extent this heritage is a conspicuously French or French-language heritage.

Scholars have questioned why, for example, early German sociological thought was markedly antipositivist. Zeitlin, Hughes, and other scholars have indicated that German social thought has traditionally had antipositivist leanings, largely because of the influence of the idealist philosophers Emmanuel Kant (1724–1804) and G.W.F. Hegel (1770–1831).[10] These two great philosophers had a profound influence on those social philosophers and philosophical historians of the last half of the nineteenth century who were precursors of a German sociology.

German philosophers of history, such as Windelband, Dilthey, and Rickert, were convinced that the human social sciences, or "cultural studies," could not be modeled along the theoretical and methodological guidelines of the natural sciences.[11] Dilthey, for example, maintained that knowledge in the cultural sciences was derived from some kind of internal process or meaningful understanding acquired through experience. Because the social investigator is also a member of the society he studies, he receives information about this cultural world through "sympathetic understanding." Ultimately, therefore, the basis for understanding the social world was *subjective,* not *objective.*[12] This is certainly a very different view from the sociologism of Durkheim. "Social facts" were not viewed as external to the individual, but as greatly contingent on subjective understandings and the shared meanings constructed by members of society.

The concept of *sympathetic understanding,* or *Verstehen,* became an important characteristic of Max Weber's definition of the central task of sociology. Weber defined sociology as

> a science which attempts the interpretative understanding of social action in order thereby to arrive at a causal explanation of its course and effects. In "action" is included all human behavior when and in so far as the acting individual attaches a subjective meaning to it.[13]

The suggestion that sociologists look to the meaningful interpretations of reality for their basic units of analysis or the fundamental building blocks of social order, was to have important ramifications for the development of social philosophy, sociological theory, and sociological perspectives on deviant behavior. These views were the rudiments of a subjectivist sociology, which took decidedly different paths toward the study of social behavior and society from those suggested by the positivist heirs of the Enlightenment.

SYMBOLIC INTERACTION AND SOCIAL LEARNING:
THE AMERICAN REACTION TO OBJECTIVIST SOCIOLOGY

Among those influenced by the "Heidelberg School,"—the group of social philosophers that included Windelband, Dilthey, and Rickert—were the American pragmatist philosophers William James and John Dewey.[14] James and Dewey had, among their numerous interests, a concern for child development and, more specifically, an interest in what we would now call "socialization." Dewey's interest was combined with his concern with education and his belief that education was a general process through which a child learns to become a member of his culture.[15] James was concerned with the process by which a member of society learns social consciousness and becomes a normal member of that society. He was one of the first social philosophers to analyze the acquisition of the "social self," an end product of socialization. In a passage from *The Principles of Psychology* (1890), James outlined his principle of the "pluralism of selves":

> Properly speaking, *a man has as many social selves as there are individuals who recognize him* and carry an image of him in their mind. . . . But as the individuals who carry the images fall naturally into classes, we may practically say that he has as many different social selves as there are distinct *groups* of persons about whose opinions he cares. He generally shows a different side of himself to each of these different groups. . . .[16]

Thus, the acquisition of the social self, of self-consciousness, was said to be contingent on the reactions of various other individuals. For the first time self was viewed as a *social* object and thus as a primary social fact. The social and behavioral scientist was urged to regard the acquisition of selfhood as a fundamental problem.

"The Looking-Glass Self"

James's conception of the "pluralism of selves" had a significant influence on the writings of the American sociologist and social psychologist Charles Horton Cooley. Cooley was one of the first American sociologists to break with the Durkheimian directive for sociological analysis and definition of social facts. In Chapter 3 of his *Human Nature and the Social Order* (1909), Cooley states that

> the imaginations which people have of one another are the *solid facts* of society, and that to observe and interpret these

> must be a chief aim of sociology. . . . The intimate grasp of any social fact will . . . require that we divine what men think of one another.[17]

In this same treatise, Cooley furthered the task of carefully specifying the components of acquiring selfhood. He writes:

> In a very large and interesting class of cases the social reference takes the form of a somewhat definite imagination of how one's self—that is any idea he appropriates—appears in a particular mind, and the kind of self-feeling one has is determined by the attitude toward this attributed to that other mind. A social self of this sort might be called the reflected or looking-glass self:
>
> > "Each to each a looking-glass
> > Reflects the other that doth pass."
>
> As we see our face, figure, and dress in the glass, and are interested in them because they are ours, and pleased or otherwise with them according as they do or do not answer to what we should like them to be; so in imagination we perceive in another's mind some thought of our appearance, manners, aims, deeds, character, friends, and so on, and are variously affected by it.[18]

Finally, Cooley indicated that the development of a self-concept has three principal elements:

1. the imagination of our appearance to the other person
2. the imagination of his judgment of that appearance
3. some sort of self-feeling, such as pride or mortification.[19]

James's "pluralism of selves" and Cooley's "looking-glass" theory of self, along with the theoretical–philosophical assumptions from which they developed, were to have a significant influence on the Chicago School sociologists from the turn of the century to the late 1920s.

"The Definition of the Situation"

William Isaac Thomas was convinced of the inseparability of social psychology and sociology. Like Cooley, he believed that the solid facts of society and, thereby, the fundamental data for sociological analysis were the *imaginations* that people had of one another and of the social worlds they lived in. In their introduction to Part IV of

The Polish Peasant in Europe and America, Thomas and Znaniecki echo the basic theme of a subjectivist sociology:

> We must put ourselves in the position of the subject who tries to find his way in this world, and we must remember, first of all, that the environment by which he is influenced and to which he adapts himself, is *his* world, not the objective world of science —is nature and society as he sees them, not as the scientist sees them. The individual subject reacts only to his experience, and his experience is not everything that an absolutely objective observer might find in the portion of the world within the individual's reach, but only what the individual himself finds.[20]

Thomas later encapsulated these ideas in his "principle of the definition of the situation":

> If men define situations as real, they are real in their consequences.[21]

This fundamental idea was later to have a significant impact on the sociological understanding of deviant behavior, for it directed attention to the definitions and meaningful understandings of that behavior; that is, to its *evaluation,* which would ostensibly explain the consequences of such behavior for the actors. But let us return to the development of the model of socialization that members of this Chicago School were concerned with.

Symbolic Interaction: George Herbert Mead

George Herbert Mead came to the University of Chicago in 1894 at the behest of his colleague and close friend John Dewey.[22] In the 37 years of his professorship at Chicago, he became one of the most important influences on generations of graduate students and, through them, on countless numbers of American sociologists and social psychologists. Mead seems to have taken upon himself the task of integrating many of the theoretical contributions of his teachers William James and Josiah Royce and his colleagues Dewey, Cooley, and another pragmatist philosopher and social psychologist, James Mark Baldwin. He was especially interested in socialization and the role of the individual in society. But his contribution to these discussions were also highly original, for he specified the theoretical components of socialization and, from these, was able to construct a more general model of society and social interaction.

Mead, like Cooley and James, was concerned with the *process* by which the social self emerged. According to Mead, self-consciousness is initially a product of the symbolic interaction between the child and the "significant others" in his life—mother, father, and other relatives. Through the acquisition of language and the learning of gestures and expressions, the child inherits the symbolic culture of his society. These symbols mediate the very interaction between his self and the significant others.

At first, the child learns that he is an object responded to by significant others. These responses are often laden with implicit and explicit evaluations of himself as object: Johnny is a bad boy, Mary is a nice girl; or, at the level of gestures a slap on the fanny or a broad smile on mother's face becomes associated with a certain evaluation of "self." Mead indicates that the learning of self as object can be observed when the young child no longer "haphazardly emulates" mother's or father's behavior, but begins responding to himself as he has experienced significant others responding. For example, when the child, playing with his father's hammer, says, "Johnny [the child] shouldn't play with the hammer . . . it hurt him," he is *taking the role of the significant other* toward himself as object. Here we see the initial internalization of social controls. Mother and father, because they become the primary sources of rewards and punishments for the child, are the significant others. For this reason, this basic model of socialization is also a primary model of social control.

Mead likened this process of taking the role of the significant other to the "play" activity of children: the child plays at taking the role of a discreet series of significant others and views himself as an *object* to those significant others. Mead, in referring to the child, notes that he

> plays that he is, for instance, offering himself something, and he buys it; he gives a letter to himself and takes it away; he addresses himself as a parent or as a teacher; he arrests himself as a policeman. He has a set of stimuli which call out in himself the sort of responses they call out in others. He takes this group of responses and organizes them into a certain whole. Such is the simplest form of being another to one's self.[23]

As the child develops his facility with role taking and role playing and learns to take into account the reactions of specific others toward him, he begins to find himself in situations in which there are a multiplicity of demands and expectations that he must live up to. The child must learn to organize these attitudes of others into a *generalized* expectation for behavior in particular situations, and for a unified conception of self vis-à-vis those others.

To illustrate the change in this new developmental phase of

socialization, Mead employs the illustration of children playing a game and contrasts this with their earlier play activity. In a game like baseball, for instance—with specific rules, roles, and thus more explicit mutual expectations—the child/player must learn not only to take into account the attitudes of others toward himself and other players, but also to

> take their attitudes toward the various . . . aspects of the common social activity . . . in which, as members of an organized society or social group, they are all engaged.[24]

The child learns to take into account the "generalized other," as well as the discreet sets of "significant others." The social collective now exercises sufficient control to influence the individual member's thinking and behavior. In his abstract thought, the individual

> takes the attitude of the generalized other toward himself, without reference to its expression in any particular other individuals; and in concrete thought, he takes that attitude insofar as it is expressed in the attitudes toward his behavior of those other individuals with whom he is involved in the given social situation or act.[25]

Thus, through role playing or taking the roles of significant others toward himself, as well as taking into account the "generalized others," the individual develops a consciousness of self and an understanding of his role vis-à-vis the social "others."

In extending and refining this model of socialization, Mead stressed the importance of language and communication as the media through which the content of the self was acquired. He emphasized the significance of studying socialization and social behavior as an emerging process, as a fluid, changing, dynamic reality in which members of society develop meaningful understandings of their social roles and participation in group behavior. *Situated interaction* (interaction in a specific time and place) became a principal object of sociological analysis. *Negotiated reality*—the shared understanding of the situation in which individuals find themselves—was seen as the mechanism that made possible the ordinary social behavior between members of society.

Symbolic Interaction

Herbert Blumer, a principal disciple of Mead, indicates that Mead saw symbolic interaction as involving *interpretation*—"ascertaining the meaning of the actions or remarks of the other person"—

and *definition*—"conveying indications to another person as to how he is to act"[26] Mead's fundamental unit of analysis was *joint action*—"fitting together . . . the lines of behavior of the separate participants."[27] Society was composed of "joint actions" and was itself, therefore, a *dynamic,* rather than a static, reality as structural theorists had characterized it. Society and social behavior were seen as intersubjective realities.

Mead challenged the traditional conception of human society as an established structure. He saw social behavior and society as constructions made by actors; as realities to which actors assigned meanings and to which they accordingly established lines of behavior. Above all, Mead stressed the learning of behavior as a primary topic for sociological analysis. Human behavior was ultimately characterized by the fact that it was learned and continually relearned through a process of symbolic interaction and the intersubjective construction of definitions of the situation.

Mead's view of society and social behavior as symbolic interaction was to have a significant impact on many generations of graduate students at the University of Chicago. Since he did not publish extensively, Mead's social psychology and sociology were largely compiled by these students, from unpublished papers and the lecture notes, after his death in 1931.[28] In Chapter 4, we referred to those who were concerned with analyzing the influence of ecological factors on social disorganization and social deviance as the Chicago School. To a great extent the disciples of Mead and W. I. Thomas formed another "Chicago School," a distinctive social-psychological school of thought. Their conceptual framework has had an important influence when applied to several different areas of sociological analysis. But its application to the study of social deviation and deviant careers has produced perhaps one of the most extensive literatures. Both Chicago Schools found the study of deviant behavior conducive to the testing of their theoretical assumptions. Their insights into the nature of deviant behavior were, however, substantially different, as were the assumptions about human behavior and society with which they began.[29]

SUBJECTIVIST SOCIOLOGY: THEORIES OF ACTUALIZATION AND DEVIANT BEHAVIOR

A principal problem with causal or predispositional theories of deviant behavior and crime was that they did not seem to identify the factors that were most *commonly* associated with those behaviors. Sociological theories of predisposition (e.g., differential access to the opportunity structure, anomie, ecological area, and status deprivation) could be challenged on the basis of deviant behavior in which none of these factors exists or is demonstrably important, or in which these factors are clearly present but deviant behavior is not.

It took social scientists a while to realize that the analysis of the *actualization* of deviant behavior—its becoming a reality to the deviant and those around him—might be an important starting point for sociological investigation. Unless one took a completely deterministic view of the role of these predisposing variables, an accounting of deviant behavior would also have to look at how such behavior was *acquired.*

Deviant Behavior and Redefinitions of the Situation

Students of deviant behavior in the United States began the initial application of subjectivist sociological themes to such behavior in the early 1920s. Among the most influential scholars to underscore the importance of examining the actualization of deviant behavior was the University of Chicago sociologist W. I. Thomas. In *The Unadjusted Girl* (1923), Thomas focused on "the central influence of cultural *definitions* and *meanings* in structuring human action."[30] He analyzed how girls turned to such delinquent activities as stealing, prostitution, and vagrancy and examined the attempted rehabilitation of these girls by various social agencies.

Although Thomas began his analysis with the assumption that all behavior was influenced by one or more of four basic "wishes" or desires— for new experience, for security, for response, and for recognition[31]—he believed that these desires were regulated by *learned* cultural standards or conventions and by the *experiences* of individuals in interaction with others. Society, through its rules and laws, designated the proper channeling of these desires. The question of how delinquents chose unacceptable or deviant means to attain these desires could only be answered by examining the process whereby meaning was attached to such behavior. Thomas notes:

> Preliminary to any self-determined act of behavior there is always a stage of examination and deliberation which we may call *the definition of the situation.* And actually not only concrete acts are dependent on the definition of the situation, but gradually a whole life-policy and the personality of the individual himself follow from a series of such definitions.[32]

Thomas initially focused on the family and the community as the primary sources of the child's definitions of self and of proper and improper behavior. Using personal letters, letters to newspaper per-

sonal-advice columnists, and autobiographical materials, he illustrated how the family and the community exercise control over the
desires of individuals. The requests for advice from those experienc-
ing family and sexual problems (very much like letters to Dear Abby
or Ann Landers) indicated the extent to which the community's definitions of morality were inculcated in these individuals. Thomas,
however, believed that an "individualization of behavior" often occurs, whereby a person begins to define the situation independent of
the community.[33] This departure from community expectations and
definitions results from a *re*definition of the situation: a girl, forced by
a male neighbor to submit to his sexual advances, believes that she has
now lost her sense of worth, feels herself socially isolated, feels economically disadvantaged because she cannot find a good husband,
and therefore decides that there are no alternatives for her except
prostitution. Another girl, seeking adventure, nice clothes, amuse-
ment, and the attention of others, decides that these are obtainable if
she "exchanges" sexual favors; she determines that most women do
this anyway, and therefore rationalizes that there is nothing wrong
with prostitution.

Thomas presents illustration after illustration in which the redefinition of the situation is said to be the critical turning point in
one's *becoming* delinquent. He indicates that the girls' specific social
circumstances vary: some feel forced into prostitution for various
reasons; some like the economic advantages; some feel they truly help
the men they do business with; some enjoy the constant attention of
men. But common to all these cases is the redefinition of the situation,
the change in meaning that the girl attaches to her behavior. These
redefinitions are always in response to some problem, whatever the
individual might perceive it to be.

Thomas points out that *becoming* delinquent follows a normal,
nonpathological process of individualized problem solving:

> When, for example, children have escapades, run away, lie,
> steal, plot, etc., they are following some plan, pursuing some
> end, solving some problem as a result of their own definition of
> the situation. The naughtiness consists in doing something
> which is not allowed, or in ways which are not allowed. The
> intellectual pattern is the same whether they are solving a
> problem in arithmetic, catching a fish, building a dog house, or
> planning some deviltry.[34]

In other words, the learning, decision making, or redefinitions
of the situation stem not from some disordered feature or characteristic of personality; rather the learning of deviant behavior "involves all
of the mechanisms that are involved in any other learning."[35]

Analytic Induction

It is important to note the approach that Thomas takes in his efforts to explain deviant behavior. He seeks to discover the most *general* and *invariable* characteristics of this phenomenon, their common features. This is a far different strategy for constructing a theoretical framework than had been followed by other sociologists. This method of *analytic induction* was later used by other students interested in analyzing the actualization of deviant behavior.

Florian Znaniecki, coauthor with Thomas of *The Polish Peasant*, is generally given credit for popularizing the use of analytic induction in sociology. In *The Method of Sociology* (1934), Znaniecki states that sociologists should

> first, discover which characters in a given datum of a certain class are more, and which are less essential; secondly, abstract these characters, and assume hypothetically that the more essential are more general than the less essential, and must be found in a greater variety of classes; thirdly, test this hypothesis by investigating classes in which the latter characters are found; fourthly, establish a classification, i.e., organize all these classes in a scientific system based on the functions the respective characters play in determining them. This would be a proper analytic induction.[36]

The hypothesis stemming from such an inductive analysis stands until a case is found that does not share these general or common properties. In this event, the hypothesis must be reformulated to account for the deviant case.

Differential Association and the Actualization of Deviant Behavior

Thomas's method of analysis, as well as his theoretical assumptions about deviant behavior, influenced a number of his students at the University of Chicago. Edwin H. Sutherland, in particular, was greatly impressed with Thomas's emphasis on studying social processes. Like Thomas, Sutherland became interested in the fundamental processes of delinquent and criminal behavior. He was drawn to the process of learning and of acquiring definitions of the situation.

Advancing by the method of analytic induction, which he learned in part from Thomas and Znaniecki, and in part from his new colleague at the University of Indiana, Alfred Lindesmith, Sutherland concluded that a theory of crime *must* begin with the proposition that it was learned.[37] Sutherland had already put other "variables" to the test of the analytic-induction principle and had found them inadequate:

> Some Negroes commit crimes, some do not; some people who reside in delinquency areas commit crimes, some do not. Any concrete condition is sometimes associated with criminal behavior and sometimes not. Perhaps there is nothing that is so frequently associated with criminal behavior as being a male. But it is obvious that maleness does not explain criminal behavior. I reached the general conclusion that a concrete condition cannot be a cause of crime, and that the only way to get a causal explanation of criminal behavior is by abstracting from the varying concrete conditions things that are universally associated with crime.
>
> With the general point of view which I had acquired as a sociologist and used particularly in relation to criminal behavior, it seemed to me that learning, interaction, and communication were the processes around which a theory of criminal behavior should be developed. The theory of differential association was an attempt to explain criminal behavior in that manner.[38]

Sutherland explicitly presented his theory of differential association in the third edition of his *Principles of Criminology,* published in 1939. In the 4th edition (1947) the theory of differential association was redrafted to what remains its present form:

1. *Criminal behavior is learned.* Negatively, this means that criminal behavior is not inherited, as such; also, the person who is not already trained in crime does not invent criminal behavior, just as a person does not make mechanical inventions unless he has had training in mechanics.
2. *Criminal behavior is learned in interaction with other persons in a process of communication.* This communication is verbal in many respects but includes also "the communication of gestures."
3. *The principal part of the learning of criminal behavior occurs within intimate personal groups.* Negatively, this means that the impersonal agencies of communication, such as movies and newspapers, play a relatively unimportant part in the genesis of criminal behavior.
4. *When criminal behavior is learned, the learning includes (a) techniques of committing the crime, which are sometimes very complicated, sometimes very simple; (b) the specific direction of motives, drives, rationalizations, and attitudes.*

5. *The specific direction of motives and drives is learned from definitions of the legal codes as favorable or unfavorable.* In some societies an individual is surrounded by persons who invariably define the legal codes as rules to be observed, while in others he is surrounded by persons whose definitions are favorable to the violation of the legal codes. . . .

6. *A person becomes delinquent because of an excess of definitions favorable to violation of law over definitions unfavorable to violation of law.* This is the principle of differential association. It refers to both criminal and anti-criminal associations and has to do with counteracting forces. When persons become criminal, they do so because of contacts with criminal patterns and also because of isolation from anti-criminal patterns. . . .

7. *Differential associations may vary in frequency, duration, priority, and intensity.* This means that associations with criminal behavior and also association with anti-criminal behavior vary in those respects. "Frequency" and "duration" as modalities of associations are obvious and need no explanation. "Priority" is assumed to be important in the sense that lawful behavior developed in early childhood may persist throughout life, and also that delinquent behavior developed in early childhood may persist throughout life. . . . "Intensity" is not precisely defined but it has to do with such things as the prestige of the source of a criminal or anti-criminal pattern and with emotional reactions related to the associations. . . .

8. *The process of learning criminal behavior by association with criminal and anti-criminal patterns involves all of the mechanisms that are involved in any other learning.* Negatively, this means that the learning of criminal behavior is not restricted to the process of imitation. . . .

9. *While criminal behavior is an expression of general needs and values, it is not explained by those general needs and values since non-criminal behavior is an expression of the same needs and values.* Thieves generally steal in order to secure money, but likewise honest laborers work in order to secure money. The attempts by many scholars to explain criminal behavior by general drives and values, such as the happiness principle, striving for social status, the money motive, or frustration, have been and must continue to be futile since they explain lawful behavior as completely as they explain criminal behavior. They

are similar to respiration, which is necessary for any behavior but which does not differentiate criminal from non-criminal behavior. . . .[39]

The influence of Thomas, Cooley, and Mead can be discerned in Sutherland's propositions. Sutherland, however, believed that many other students of deviation and crime who took their orientation from these social-psychological theorists did not sufficiently stress the *process* of learning. In discussing the work of other adherents to the Chicago School tradition, he stated that they considered

> the development of criminal behavior . . . as involving the same learning processes as does the development of the behavior of a banker, waitress, or doctor. The content of learning, not the process itself, is considered as the significant element determining whether one becomes a criminal or a non-criminal.[40]

It is difficult to assess this attempt by Sutherland to differentiate his theory of *becoming* a criminal from attempts by others of the subjectivist orientation.[41] The important point remains that his was one of the first extensive formulations of a perspective on deviant behavior to couch its explanation in an interactionist–subjectivist framework. For this reason, it was a major departure from the theories of predisposition, which had dominated the field until then. Sutherland, through a careful explanation of the ideas that had brought him to his formulation, was influential in leading numerous students of deviation and crime to an analysis of the process of "actualization."

Differential Association: Some Problems

The theory of differential association has sparked considerable criticism and controversy in the decades since its original presentation. A comprehensive review of this controversy would lead us well beyond the scope of this chapter. However, a few examples of the criticisms leveled at this perspective will reveal some of its major problems. The student is also directed to many excellent reviews of this long and very interesting debate.[42]

A major criticism and a continuing topic of debate between opponents and proponents of this perspective is that it fails to live up to the principle of analytic induction: there are, critics claim, a number of exceptions or negative cases that the theory cannot explain. In particular, crimes of passion or of compulsion, such as murder or kleptomania (compulsive stealing), have been pointed to as exceptions since they do not seem to be learned and do not, supposedly, involve definitions of the situation or differential association.[43]

Donald Cressey, Sutherland's principal disciple and, since the 5th edition, the coauthor of *Principles,* has attempted to counter some of these criticisms through research findings, both his own and others, which show that even compulsive crimes manifest the kinds of thought processes implied by the theory. Using C. Wright Mills's conception of motivation as typical vocabularies or linguistic constructs that rationalize the behavior in question,[44] Cressey points out that crimes of compulsion, such as kleptomania and pyromania (compulsive fire setting), involve a very specific motivational set. Some "compulsive" shoplifters, for example, are quite able to rationalize their behavior and even to explain the development of their activities:

> For example, one might say, as did a criminal who had stolen a whole truck-load of groceries, "I didn't want to take them but I had to because I was hungry." This response may be compared with that of a person arrested for taking small objects from a store: "I didn't want to take them but I just had to take them," and with that of a person who had burned an automobile, "I just wanted to stir up some excitement." As indicated above, such rationalizations are not necessarily *ex post facto* justifications for acts—and if they are not, then there is no logical justification for classifying one person as a "thief" and the others as "compulsive." Motives are circumscribed by the actor's learned vocabulary.[45]

Cressey argues that compulsive criminal behavior displays learned thought processes and definitions of the situation through the rationalizations the criminal develops for his behavior. These rationalizations become the major "motivations" for the behavior in question. He adds that these individuals often define themselves as "kleptomaniacs" or as some other form of compulsive criminal; in other words, they have internalized the role definition of themselves as people who cannot stop what they are doing. This definition of self adds to the vocabulary of motives a major rationalization for continuing such behavior. Cressey concludes that because

> the development processes in so-called "compulsive criminality" are the same as the processes in other criminality, "compulsive crimes" are not, because of something in their nature, exceptional to the differential association theory. Upon closer empirical examination it probably will be demonstrated that criminality which traditionally has been assumed to be "personal" is actually a group product, and this criminality will become of more concern to the sociologist than has been the case in the past.[46]

A significant problem exists with Cressey's defense of the theory. Although he has made an ingenious point about the relationship of learning and motivation to behaviors formerly considered "pathological," he has not clearly demonstrated how this behavior is "learned in interaction with others," through a process of differential association. Although he points to *a* process of learning, he does not point to *the* process of learning predicted by the theory.[47]

The same problem is found in Cressey's explanation of "trust violation" (the crime of embezzlement). He indicates that the embezzler typically learns the skills needed for embezzlement as a normal course of learning to be an accountant or financial expert.[48] When this person is confronted with a situation in which he feels that a "non-shareable financial problem" exists (a problem that cannot be discussed with anyone), finds an opportunity for trust violation, and at the same time can redefine the situation as one in which he is only "borrowing" the money, the embezzlement will be more likely. The problem, again, is that the predicted pattern of learning is not found in embezzlement. Cressey himself has stated that although

> the general contention of the differential association theory, that criminality is learned, cannot be disputed, the more specific idea that criminality and non-criminality depend upon a ratio of contacts with criminal and anti-criminal behavior patterns is open to question in cases of crimes involving violation of financial trust. In the first place, contacts with criminal behavior patterns are not necessary to the learning of the technique or skill used in trust violation. Second, while the present research has not indicated definitely that such contacts cannot be precisely identified and weighted, it does appear that there is no practical way that known violators' prior contacts with the rationalizations necessary to trust violation can be observed so that one could develop a formula to be used in either the determination or prediction of trust violation in other cases.[49]

Cressey's second point above, concerning the impracticality of identifying the violator's prior contacts with definitions favorable or unfavorable to violation of law, has also been the subject of much discussion. Many critics have agreed with Cressey's conclusions, but have gone further to claim that the most significant problem with the theory is that its major concepts cannot be operationalized. They point out that such key concepts as "excess of definitions," "favorable or unfavorable," "differential" are very difficult to find indicators for.[50] Because Cressey seems to agree with a significant portion of these critics, some have found it disappointing that the theory has not been substantially revised to take these problems into account. Cressey explains that his reasons for not doing so have to do with the difference in the theory of differential association considered as a general principle which organizes and makes good sense of the data on crime and delinquency rates, as compared to the theory considered only as a statement of the precise mechanism by which a person becomes a criminal or a delinquent.[51]

In this defense, Cressey has nicely summed up the benefits and limitations of differential-association theory. As a principle that defines the general processes involved in someone's becoming deviant or criminal, the theory remains an important model for sociological investigation. As a theory that attempts a precise explanation of the specific mechanisms involved in learning to be a criminal, it has severe limitations. This has led many sociologists, including such adherents to the theory as Cressey, in search of a far less mechanistic and more precise model for explaning the learning or actualization of deviant behavior. These will be discussed in the next few chapters.

Sutherland's theory of differential association stands as a significant early application of basic symbolic-interactionist principles to the study of deviant behavior. This application was understandably very limited: it could apply only the bare framework of the interactionist perspective to this behavior. The richness of ideas contained in the thought of G. H. Mead, W. I. Thomas, and C. H. Cooley could not entirely be contained in a theory whose original intentions were to establish the rudimentary framework for explaining the social base of criminal behavior. The elaboration of this model, based on the more detailed and multifaceted symbolic-interactionist perspective, would occupy the attention of sociologists in decades to come.

The symbolic-interactionist perspective stressed above all, the *reciprocity* and *reflexiveness* of human behavior and interaction. The actions of one individual were often the basis of another's action. Actors continually consider the "other" in designing their own lines of behavior. Thus, comprehensive interactionist analysis must explain the behavioral dynamics between self and others. To use Blumer's term, the interactionist model forces us to consider the *joint actions* of the participants in a behavioral scene. To analyze the *action* of the "other" becomes as significant as to analyze the *action* of some primary person whose life experiences and definitions we are more interested in. The analysis of the "other's" action becomes particularly important when the relationship between actor and the "other" is one of unequal power or authority; when the "significant other" holds some power to control the life chances and self-regarding attitudes of the individual.

Sutherland's differential-association theory certainly implied the importance of key "others" in shaping the behavior of the individual engaged in criminal behavior. Most significantly, these "others" were

assumed to be the major suppliers of "definitions favorable to violation of the criminal law." However, Sutherland did not clearly account for the *range* of significant others who might potentially influence the deviant behavior or self-regarding attitudes of the individual, nor did he fully envisage the more particular characteristics of
the other's *actions* toward the deviant that could account for these
behavior and attitudes.

THE ACTUALIZATION OF DEVIANCE

Frank Tannenbaum, who was a disciple of John Dewey and was
influenced by Thomas and the Chicago School's social-psychological
and ecological traditions, was interested in juvenile delinquency and
the formation of delinquent subcultures. His text *Crime and the Community* (1938) not only focused on the primary actualization of deviant
behavior—the education of the delinquent into the delinquent role—
but also significantly extended the notion of "actualization" to include
those actions of significant others that increased the likelihood of
delinquent behavior and the formation of delinquent subcultures. In
other words, Tannenbaum recognized that the actualization of deviant behavior was the result of both the joint actions of certain juveniles and the various community-control agent who reacted to them
in various ways.

Tannenbaum, like Sutherland, was especially disenchanted with
theories of crime and delinquency that emphasized the pathological,
unsocial, or "maladjusted" nature of the behavior in question. According to Tannenbaum, crime and delinquency were best viewed as
normal reactions to certain life situations and problems. The delinquent gang was the outgrowth of the neighborhood play group,
which emphasized adventure, excitement, annoying others, climbing
over roofs, playing truant, "horsen around" and "goofing off."[52] "The
play group becomes a gang through coming into conflict with some
element in the environment."[53] The question becomes specifically *how*
are these "normal" children's activities, and the social organization
that supports them, transformed into delinquency by means of this
"conflict"? The conflict arises from the opposing definitions of the
situation, as held by the group of children or adolescent and others
within the community. What the juvenile defines as play, adventure,
and excitement are not defined as such by the community.

> To the community, however, these activities may and often do
> take on the form of a nuisance, evil, delinquency, with the
> demand for control, admonition, chastisement, punishment,
> police court, truant school. This conflict over the situation is

one that arises out of a divergence of values. As the problem develops, the situation gradually becomes redefined. The attitude of the community hardens definitely into a demand for suppression. There is a gradual shift from the definition of the specific acts as evil to a definition of the individual as evil, so that all his acts come to be looked upon with suspicion. In the process of identification his companions, hangouts, play, speech, income, all his conduct, the personality itself, become subject to scrutiny and question. From the community's point of view, the individual who used to do bad and mischievous things has now become a bad and unredeemable human being. From the individual's point of view there has taken place a similar change. He has gone slowly from a sense of grievance and injustice, of being unduly mistreated and punished, to a recognition that the definition of him as a human being is different from that of other boys in his neighborhood, his school, street, community. This recognition on his part becomes a process of self-identification and integration with the group which shares his activities. It becomes, in part, a process of rationalization; in part, a simple response to a specialized type of stimulus. The young delinquent becomes bad because he is defined as bad and because he is not believed if he is good. There is a persistent demand for consistency in character. The community cannot deal with people whom it cannot define. Reputation is this sort of public definition. . . .[54]

Tannenbaum goes on to describe the child's response to this evaluation of self as of defiance and escape.[55] The gang gives the juvenile the opportunity for expressing this defiance and provides the social context for "escape, security, pleasure, and peace."[56] He concludes that the transformation of "goofing-off" behavior into "juvenile delinquency" is caused by the initial "dramatization of evil," and the community's early negative reactions to the juvenile and his group.

The process of making the criminal, therefore, is a process of tagging, defining, identifying, segregating, describing, emphasizing, making conscious and self-conscious; it becomes a way of stimulating, suggesting, emphasizing, and evoking the very traits that are complained of. . . . The person becomes the thing he is described as being. . . .
The dramatization of the evil therefore tends to precipitate the conflict situation which was first created through some innocent maladustment.[57]

Tannenbaum's analysis of the dramatization of evil was a precursor of the *labeling,* or *societal-reaction* perspective. More specifically, it established the societal reactions of significant others to deviance as equally significant a subject for sociological analysis as the behavior of the deviant. Tannenbaum was one of the first analysts of deviant behavior to incorporate the notion of what Merton later called the "self-fulfilling prophecy" into his explanation of such behavior.[58] Initial evaluations, prophecies, or predictions of deviant character or actions have a tendency to fulfill themselves. The reason (beyond individual defiance) for the person's becoming "the thing he is described as being" were not fully specified by Tannenbaum. But his notion of the dramatization of evil opened the door to a new area of sociological exploration. This was the first in a series of concepts— "self-fulfilling prophecy," "secondary deviation," "deviance feedback and amplifying systems"—that characterized deviance as a reactive and eventually self-sustaining process.[59]

In his analysis of the learning of criminal behavior, Tannenbaum emphasized the role of "habituation" to a certain way of life. Learning to be a deviant involved a socialization process in which "instruction, stimulus, approval, companionship, conversation"[60] all combine to "normalize" a lifestyle that the deviant himself begins to define as usual; as not really an alternative lifestyle but as *the* lifestyle, his everyday reality.

Although couched in a peculiarly behavioristic language, Tannenbaum's explanation of learning went well beyond the examination of "objective" schedules of positive and negative reinforcements and dealt with the significant meanings and definitions of the situation that the deviant attached to the actions and attitudes of others. He was especially interested in the impact of these reactions by peers, older deviants, and control agents on the self-fulfilling lifestyle of the juvenile. The crystalization of these self-definitions and the development of social actions and reactions needed to sustain them would mark the juvenile's entrance into and passage through a deviant, or criminal, career.

THE EARLY INTERACTIONISTS: A SUMMARY

The combined contributions of Thomas, Sutherland, and Tannenbaum to a new model of analyzing deviation and crime are formidable. Each of these scholars added analytic aspects to an interactionist framework for the study of social deviation. Thomas provided both a theoretical and methodological model for analyzing the actualization of such behavior. Through the use of case histories, autobiographies, diaries, and letters, he explored attributes that were universally associated with deviant behavior. His preliminary analysis of socialization into the deviant role and his development of meaningful understandings and definitions of deviant behavior opened an area of sociological investigation that has yet to be adequately explored. Thomas's early exploration of the rationalization developed by deviants to explain their behavior and social status became a significant precursor of a sociological model of motivation that still influences the sociology of deviant behavior.

Sutherland offered students of crime a general but basic theoretical platform from which the *actualization* of such behavior could be viewed. His was the strongest argument for a refocusing of emphasis from theories of predisposition of either the uni- or multifactor variety to theories that explained deviant behavior as a process of becoming. Crime and delinquency, regardless of the social contexts in which they were found and the background characteristics of individuals engaged in these activities, were *learned;* and, specifically, were learned in a process of interaction. The task of the sociologist was to explore exactly how this learning took place—to specify the ways in which symbolic interaction, differential association, and the development of meaningful understandings led to deviant activity.

Tannenbaum helped to complete this analytic framework by drawing attention to the reactions of key "significant others" in crystallizing the deviation for the community and the deviant. Above all, Tannenbaum's description of the "dramatization of evil" was one of the most perceptive demonstrations of the idea that deviation, no matter what else it entailed, was a phenomenon subject to *evaluation.* No matter what the "causes" of deviant behavior, delinquency, or crime were said to be, its *determination* and dramatization by significant others played a major role in its actualization. Tannenbaum's formulation underscored the fact that deviation was a moral–ethical reality contingent on the judgments of goodness, badness, evil, and righteousness, and that these ethical pronouncements could have a significant impact on the indivdual or group being judged.

A PERSPECTIVE ON CRIMINAL OR ON DEVIANT BEHAVIOR?

The interactionist analysis of deviant behavior did not make significant progress beyond these early formulations until after World War II. Although some research pursued the ideas that we have just discussed,[61] no major theoretical integration was made until the early 1950s. Most significantly, there was no attempt to go beyond the specific subject matter of crime and delinquency to other varieties of deviant behavior. It might be obvious to the reader that the attention of sociologists who studied "social control" and the violation of social norms was focused, with few exceptions, on formal and official control systems and on violation of *legal* norms. Of the major sociological schools of thought that were applied to the study of deviant behavior, the disciples of Park and Burgess (students of the ecological distribution of social disorganization) were the most successful at extending their analyses beyond specifically criminal and delinquent behavior.[62]

Sociologists who took an interactionist perspective in studying the violation of norms confined themselves to clear-cut cases of legal infraction. The awareness that their assumptions on socialization, the learning of meaningful understandings, deviant self-identities, deviant motivations, the influence of societal reactions, and the "dramatizations of evil" could be applied to such phenomena as mental illness, alcoholism, eccentricity, physical disabilities, and other stigmatized conditions did not clearly develop until the 1950s. For this reason, it is difficult to speak of an interactionist theory of *deviant behavior* before this period.[63] A theory of criminal and delinquent activity differs from one of deviant behavior for the simple reason that it confines itself to more limited phenomena. A theory of deviant behavior would have to extend itself to other behaviors and actors perceived to be in violation of the normative expectations of a group.

Some scholars, no doubt, saw problems in extending these ideas in this way. After all, does mental illness, physical disability, or alcoholism really involve the same processes of actualization as criminal behavior or delinquency? *Based on prevailing understandings* of these behaviors, there was every reason to believe that they were illnesses or conditions for which personal responsibility was entirely or partially lacking. Could one really speak of "motivations" for becoming mentally ill or an alcoholic? Did a physically disabled individual really learn to become such in the same way as a burglar learned to steal? Did the societal reaction to mental illness, unwed mothers, or transvestites evidence the same "dramatization of evil" as found for juvenile delinquency? These were certainly crucial questions for the development of a perspective on deviant behavior. Even partial solutions to such questions were not realized until the decades of the 1950s and even the 1960s. The understanding that each of these behaviors involved a socialization process in which role playing, the development of self-identity, and the learning of interactional skills were necessary; that these behaviors were influenced by societal reactions to them in many of the same ways that had been found for delinquency and crime; and that each of these was subject to processes of stigmatization and evaluation—these were insights slow in developing.

OTHER SOCIOLOGICAL INFLUENCES ON THE STUDY OF THE ACTUALIZATION OF DEVIANT BEHAVIOR

The analysis of the actualization of deviant and, in particular, criminal behavior was enhanced by developments in other fields of sociological investigation. The growth of the sociology of occupations and professions, and the interest of sociologists in the formation and functioning of various types of urban subcultures, brought to the study of crime and delinquency an added emphasis on the analysis of "behavior systems."[64] With the increasing popularity of participant observation and the interest in an ethnographic sociology whose prime goal was the detailed description of situated social behavior, sociologists began to analyze what criminals and delinquents *did,* what they thought about themselves and others, and how they went about learning all of this.

Behavior Systems and the Sociology of Occupations

The interest in describing the behavior systems in crime was based on the dual assumption of *homogeneity* and *normality* in the activities and characteristics of those engaged in various types of crime or delinquency. To see the similarities in attitude, values, goals, practices, and interactional strategies of between criminals and delin-quents, the sociologist would have to view both in the context of their normal, day-to-day lives. Thus, a thorough examination of the life-styles and "life careers" of criminals and delinquents was needed. The developing field of the sociology of occupations and professions was influential in this effort. A great deal of credit for this interest must be given to Robert Park, Ernest Burgess, and other members of the Chicago ecological school. Their students were among the first to systematically study the occupational careers of such urban inhabit-ants as the taxi dance-hall girl, the jackroller, prostitute, saleslady, waitress, professional thief, teacher, doctor, and hobo. This tradition was continued and given broader theoretical meaning by a disciple of Park's and a professor at Chicago from 1938 to 1961, Everett C. Hughes.

Hughes was instrumental in developing a conceptual framework permitting the comparative analysis of various occupations and pro-fessions. Beginning with the following premise—

> I think it a good rule to assume that a feature of work behavior found in one occupation, even a minor or an odd one, will be found in others[65]

—Hughes and his students became interested in the common inter-actional strategies of doctors, schoolteachers, janitors, cabdrivers, musicians, barbers, and the publics that they serviced. They were especially interested in the detailed description of the social meaning of work as defined by the workers themselves.

Like the earlier wave of Chicago School sociologists, Hughes and his students were as interested in the illegitimate occupations as in the legitimate. Hughes himself was interested in the "bastard institutions"[66] and professions (because they were said to lie outside the realm of respectability)—gambling, prostitution, the black market, rackets, homosexual clubs and cabarets—and he encouraged the comparative analysis of these occupational enterprises with one another and with their more respectable neighbors.

In these various investigations, the students of occupations and professions began to study the preparation and education for the work role, the important later aspects of the workers' careers, and the special and routine problems and dilemmas associated with various types of work. The social-psychological dynamics of work deemed particularly important:

> Our aim is to *penetrate more deeply* into the personal and social drama of work to understand the social and social-psychological arrangements and devices by which men make their work tolerable, or even make it glorious to themselves and others. . . .Specifically we need to rid ourselves of any concepts which keep us from seeing that the essential problems of men at work are the same whether they do their work in the laboratories of some famous institution or in the messiest vat room of a pickle factory.[67]

This perspective, when applied to both legitimate and illegitimate enterprises, greatly enhanced the *demystification* of these activities and of those engaged in them. No matter what the status of the worker, the common, everyday properties of work and social identity became the subject for sociological examination. Stereotyped, romanticized, idealized, and overly-moralistic conceptions of these phenomena were (for the first time, in some cases) countered by rigorous and detailed analyses of their constitutive, everyday properties.

Urban Ethnography

Another contributing influence to and a partial development of this concern with the description of behavior systems and the routine or normal properties of everyday life and lifestyles was the growing popularity of ethnographic studies. A contribution of great importance was William Foote Whyte's study of the social organization of an Italian slum, *Street Corner Society*.[68]

In this study of "Cornerville," Whyte demonstrated the potential of a participant-observation methodology for depicting both the structural and interactional characteristics of Italian street culture. Throughout this field study, his primary concern was to characterize the world of Cornerville as it appears to those who live their lives within it. What are their standards for group acceptance of individuals in this society? What are the obligations of group members to one another? What are the typical life problems and conflicts experienced by these individuals? How do they define the role of work, family, recreation, and friendship in their lives? How is leadership developed and maintained in a group of streetcorner men? For all of these questions Whyte provided a carefully constructed explanation based upon field data.

In the enlarged edition of *Street Corner Society* (1955) Whyte added a methodological appendix, which went far beyond the recitation of rules and procedures for doing this type of field work. He shared with readers his experiences in doing this study, the decisions that had to be made as the study progressed and the advantages and shortcomings of this particular strategy. In short, he was able to give an informative accounting of fieldwork as a social process and of the researcher as social actor.

The importance of this book is its demonstration that the analysis of urban subcultures could best proceed by methods that preserved the integrity of the natural and routine settings in which they were found. Lifestyles that appeared to others as deviant, strange, disorganized, or unproductive looked very different when seen from the perspective of those that lived them. In the analysis of deviant behavior, as in the study of all social behavior, the subjects of our investigation must be accepted on their own terms. This is also the assumption underlying the sentiments of such analysts of deviation as David Matza, in his statement that

> there is a subculture of delinquency, but it is not a delinquent subculture.[69]

Matza points out that there is a long and strong tradition within sociology that views delinquent and other deviant subcultures as the immediate cause of delinquent or deviant behavior or acts. Deviation is explained by the reaction formations of members of oppositional subcultures (Cohen); or by the peculiarly different class and cultural values and standards of such subcultures as compared with those of conventional society (Miller); or by the common alienation of subcultural group members because of differential access to both legitimate- and illegitmate-opportunity structures (Cloward and Ohlin). These perspectives share the view that the delinquent subculture is somehow inherently different from, opposed to, and nonintegrated with the conventional order, and that these characteristics provide the structural context for delinquency.

Matza indicates that the delinquent subculture, when seen from the vantage point of its members, is far more integrated into the conventional order than assumed, and that the actions, values, and attitudes of supposedly delinquent group members do not evidence the kinds of commitments to delinquency that the theories imply. Not to realize that belonging to a gang is "recreational," "thrilling," "fun," "something to do," "something the rest of the guys do all the time," and that *delinquents would rather define it in these terms than in terms of moral or legal approbation,* is to miss the social meaning of delinquent behavior to the participants. To accentuate the differences of delinquent subcultures from conventional society and to overemphasize the sociocultural conditions that predispose one toward delinquency merely creates a mystique around the everyday reality of "delinquency" for those whose behaviors are judged as such.[70]

What Matza has said about delinquency applies with equal force to other forms of subcultural deviation. Before we concern ourselves with what causes or predisposes one toward deviation, we should analyze how those subcultures, behaviors, societal reactions, and counterreactions appear to those involved in the joint or collective action called social deviation. This analysis might very well inform our quest for why deviant behavior comes about.

Argot Analysis

Still another contribution to the study of the routine grounds and everyday reality of deviant behavior and individuals was the developing interest in the deviants' language, or "argot." Linguistic analysis was elevated to the status of a major technique in criminological investigation through the almost singular efforts of David Maurer, a professor of English and sociolinguistics. Maurer analyzed the special languages used by drug addicts, con artists, and pickpockets within their own deviant subcultures. Through the analysis of argot, Maurer was able to reveal, with acumen, the social worlds of these individuals; for the categories and meanings attached to these social realities were their very own. Maurer believed that

> argots originate in tightly closed cliques, in groups where there is a strong sense of camaraderie and highly developed group solidarity based primarily on community of occupation.[71]

The greater the extent to which the subculture is socially distant from the dominant culture, evidences this camaraderie and solidarity, develops specialized needs and specialized technical skills, the more likely that an argot will be developed. For this reason, Maurer claimed, con artists and pickpockets have a well-developed criminal argot, while prostitutes have one of the *least* developed.[72] Prostitutes do not need to learn specialized technical skills and do not, as a group, possess the camaraderie and solidarity that more professionalized criminals exhibited.

Among highly skilled professional thieves, argot is related to the complexity of their social organization and to the differential categories of task performance and experience. Without knowledge of these categories and of their usage by members of deviant subcultures, the investigator is incapable of understanding the fundamental meaning of their daily activities; in addition, his perspective will always be that of an outsider witnessing a mysterious, strange, and sometimes even threatening melange of activities and people. The social scientist is in much the same position as the judge trying to understand the admitted professional pickpocket in this passage from Maurer's *Whiz Mob*:

> *Judge:* Now you just tell the Court in your own way what you were doing.
>
> *Me:* Well, Judge, your honor; I was out gandering around for a soft mark and made a tip that was going to cop a short. I eased myself into the tip and just topped a leather in Mr. Bate's left prat when I blowed I was getting a jacket from these two honest bulls. So I kick the okus back in his kick and I'm clean. Just then this flatfoot nails me, so here I am on a bum rap. All I crave is justice, and I hope she ain't blind.[73]

Although this illustration is, no doubt, an extreme one, it serves to show the importance of understanding the categories of meaning used by the subjects we study.

For Maurer, the benefit of sociolinguistic, or argot, analysis was not only that it offered the student of crime another inroad to understanding the social and social-psychological reality of crime, but also that it was essential in the demystification of the criminal and his activities. Without this demystification, the routine properties of many varieties of deviant behavior are unfathomable. In short, if the student of deviant behavior wants to fully understand these phenomena, he must at some point study the categories of meaning used by his subjects in reference to their activities. Maurer was influential in bringing other students of crime and deviant behavior to the study of argot and, through this analysis, to the routine, everyday characteristics of deviant activities and lifestyles.[74]

SUMMARY

The introduction into sociology of a subjectivist perspective marked the development of a concern for the thorough analysis of the actualization of human behavior. Among American social scientists, the work of Thomas, Cooley, and Mead emphasized the need for an examination of socialization, human communication, situated social interaction, and definitions of the situation. Social reality was viewed as an emergent reality, *constructed* by the members of society in their daily encounters with one another. Through an examination of situated social behavior and the development of intersubjective or shared definitions of the situation, the sociologist could come to understand this *process* by which social reality was constructed. The meanings that actors attached to their daily social activities with and among fellow actors were made the focal points of sociological attention.

This shift in perspective among American sociologists had a significant effect on the study of deviant behavior. Students of crime and delinquency began moving away from uni- and multifactor theories of crime causation and predisposition to an examination of the *actualization* of those behaviors. No matter what social-structural or ecological factors characterized the alleged deviants, sociologists still had to explain *how* these individuals went about learning and doing what they did. It might well be said that subjectivist sociology forced students of human behavior to turn their attention to questions of *how*, and not only of *why*. *How*-questions inevitably lead to the description of a process. Deviant behavior, it was believed, was best viewed as just such a process; as an evolving phenomenon subject to the interpretations, evaluations, and definitions of both the deviant and others who were involved in the joint activity.

Thomas and Sutherland each emphasized the significance of definitions and subjective interpretations as motivational factors toward delinquency and crime—as the deviants' commonsensical rationalizations and attempts to come to grips with how they have become deviant. These "vocabularies of motive," as well as attitudes, values, techniques, and skills, were seen as learned in a process of "differential association." It became necessary to specify the precise mechanisms of learning and the patterns of interaction that allowed for the development of factors integral to one's becoming deviant.

Still another perspective on this process of *becoming* deviant was Tannenbaum's. Seeing that the reactions of the community to delinquency were vital to its actualization, he characterized this form of deviation as truly a *joint activity* involving both the alleged deviant and those given to the dramatization of the deviant's evil ways. Tannenbaum, more than other analysts of deviant behavior, realized the essential *reflexiveness* of such behavior and warned against the danger of viewing delinquency as a pathological phenomenon within a social vacuum. Delinquency and the delinquent subculture were best understood as normal or routine activities and as forms of social organization, respectively. The actions of both the deviant and the community-control agents should be analyzed for their constitutive properties; but this analysis was threatened by sociological perspectives that began with the assumption of inherent pathology and disorganization in the initial actions of the youth. Above all, Tannenbaum was one of the first students of deviant behavior to clearly emphasize the role of "evaluation" in its actualization: deviance was an *evaluative* reality.

The study of deviant behavior as an evolving process required firsthand observation of what exactly was evolving. The detailed, descriptive accounting of deviant lifestyles and the routine and normal characteristics of deviant behavior became more popular as a result of developments in other sociological disciplines. Students of occupations and professions were influential in developing a conceptual framework that greatly aided the demystification of various careers, both legitimate and illegitimate. Emphasis was placed on the routine properties of career roles: problems of entrance into a career, socialization into a career role, learning to deal with typical career problems and difficulties, factors influential in advancing through stages of a career, and so on. The applicability of this analytic framework to deviant careers was later demonstrated by the work of sociologists in the 1950s and 1960s. Again, the major contribution of this perspective for the advancement of a sociology of deviant behavior was its framework, through which the routine, everyday properties of deviant behavior could be understood *from the perspective of the alleged deviant.*

Finally, the analysis of deviant behavior *on its own terms* was given a special emphasis through the efforts of urban ethnographers like William F. Whyte and sociolinguists like David Maurer. In his own way and through his own methods of analysis, each was able to reveal the social organization and cultural characteristics of groups that sizeable segments of our society consider outsiders or deviants. Their impact on students of deviant behavior and crime was and remains considerable.

---

[1]The debate seems to have functioned as an arena in which the substantive domain boundaries of the new and old disciplines could be established.

[2]See H. Stuart Hughes, *Consciouness and Society: The Reorientation of European Social Thought* 1890–1930. New York: Knopf, 1958. Durkheim, unlike the others, would have been very much against the sociological analysis of "individual consciousness," for he saw this as a purely psychological problem. He was, however, concerned with the development of group, or "collective," conscience and consciousness. See, for example, *The Division of Labor in Society.*

[3]As we will show, a well-formulated theoretical/conceptual model of some variety of deviant behavior based on the principle of learning emerged in the late 1930s

with the work of Sutherland, Tannenbaum, and other criminologists influenced by a subjectivist sociological perspective.

[4]The sociology of Emile Durkheim most clearly embodied these two major characterizing themes. The reader should review the discussions of these themes in Chapter 2 of this book. The view of social facts as *external* to the individual (the sociologism of Durkheim's sociology) is essentially what is meant by an objectivist position.

[5]This, again, is the belief in a causal analysis that proceeds from the explanation of "objective" social facts by other "objective" social facts, and a renunciation of what proponents referred to as psychological reductionist explanations and concerns with "subjective reality."

[6]Robert M. MacIver, *Social Causation.* New York: Harper Torchbooks, 1964, pp. 371–72. Originally published by Ginn, 1942.

[7]Although a full analysis of the intellectual antecedents of subjectivist sociology would be quite out of place in a text on prespectives on social deviation, a short discussion cannot be avoided because of the fundamental relevance of these sociological frameworks to contemporary perspectives on deviation.

[8]The Enlightenment period extended roughly from the late seventeenth century to the period just before the French Revolution.

[9]See Irving Zeitlin, *Ideology and the Development of Sociological Theory.* Englewood Cliffs, N.J.: Prentice-Hall, 1968

[10]See, for example, Hughes, *Consciousness and Society,* Ch. 6, "Neo-Idealism in History," pp. 183–92.

[11]In many cases, these were the major professors of future sociologists like Weber, Simmel, Mannheim and an influence on American social philosophers and sociologists like William James, Dewey, G. H. Mead, and C. H. Cooley.

[12]It is contingent on the subjective interpretations of reality by the social scientist in the same way that all understanding of the social world is contingent on the actor's subjective interpretation of it. The understanding of the social scientist is not based on a categorically different process of knowing from that of other social actors.

[13]Max Weber, *The Theory of Social and Economic Organizations,* trans. by A. M. Henderson and Talcott Parsons. Glencoe, Ill.: Free Press, 1947, p. 88.

[14]See Hughes, *Consciousness and Society,* p. 197. James and Dilthey had a good many ideas in common. Hughes quotes Albert Saloman as describing Dilthey as "the German William James."

[15]See, especially, John Dewey, *Human Nature and Conduct.* New York: Henry Holt, 1922.

[16]William James, *The Principles of Psychology,* Vol. 1. London: Macmillan, 1901, Ch. 10, p. 294. Originally published by Henry Holt, 1890.

[17]Charles Horton Cooley *Human Nature and the Social Order.* Glencoe, Ill.: Free Press, 1909, pp. 121–22.

[18]Ibid., pp. 183–84.

[19]Ibid., p. 184.

[20]W. I. Thomas and Florian Znaniecki, *The Polish Peasant in Europe and America.* New York: Dover, 1958. Originally published by Knopf, 1927.

[21]W. I. Thomas and Dorothy S. Thomas, *The Child in America.* New York: Knopf, 1928.

[22]Anselm Strauss, (ed.) *G. H. Mead On Social Psychology.* Chicago: University of Chicago Press, Phoenix Ed. 1964, p. viii.

[23]Ibid., p. 215.

[24]Ibid., p. 219.

[25]Ibid., p. 220.

[26]Herbert Blumer, "Sociological Implications of the Thought of George Herbert Mead," *The American Journal of Sociology*, Vol. 71 (March 1966), p. 537.

[27]Ibid., p. 540.

[28]Strauss, *G. H. Mead.*

[29]There is much that these two schools have in common. In particular, the methodological strategies employed by members of the ecological school—field studies, and the use of biographical data, life histories, and descriptive analysis—were also used by "symbolic interactionists." As we will see later in the chapter, there were mutual interests in the study of occupations and professions and in the study of urban lifestyles and urban subcultures.

[30]Michael Parenti, Introduction to W. I. Thomas, *The Unadjusted Girl.* New York: Harper Torchbooks, 1967, p. xi. Originally published by Little, Brown, 1923.

[31]Ibid., p. 5.

[32]Ibid., p. 42.

[33]Ibid., Ch. 3, pp. 70–97.

[34]Ibid., pp. 234–35.

[35]Edwin Sutherland and Donald Cressey, *Principles of Criminology*, 6th ed. Philadelphia: Lippincott, New York: p. 79.

[36]Florian Znaniecki, *The Method of Sociology.* New York: Farrar and Rinehart, 1934, pp. 259–60.

[37]Karl Schuessler, ed., *Edwin H. Sutherland On Analyzing Crime.* Chicago: University of Chicago Press, 1973. See "Field of Interest," p. 17.

[38]*Edwin H. Sutherland,* Development of the Theory" in Schuessler, *Edwin H. Sutherland*, p. 19.

[39]Edwin H. Sutherland and Donald Cressey, *Principles of Criminology*, 6th ed. Philadelphia: Lippincott, 1955, pp. 77–79.

[40]Ibid., p. 58.

[41]From the text and other papers that he has written, it is difficult to understand precisely who were these "others" who emphasized the *content* of learning over the *process* of learning.

[42]See, especially, Donald Cressey, "Some Popular Criticisms of Differential Association," in Cressey, *Delinquency, Crime and Differential Association.* The Hague: Martinus Nijhoff, 1964. Cressey gives a thorough listing of the major criticisms of the theory.

[43]See Cressey, Ibid., "Differential Associations and Compulsive Crimes," pp. 90–107.

[44]For example, a prostitute might claim that *all* women are made to be prostitutes in one way or another and that her own prostitution is therefore not really deviant. These are "after-the-act" motivations to continue on with behavior in question. These will be discussed in greater depth in the next chapter.

[45]Cressey, *Delinquency*, p. 104.

[46]Ibid., p. 107.

[47]The theory specifically says that the learning takes place in "differential association" with others, and it implies that motivation as a learned definition of the situation ought to precede the behavior in question.

[48]Donald R. Cressey, *Other People's Money: A Study in the Social Psychology of Embezzlement.* Glencoe, Ill.: Free Press, 1953.

[49]Cressey, *Delinquency*, pp. 117–18.

[50]Ibid., pp. 86–87.

[51]Ibid., p. 88.

[52]Frank Tannenbaum, *Crime and the Community*. Cincinnati: Ginn, 1938, p. 17.

[53]Ibid., p. 10.

[54]Ibid., p. 18.

[55]Ibid.

[56]Ibid., p. 19.

[57]Ibid., pp. 19–20.

[58]Robert K. Merton, "The Self-fulfilling Prophecy," in Merton, *Social Theory and Social Structure,* revised and enlarged ed. New York: Free Press of Glencoe, 1957, pp. 421–36.

[59]For "secondary deviation" see Edwin Lemert, *Social Pathology*. New York: McGraw-Hill, 1951, pp. 75ff; also Lemert, "The Concept of Secondary Deviation," in Lemert *Human Deviance, Social Problems, and Social Control,* Englewood Cliffs, N.J.: Prentice-Hall, 1967, pp. 40–64. For "deviance-feedback and amplifying systems" see Magorah Maruyama, "The Second Cybernetics: (Deviation-Amplifying-Mutual Causal) Processes," in Walter Buckley, ed., *Modern Systems Research for the Behavioral Scientists*. Chicago: Aldine, 1968, also Thomas Scheff, *Mental Ilness: A Sociological Theory*. Chicago: Aldine, 1966, pp. 97–101.

[60]Tannenbaum, *Crime,* Ch. 3 "Education for Crime," p. 51.

[61]Most notably, research by Sutherland and students of his interested in substantiating the assumptions of the differential-association theory.

[62]As we have already noted, these sociologists, in addition to sudying delinquency and crime, also analyzed mental illness, hobos, alcholism, and suicide.

[63]I have until now been referring to "theories of deviant behavior," knowing that these ideas were eventually applied successfully to other forms of deviant behavior.

[64]The term *behavior system* was used by Sutherland to illustrate that criminal behavior often showed a significant amount of integration and unity and that it was common to an entire category of criminal activity. Professional theft, racketeering, corporate security swindlers, and con artists manifest a *system* of behavior, values, attitudes, and skills. For a description of criminal behavior systems, see Sutherland and Cressey *Principles of Criminology,* Ch. 13, and Marshall Clinard and Richard Quinney, *Criminal Behavior Systems: A Typology*. New York: Holt, Rinehart and Winston, 1967.

[65]Everett C. Hughes, *The Sociological Eye: Selected Papers*. Chicago: Aldine-Atherton, 1971, p. 301.

[66]Ibid., pp. 98–105.

[67]Ibid., p. 342.

[68]William Foote Whyte, *Street Corner Society*. Chicago: University of Chicago Press, 1943.

[69]David Matza, *Delinquency and Drift*. New York: Wiley, 1964, p. 33.

[70]This is not to say that there are no significant differences between deviant subcultures and the dominant culture. But the important question is whether we should attribute a deterministic role to these factors, as other theorists have done. For a discussion of the need to demystify explanations of deviant behavior, see Howard S. Becker, "Labelling Theory Reconsidered," in Becker, *Outsiders,* rev. ed. New York: Free Press, 1973.

[71]David Maurer, "Prostitutes and Criminal Argot," *American Journal of Sociology,* Vol. 44 (January 1939), pp. 546–50, 547. See also David Maurer, *The Big Con*. Indianapolis: Bobbs-Merrill, 1940.

[72]Maurrer's analysis of prostitution is heavily biased by certain assumptions about the morals of women who have become prostitutes.

[73]David Maurer, *Whiz Mob*. New Heaven: New Haven College and University Press, 1964, p. 55.

[74]See, for example, Ned Polsky, *Hustlers, Beats and Others*. Chicago: Aldine, 1967, and Peter Letkemann *Crime As Work*. Englewood Cliffs, N.J.: Prentice-Hall, 1973.

SELECTED READINGS

1966 Herbert Blumer, "Sociological Implications of the Thought of George Herbert Mead," *The American Journal of Sociology*, Vol. 71 (March 1966), pp. 535-44.

1967 W. I. Thomas, *The Unadjusted Girl*. New York: Harper Torchbook ed.

1973 Karl Schuessler, *Edwin H. Sutherland on Analyzing Crime*. Chicago: University of Chicago Press.

1974 Edwin Sutherland and Donald Cressey, *Criminology*, 9th ed. Philadelphia: Lippincott.

1938 Frank Tannenbaum, *Crime and Community*. Cincinnati: Ginn.

1964 David Maurer, *Whiz Mob*. New Haven: New Haven College and University Press.

SELECTED APPLICATIONS

The article by Chambliss illustrates some of the important factors that influence the societal reaction to delinquency. The "dramatization of evil" appears to be contingent on the perceived seriousness, threat, and visibility of the individuals and behaviors in question. The selection also indicates how the different social identities of the youths, as maintained by members of the community, made for a difference between pronouncements of "delinquency" and "sowing wild oats."

THE SAINTS AND THE ROUGHNECKS
William J. Chambliss

Eight promising young men—children of good, stable, white upper-middle-class families, active in school affairs, good pre-college students—were some of the most delinquent boys at Hanibal High School. While community residents and parents knew that these boys occasionally sowed a few wild oats, they were totally unaware that sowing wild oats completely occupied the daily routine of these young men. The Saints were constantly occupied with truancy, drinking, wild driving, petty theft and vandalism. Yet not one was officially arrested for any misdeed during the two years I observed them.

This record was particularly surprising in light of my observations during the same two years of another gang of Hanibal High School students, six lower-class white boys known as the Roughnecks. The Roughnecks were constantly in trouble with police and community even though their rate of delinquency was about equal with that of the Saints. What was the cause of this disparity? the result? The following consideration of the activities, social class and community perceptions of both gangs may provide some answers.

The Saints from Monday to Friday   The Saints' principal daily concern was with getting out of school as early as possible. The boys managed to get out of school with minimum danger that they would be accused of playing hookey through an elaborate procedure for obtaining "legitimate" release from class. The most common procedure was for one boy to obtain the release of another by fabricating a meeting of some committee, program, or recognized club. Charles might raise his hand in his 9:00 chemistry class and ask to be excused—a euphemism for going to the bathroom. Charles would go to Ed's math class and inform the teacher that Ed was needed for a 9:30 rehearsal of the drama club play. The math teacher would recognize Ed and Charles as "good students" involved in numerous school activities and would permit Ed to leave at 9:30. Charles would return to his class, and Ed would go to Tom's English class to obtain his release. Tom would engineer Charles' escape. The strategy would continue until as many of the Saints as possible were freed. After a stealthy trip to the car (which had been parked in a strategic spot), the boys were off for a day of fun.

Over the two years I observed the Saints, this pattern was repeated nearly every day. There were variations on the theme, but in one form or another, the boys used this procedure for getting out of class and then off the school grounds. Rarely did all eight of the Saints manage to leave school at the same time. The average number avoiding school on the days I observed them was five.

Having escaped from the concrete corridors the boys usually

Reprinted by permission of Transaction, Inc., from *Society*, Vol. II, no. 1. © 1973 by Transaction, Inc.

went either to a pool hall on the other (lower-class) side of town or to a cafe in the suburbs. Both places were out of the way of people the boys were likely to know (family or school officials), and both provided a source of entertainment. The pool hall entertainment was the generally rough atmosphere, the occasional hustler, the sometimes drunk proprietor and, of course, the game of pool. The cafe's entertainment was provided by the owner. The boys would "accidentally" knock a glass on the floor or spill cola on the counter—not all the time, but enough to be sporting. They would also bend spoons, put salt in sugar bowls and generally tease whoever was working in the cafe. The owner had opened the cafe recently and was dependent on the boys' business which was, in fact, substantial since between the horsing around and the teasing they bought food and drinks.

The Saints on Weekends   On weekends the automobile was even more critical than during the week, for on weekends the Saints went to Big Town—a large city with a population of over a million 25 miles from Hanibal. Every Friday and Saturday night most of the Saints would meet between 8:00 and 8:30 and would go into Big Town. Big Town activities included drinking heavily in taverns or nightclubs, driving drunkenly through the streets, and committing acts of vandalism and playing pranks.

By midnight on Fridays and Saturdays the Saints were usually thoroughly high, and one or two of them were often so drunk they had to be carried to the cars. Then the boys drove around town, calling obscenities to women and girls; occasionally trying (unsuccessfully so far as I could tell) to pick girls up; and driving recklessly through red lights and at high speeds with their lights out. Occasionally they played "chicken." One boy would climb out the back window of the car and across the roof to the driver's side of the car while the car was moving at high speed (between 40 and 50 miles an hour); then the driver would move over and the boy who had just crawled across the car roof would take the driver's seat.

Searching for "fair game" for a prank was the boys' principal activity after they left the tavern. The boys would drive alongside a foot patrolman and ask directions to some street. If the policeman leaned on the car in the course of answering the question, the driver would speed away, causing him to lose his balance. The Saints were careful to play this prank only in an area where they were not going to spend much time and where they could quickly disappear around a corner to avoid having their license plate number taken.

Construction sites and road repair areas were the special province of the Saints' mischief. A soon-to-be-repaired hole in the road inevitably invited the Saints to remove lanterns and wooden barricades and put them in the car, leaving the hole unprotected. The boys would find a safe vantage point and wait for an unsuspecting motorist to drive into the hole. Often, though not always, the boys would go up to the motorist and commiserate with him about the dreadful way the city protected its citizenry.

Leaving the scene of the open hole and the motorist, the boys would then go searching for an appropriate place to erect the stolen barricade. An "appropriate place" was often a spot on a highway near a curve in the road where the barricade would not be seen by an oncoming motorist. The boys would wait to watch an unsuspecting motorist attempt to stop and (usually) crash into the wooden barricade. With saintly bearing the boys might offer help and understanding.

A stolen lantern might well find its way onto the back of a police car or hang from a street lamp. Once a lantern served as a prop for a reenactment of the "midnight ride of Paul Revere" until the "play," which was taking place at 2:00 AM in the center of a main street of Big Town, was interrupted by a police car several blocks away. The boys ran, leaving the lanterns on the street, and managed to avoid being apprehended.

Abandoned houses, especially if they were located in out-of-the-way places, were fair game for destruction and spontaneous vandalism. The boys would break windows, remove furniture to the yard and tear it apart, urinate on the walls and scrawl obscenities inside.

Through all the pranks, drinking and reckless driving the boys managed miraculously to avoid being stopped by police. Only twice in two years was I aware that they had been stopped by a Big City policeman. Once was for speeding (which they did every time they drove whether they were drunk or sober), and the driver managed to convince the policeman that it was simply an error. The second time they were stopped they had just left a nightclub and were walking through an alley. Aaron stopped to urinate and the boys began making obscene remarks. A foot patrolman came into the alley, lectured the boys and sent them home. Before the boys got to the car one began talking in a loud voice again. The policeman, who had followed them down the alley, arrested this boy for disturbing the peace and took him to the police station where the other Saints gathered. After paying a $5.00 fine, and with the assurance that there would be no permanent record of the arrest, the boy was released.

The boys had a spirit of frivolity and fun about their escapades. They did not view what they were engaged in as "delinquency," though it surely was by any reasonable definition of that word. They simply viewed themselves as having a little fun and who, they would ask, was really hurt by it? The answer had to be no one, although this fact remains one of the most difficult things to explain about the gang's behavior. Unlikely though it seems, in two years of drinking, driving, carousing and vandalism no one was seriously injured as a result of the Saints' activities.

The Saints in School   The Saints were highly successful in school. The average grade for the group was "B," with two of the boys having close to a straight "A" average. Almost all of the boys were popular and many of them held offices in the school. One of the boys was vice-president of the student body one year. Six of the boys played on athletic teams.

At the end of their senior year, the student body selected ten seniors for special recognition as the "school wheels"; four of the ten were Saints. Teachers and school officials saw no problem with any of these boys and anticipated that they would all "make something of themselves."

How the boys managed to maintain this impression is surprising in view of their actual behavior while in school. Their technique for covering truancy was so successful that teachers did not even realize that the boys were absent from school much of the time. Occasionally, of course, the system would backfire and then the boy was on his own. A boy who was caught would be most contrite, would plead guilty and ask for mercy. He inevitably got the mercy he sought.

Cheating on examinations was rampant, even to the point of orally communicating answers to exams as well as looking at one another's papers. Since none of the group studied, and since they were primarily dependent on one another for help, it is surprising that grades were so high. Teachers contributed to the deception in their admitted inclination to give these boys (and presumably others like them) the benefit of the doubt. When asked how the boys did in school, and when pressed on specific examinations, teachers might admit that they were disappointed in John's performance, but would quckly add that they "knew that he was capable of doing better," so John was given a higher grade than he had actually earned. How often this happened is impossible to know. During the time that I observed the group, I never saw any of the boys take homework home. Teachers may have been "understanding" very regularly.

One exception to the gang's generally good performance was Jerry, who had a "C" average in his junior year, experienced disaster the next year and failed to graduate. Jerry had always been a little more nonchalant than the others about the liberties he took in school. Rather than wait for someone to come get him from class, he would offer his own excuse and leave. Although he probably did not miss any more classes than most of the others in the group, he did not take the requisite pains to cover his absences. Jerry was the only Saint whom I ever heard talk back to a teacher. Although teachers often call him a "cut up" or a "smart kid," they never referred to him as a troublemaker or as a kid headed for trouble. It seems likely, then, that Jerry's failure his senior year and his mediocre performance his junior year were consequences of his not playing the game the proper way (possibly because he was disturbed by his parents' divorce). His teachers regarded him as "immature" and not quite ready to get out of high school.

The Police and the Saints The local police saw the Saints as good boys who were among the leaders of the youth in the community. Rarely, the boys might be stopped in town for speeding or for running a stop sign. When this happened the boys were always polite, contrite and pled for mercy. As in school, they received the mercy they asked for. None ever received a ticket or was taken into the precinct by the local police.

The situation in Big City, where the boys engaged in most of their delinquency, was only slightly different. The police there did not know the boys at all, although occasionally the boys were stopped by a patrolman. Once they were caught taking a lantern from a construction site. Another time they were stopped for running a stop sign, and on several occasions they were stopped for speeding. Their behavior was as before: contrite, polite and penitent. The urban police, like the local police, accepted their demeanor as sincere. More important, the urban police were convinced that these were good boys just out for a lark.

The Roughnecks Hanibal townspeople never perceived the Saints' high level of delinquency. The Saints were good boys who just went in for an occasional prank. After all, they were well dressed, well mannered and had nice cars. The Roughnecks were a different story. Although the two gangs of boys were the same age, and both groups engaged in an equal amount of wild-oat sowing, everyone agreed that the not-so-well-dressed, not-so-well-mannered, not-so-rich boys were heading for trouble. Townspeople would say, "You can see the gang members at the drugstore, night after night, leaning against the storefront (sometimes drunk) or slouching around inside buying cokes, reading magazines, and probably stealing old Mr. Wall blind. When they are outside and girls walk by, even respectable girls, these boys make suggestive remarks. Sometimes their remarks are downright lewd."

From the community's viewpoint, the real indication that these kids were in for trouble was that they were constantly involved with the police. Some of them had been picked up for stealing, mostly small stuff, of course, "but still it's stealing small stuff that leads to big time crimes." "Too bad," people said. "Too bad that these boys couldn't behave like other kids in town; stay out of trouble, be polite to adults, and look to their future."

The community's impression of the degree to which this group of six boys (ranging in age from 16 to 19) engaged in delinquency was somewhat distorted. In some ways the gang was more delinquent than the community thought; in other ways they were less.

The fighting activities of the group were fairly readily and accurately perceived by almost everyone. At least once a month, the boys would get into some sort of fight, although most fights were scraps between members of the group or involved only one member of the group and some peripheral hanger-on. Only three times in the period of observation did the group fight together: once against a gang from across town, once against two blacks and once against a group of boys from another school. For the first two fights the group went out "looking for trouble"— and they found it both times. The third fight followed a football game and began spontaneously with an argument on the football field between one of the Roughnecks and a member of the opposition's football team.

Jack had a particular propensity for fighting and was involved in most of the brawls. He was a prime mover of the escalation of arguments into fights.

More serious than fighting, had the community been aware of it, was theft. Although almost everyone was aware that the boys occasionally stole things, they did not realize the extent of the activity. Petty stealing was a frequent event for the Roughnecks. Sometimes they stole as a group and coordinated their efforts; other times they stole in pairs. Rarely did they steal alone.

The thefts ranged from very small things like paperback books, comics and ballpoint pens to expensive items like watches. The nature of the thefts varied from time to time. The gang would go through a period of systematically shoplifting items from automobiles or school lockers. Types of thievery varied with the whim of the gang. Some forms of thievery were more profitable than others, but all thefts were for profit, not just thrills.

Roughnecks siphoned gasoline from cars as often as they had access to an automobile, which was not very often. Unlike the Saints, who owned their own cars, the Roughnecks would have to borrow their parents' cars, an event which occurred only eight or nine times a year. The boys claimed to have stolen cars for joy rides from time to time.

Ron committed the most serious of the group's offenses. With an unidentified associate the boy attempted to burglarize a gasoline station. Although this station had been robbed twice previously in the same month, Ron denied any involvement in either of the other thefts. When Ron and his accomplice approached the station, the owner was hiding in the bushes beside the station. He fired both barrels of a double-barreled shotgun at the boys. Ron was severely injured; the other boy ran away and was never caught. Though he remained in critical condition for several months, Ron finally recovered and served six months of the following year in reform school. Upon release from reform school, Ron was put back a grade in school, and began running around with a different gang of boys. The Roughnecks considered the new gang less delinquent than themselves, and during the following year Ron had no more trouble with the police.

The Roughnecks, then, engaged mainly in three types of delinquency: theft, drinking and fighting. Although community members perceived that this gang of kids was delinquent, they mistakenly believed that their illegal activities were primarily drinking, fighting and being a nuisance to passersby. Drinking was limited among the gang members, although it did occur, and theft was much more prevalent than anyone realized.

Drinking would doubtless have been more prevalent had the boys had ready access to liquor. Since they rarely had automobiles at their disposal, they could not travel very far, and the bars in town would not serve them. Most of the boys had little money, and this, too, inhibited their purchase of alcohol. Their major source of liquor was a local drunk who would buy them a fifth if they would give him enough extra to buy himself a pint of whiskey or a bottle of wine.

The community's perception of drinking as prevalent stemmed from the fact that it was the most obvious delinquency the boys engaged in. When one of the boys had been drinking, even a casual observer seeing him on the corner would suspect that he was high.

There was a high level of mutual distrust and dislike between the Roughnecks and the police. The boys felt very strongly that the police were unfair and corrupt. Some evidence existed that the boys were correct in their perception.

The main source of the boys' dislike for the police undoubtedly stemmed from the fact that the police would sporadically harass the group. From the standpoint of the boys, these acts of occasional enforcement of the law were whimsical and uncalled for. It made no sense to them, for example, that the police would come to the corner occasionally and threaten them with arrest for loitering when the night before the boys had been out siphoning gasoline from cars and the police had been nowhere in sight. To the boys, the police were stupid on the one hand, for not being where they should have been and catching the boys in a serious offense, and unfair on the other hand, for trumping up "loitering" charges against them.

From the viewpoint of the police, the situation was quite different. They knew, with all the confidence necessary to be a policeman, that these boys were engaged in criminal activities. They knew this partly from occasionally catching them, mostly from circumstantial evidence ("the boys were around when those tires were slashed"), and partly because the police shared the view of the community in general that this was a bad bunch of boys. The best the police could hope to do was to be sensitive to the fact that these boys were engaged in illegal acts and arrest them whenever there was some evidence that they had been involved. Whether or not the boys had in fact committed a particular act in a particular way was not especially important. The police had a broader view: their job was to stamp out these kids' crimes; the tactics were not as important as the end result.

Over the period that the group was under observation, each member was arrested at least once. Several of the boys were arrested a number of times and spent at least one night in jail. While most were never taken to court, two of the boys were sentenced to six months' incarceration in boys' schools.

The Roughnecks in School   The Roughnecks' behavior in school was not particularly disruptive. During school hours they did not all hang around together, but tended instead to spend most of their time with one or two other members of the gang who were their special buddies. Although every member of the gang attempted to avoid school as much as possible, they were not particularly successful and most of them attended school with surprising regularity. They considered school a burden—something to be gotten through with a minimum of conflict. If they were "bugged" by a particular teacher, it could lead to trouble. One of the boys, Al, once threatened to beat up a teacher and, according to the other boys, the teacher hid under a desk to escape him.

Teachers saw the boys the way the general community did, as heading for trouble, as being uninterested in making something of themselves. Some were also seen as being incapable of meeting the academic standards of the school. Most of the teachers expressed concern for this group of boys and were willing to pass them despite poor performance, in the belief that failing them would only aggravate the problem.

The group of boys had a grade point average just slightly above "C." No one in the group failed either grade, and no one had better than a "C" average. They were very consistent in their achievement or, at least, the teachers were consistent in their perception of the boys' achievement.

Two of the boys were good football players. Herb was acknowledged to be the best player in the school and Jack was almost as good. Both boys were criticized for their failure to abide by training rules, for refusing to come to practice as often as they should, and for not playing their best during practice. What they lacked in sportsmanship they made up for in skill, apparently, and played every game no matter how poorly they had performed in practice or how many practice sessions they had missed.

Two Questions Why did the community, the school and the police react to the Saints as though they were good, upstanding, nondelinquent youths with bright futures but to the Roughnecks as though they were tough, young criminals who were headed for trouble? Why did the Roughnecks and the Saints in fact have quite different careers after high school—careers which, by and large, lived up to the expectations of the community?

In the most obvious explanation for the differences in the community's and law enforcement agencies' reactions to the two gangs is that one group of boys was "more delinquent" than the other. Which group *was* more delinquent? The answer to this question will determine in part how we explain the differential responses to these groups by the members of the community and, particularly, by law enforcement and school officials.

In sheer number of illegal acts, the Saints were the more delinquent. They were truant from school for at least part of the day almost every day of the week. In addition, their drinking and vandalism occurred with surprising regularity. The Roughnecks, in contrast, engaged sporadically in delinquent episodes. While these episodes were frequent, they certainly did not occur on a daily or even a weekly basis.

The difference in frequency of offenses was probably caused by the Roughnecks' inability to obtain liquor and to manipulate legitimate excuses from school. Since the Roughnecks had less money than the Saints, and teachers carefully supervised their school activities, the Roughnecks' hearts may have been as black as the Saints', but their misdeeds were not nearly as frequent.

There are really no clear-cut criteria by which to measure qualitative differences in antisocial behavior. The most important dimension of the difference is generally referred to as the "seriousness" of the offenses.

If seriousness encompasses the relative economic costs of delinquent acts, then some assessment can be made. The Roughnecks probably stole an average of about $5.00 worth of goods a week. Some weeks the figure was considerably higher, but these times must be balanced against long periods when almost nothing was stolen.

The Saints were more continuously engaged in delinquency but their acts were not for the most part costly to property. Only their vandalism and occasional theft of gasoline would so qualify. Perhaps once or twice a month they would siphon a tankful of gas. The other costly items were street signs, construction lanterns and the like. All of these acts combined probably did not quite average $5.00 a week, partly because much of the stolen equipment was abandoned and presumably could be recovered. The difference in cost of stolen property between the two groups was trivial, but the Roughnecks probably had a slightly more expensive set of activities than did the Saints.

Another meaning of seriousness is the potential threat of physical harm to members of the community and to the boys themselves. The

Roughnecks were more prone to physical violence; they not only wel-
comed an opportunity to fight; they went seeking it. In addition, they
fought among themselves frequently. Although the fighting never included deadly weapons, it was still a menace, however minor, to the
physical safety of those involved.

The Saints never fought. They avoided physical conflict both
inside and outside the group. At the same time, though, the Saints frequently endangered their own and other people's lives. They did so almost
every time they drove a car, especially if they had been drinking. Sober,
their driving was risky; under the influence of alcohol it was horrendous.
In addition, the Saints endangered the lives of others with their pranks.
Street excavations left unmarked were a very serious hazard.

Evaluating the relative seriousness of the two gangs' activities
is difficult. The community reacted as though the behavior of the Roughnecks was a problem, and they reacted as though the behavior of the
Saints was not. But the members of the community were ignorant of the
array of delinquent acts that characterized the Saints' behavior. Although
concerned citizens were unaware of much of the Roughnecks' behavior as
well, they were much better informed about the Roughnecks' involvement
in delinquency than they were about the Saints'.

Visibility   Differential treatment of the two gangs resulted in part because one
gang was infintely more visible than the other. This differential visibility
was a direct function of the economic standing of the families. The Saints
had access to automobiles and were able to remove themselves from the
sight of the community. In as routine a decision as to where to go to have a
milkshake after school, the Saints stayed away from the mainstream of
community life. Lacking transportation, the Roughnecks could not make it
to the edge of town. The center of town was the only practical place for
them to meet since their homes were scattered throughout the town and
any noncentral meeting place put an undue hardship on some members.
Through necessity the Roughnecks congregated in a crowded area where
everyone in the community passed frequently, including teachers and law
enforcement officers. They could easily see the Roughnecks hanging
around the drugstore.

The Roughnecks, of course, made themselves even more visible by making remarks to passersby and by occasionally getting into fights
on the corner. Meanwhile, just as regularly, the Saints were either at the
cafe on one edge of town or in the pool hall at the other edge of town.
Without any particular realization that they were making themselves in-
conspicuous, the Saints were able to hide their time-wasting. Not only
were they removed from the mainstream of traffic, but they were almost
always inside a building.

On their escapades the Saints were also relatively invisible,
since they left Hanibal and travelled to Big City. Here, too, they were
mobile, roaming the city, rarely going to the same area twice.

Demeanor   To the notion of visibility must be added the difference in the responses of group members to outside intervention with their activities. If one of the Saints was confronted with an accusing policeman, even if he felt he was truly innocent of a wrongdoing, his demeanor was apologetic and penitent. A Roughneck's attitude was almost the polar opposite. When confronted with a threatening adult authority, even one who tried to be pleasant, the Roughneck's hostility and disdain were clearly observable. Sometimes he might attempt to put up a veneer of respect, but it was thin and was not accepted as sincere by the authority.

School was no different from the community at large. The Saints could manipulate the system by feigning compliance with the school norms. The availability of cars at school meant that once free from the immediate sight of the teacher, the boys could disappear rapidly. And this escape was well enough planned that no administrator or teacher was nearby when the boys left. A Roughneck who wished to escape for a few hours was in a bind. If it were possible to get free from class, downtown was still a mile away, and even if he arrived there, he was still very visible. Truancy for the Roughnecks meant almost certain detection, while the Saints enjoyed almost complete immunity from sanctions.

Bias Community members were not aware of the transgressions of the Saints. Even if the Saints had been less discreet, their favorite delinquencies would have been perceived as less serious than those of the Roughnecks.

In the eyes of the police and school officials, a boy who drinks in an alley and stands intoxicated on the street corner is committing a more serious offense than is a boy who drinks to inebriation in a nightclub or a tavern and drives around afterwards in a car. Similarly, a boy who steals a wallet from a store will be viewed as having committed a more serious offense than a boy who steals a lantern from a construction site.

Perceptual bias also operates with respect to the demeanor of the boys in the two groups when they are confronted by adults. It is not simply that adults dislike the posture affected by boys of the Roughneck ilk; more important is the conviction that the posture adopted by the Roughnecks is an indication of their devotion and commitment to deviance as a way of life. The posture becomes a cue, just as the type of the offense is a cue, to the degree to which the known transgressions are indicators of the youths' potential for other problems.

Visibility, demeanor and bias are surface variables which explain the day-to-day operations of the police. Why do these surface variables operate as they do? Why did the police choose to disregard the Saints' delinquencies while breathing down the backs of the Roughnecks?

The answer lies in the class structure of American society and the control of legal institutions by those at the top of the class structure. Obviously, no representative of the upper class drew up the operational chart for the police which led them to look in the ghettos and on streetcorners—which led them to see the demeanor of lower-class youth as troublesome and that of upper middle-class youth as tolerable. Rather, the procedures simply developed from experience—experience with irate and influential upper-middle-class parents insisting that their son's vandalism was simply a prank and his drunkenness only a momentary "sowing of wild oats"—experience with cooperative or indifferent, powerless, lower-class parents who acquiesced to the laws' definition of their son's behavior.

Adult Careers of the Saints and the Roughnecks   The community's confidence in the potential of the Saints and the Roughnecks apparently was justified. If anything, the community members underestimated the degree to which these youngsters would turn out "good" or "bad."

Seven of the eight members of the Saints went on to college immediately after high school. Five of the boys graduated from college in four years. The sixth one finished college after two years in the army, and the seventh spent four years in the air force before returning to college and receiving a B.A. degree. Of these seven college graduates, three went on for advanced degrees. One finished law school and is now active in state politics, one finished medical school and is practicing near Hanibal, and one boy is now working for a Ph.D. The other four college graduates entered submanagerial, managerial or executive training positions with larger firms.

The only Saint who did not complete college was Jerry. Jerry had failed to graduate from high school with the other Saints. During his second senior year, after the other Saints had gone on to college, Jerry began to hang around with what several teachers described as a "rough crowd"—the gang that was heir apparent to the Roughnecks. At the end of his second senior year, when he did graduate from high school, Jerry took a job as a used car salesman, got married and quickly had a child. Although he made several abortive attempts to go to college by attending night school, when I last saw him (ten years after high school) Jerry was unemployed and had been living on unemployment for almost a year. His wife worked as a waitress.

Some of the Roughnecks have lived up to community expectations. A number of them were headed for trouble. A few were not.

Jack and Herb were the athletes among the Roughnecks and their athletic prowess paid off handsomely. Both boys received unsolicited athletic scholarships to college. After Herb received his scholarship (near the end of his senior year), he apparently did an about-face. His demeanor became very similar to that of the Saints. Although he remained a member in good standing of the Roughnecks, he stopped participating in most activities and did not hang on the corner as often.

Jack did not change. If anything, he became more prone to fighting. He even made excuses for accepting the scholarship. He told the other gang members that the school had guaranteed him a "C" average if he would come to play football—an idea that seems far-fetched, even in this day of highly competitive recruiting.

During the summer after graduation from high school, Jack attempted suicide by jumping from a tall building. The jump would certainly have killed most people trying it, but Jack survived. He entered college in the fall and played four years of football. He and Herb graduated in four years, and both are teaching and coaching in high schools. They are married and have stable families. If anything, Jack appears to have a more prestigious position in the community than does Herb, though both are well respected and secure in their positions.

Two of the boys never finished high school. Tommy left at the end of his junior year and went to another state. That summer he was arrested and placed on probation on a manslaughter charge. Three years later he was arrested for murder; he pleaded guilty to second degree murder and is serving a 30-year sentence in the state penitentiary.

Al, the other boy who did not finish high school, also left the state in his senior year. He is serving a life sentence in a state penitentiary for first degree murder.

Wes is a small-time gambler. He finished high school and "bummed around." After several years he made contact with a bookmaker who employed him as a runner. Later he acquired his own area and has been working it ever since. His position among the bookmakers is almost identical to the position he had in the gang; he is always around but no one is really aware of him. He makes no trouble and he does not get into any. Steady, reliable, capable of keeping his mouth closed, he plays the game by the rules, even though the game is an illegal one.

That leaves only Ron. Some of his former friends reported that they had heard he was "driving a truck up north," but no one could provide any concrete information.

Reinforcement The community responded to the Roughnecks as boys in trouble, and the boys agreed with that perception. Their pattern of deviancy was reinforced, and breaking away from it became increasingly unlikely. Once the boys acquired an image of themselves as deviants, they selected new friends who affirmed that self-image. As that self-conception became more firmly entrenched, they also became willing to try new and more extreme deviances. With their growing alienation came freer expression of disrespect and hostility for representatives of the legitimate society. This disrespect increased the community's negativism, perpetuating the entire process of commitment to deviance. Lack of a commitment to deviance works the same way. In either case, the process will perpetuate itself unless some event (like a scholarship to college or a sudden failure) external to the established relationship intervenes. For two of the Roughnecks (Herb and Jack), receiving college athletic scholarships created new relations and culminated in a break with the established pattern of deviance. In the case of one of the Saints (Jerry), his parents' divorce and his failing to graduate from high school changed some of his other relations. Being held back in school for a year and losing his place among the Saints had sufficient impact on Jerry to alter his self-image and virtually to assure that he would not go on to college as his peers did. Although the experiments of life can rarely be reversed, it seems likely in view of the behavior of the other boys who did not enjoy this special treatment by the school that Jerry, too, would have "become something" had he graduated as anticipated. For Herb and Jack outside intervention worked to their advantage; for Jerry it was his undoing.

Selective perception and labelling—finding, processing and punishing some kinds of criminality and not others—means that visible, poor, nonmobile, outspoken, undiplomatic "tough" kids will be noticed, whether their actions are seriously delinquent or not. Other kids, who have established a reputation for being bright (even though underachieving), disciplined and involved in respectable activities, who are mobile and monied, will be invisible when they deviate from sanctioned activities. They'll sow their wild oats—perhaps even wider and thicker than their lower class cohorts—but they won't be noticed. When it's time to leave adolescence most will follow the expected path, settling into the ways of the middle class, remembering fondly the delinquent but unnoticed fling of their youth. The Roughnecks and others like them may turn around, too. It is more likely that their noticeable deviance will have been so reinforced by police and community that their lives will be effectively channelled into careers consistent with their adolescent background.

CHAPTER 6

LABELING DEVIANT BEHAVIOR

The influence of subjective perspectives on the study of social devia-tion was described in the previous chapter. These perspectives led sociologists to consider processes through which deviation was actual-ized. They marked a departure from examining the pedisposing fac-tors that led to deviant behavior. Those most responsible for taking a subjectivist, or interactionist, stance—Thomas, Sutherland, Tannen-baum—had indicated several important issues that needed empirical examination. What definitions of the situation were required to sus-tain involvement in deviant activities? What patterns of interaction, in turn, were significant in fostering the learning of definitions, motiva-tions, attitudes, and skills essential to such behavior? The investiga-tion of such sustained involvement and patterns of interaction would broaden our understanding of the development of deviant behavior and the formation of deviant subcultures.

Tannenbaum, through his description of the dramatization of evil, has emphasized the role of evaluation in the actualization of deviant behavior. Evaluation was integral to the development of de-linquent self-concepts and to the youth's continued involvement in activities that authorities defined as deviant. These sociologists viewed deviance as a nonobjective reality—one subject to the meaningful interpretations of those who found some behavior, individual, or group objectionable. These evaluations, more specifically, were viewed as "prophecies" that had an amplifying effect on the behavior in question. The delinquent became what he was described as being, ostensibly because both he and the agents who dramatized the evil of his actions needed to determine consistency in character or identity.

Control agents within the community needed to "peg" the reputation of the deviant so that his behavior would continue to be seen as evil and their negative reactions as just. The alleged deviant, as a response to the negative reactions of the community, was somehow stimulated into the castigated behavior. This reaction formation, as a defiance of established authority and conventional morality, became, in effect, a self-fulfilling prophecy. What had to be specified, however, were the varieties of reactions that might bring about such self-fulfilling prophecies and the more precise mechanisms of learning that helped mold the identity and behavior of the alleged deviant as a consequence.

The interactionist analysis of deviation in the 1950s and 1960s placed a major emphasis on the mode of actualization that Tannenbaum had initially described. However, several new and important themes appeared in the work of sociologists who pursued this line of investigation. The most significant was a reorientation from a concern with exclusively *criminal* and *delinquent* behavior to the development of a true sociology of *deviant* behavior. Sociologists came to share the belief that processes involved in the actualization of deviance were much the same as those for law-violation. The dramatization of evil, they argued, was essentially the same for alcoholism, mental illness, and child illegitimacy as for juvenile delinquency and crime. All such behaviors have in common those negative societal reactions that serve to crystallize moral indignation for the *public,* in whose interests various control agents act, and for *rule violators,* who are the targets of that indignation.

This extension of the analytic scope of deviation was considered problematic by some, for individuals who were defined as mentally ill or alcoholic were said to have an intrapersonal "condition." For these problems, analytic frameworks existed that did not couch their reactions in terms of moral indignation. Medical or psychiatric reactions to such intrapersonal conditions were felt to be value neutral and "scientific" and thus not subject to the dramatizations of evil or moral indignation that could stimulate the reaction formations and conflicts anticipated by analysts of criminal or delinquent behavior. A major goal of sociologists in the 1950s and 1960s was to demonstrate that this was not true—that a sociology of social deviation was possible. This chapter presents the basic conceptual framework developed by these labeling sociologists, and examines the tools used by students of deviance to analyze societal-reaction processes.

LEMERT ON SOCIAL PATHOLOGY AND SOCIETAL REACTIONS

The sociologist Edwin M. Lemert was influential in stimulating a concern for the systematic study of social rule violation. In an early paper and in his book *Social Pathology*, Lemert developed a "general and systematic theory of sociopathic behavior."[1] Other sociologists had attempted the construction of a general theory of social deviation but had failed to locate the significant common attributes of deviation and, thus, the *focus* of an analytical framework.

Brown, for example, had argued for a unified study of personal and social disorganization. He believed that normal and abnormal behavior were not categorically different and that each was produced in "interactive living."[2] Brown suggested that a fruitful course of investigation would be to examine the properties of interactive living through which the individual *learns* to be both normal and abnormal.[3] He suggested that an investigation emphasizing the *process* of learning and the development of multiple-interactive patterns related to "social pathology" would be more profitable than a "cause and effect" analysis.[4] Beyond these properties of "interactive living" and learning, however, Brown did not locate other specific and common attributes shared by "sex pathologies," drug addiction, emotional disorders, crime, and delinquency.

Lemert believed that a systematic theory of social pathology, or deviant behavior, must clearly define the common properties of the phenomena and indicate precisely the social factors involved in their actualization. In the introduction to *Social Pathology*, Lemert presented the "postulates" of his theory. He maintained that deviation was the outcome of culture conflict, that societal reactions to deviation varied in intensity, and that sociopathic behavior was behavior that was effectively disapproved. Lemert defined the deviant person as one whose self-concept was shaped by the behavior engaged in, its social visibility, and the influence of the societal reaction. Deviants were "individuated" (i.e., their identities were crystallized) by their differential vulnerability to the societal reaction. This individuation was said to be a function of both their personality and the nature of their behavioral participation.[5]

Lemert believed that *behaviors* and *individuals* as seemingly different from one another as blindness and the blind, radicalism and radicals, mental disorders and the mentally ill, and drunkenness and the alcoholic, all shared two interrelated processes: sociopathic *differentiation* (the process of setting the individual apart from the group) and sociopathic *individuation* (the process of identity crystallization).[6] The individual who was involved in *recurrent,* and not merely situational or "once-in-a-lifetime" varieties of deviant behavior, experienced societal reactions that set him apart from conventional members of the group. This was as true for mental illness as for criminal behavior. As he continued in his rule-violating behavior, the increasing differentiation of the deviant had the principal effect of crystallizing his deviant role and of shaping his attitudes and self-concept.

Lemert called this pattern of deviant behavior "secondary deviation." In a more recent discussion of the concept, he offers the following definition:

> Secondary deviation refers to a special class of socially defined responses which people make to problems created by the societal reaction to their deviance. These problems are essentially moral problems which revolve around stigmatization, punishments, segregation, and social control. Their general effect is to differentiate the symbolic and interactional environment to which the person responds, so that early or adult socialization is categorically affected. They become central facts of existence for those experiencing them, altering psychic structure, producing specialized organization of social roles and self-regarding attitudes.[7]

By contrast, behaviors that Lemert calls *primary deviation* have only "marginal" implications for role crystallization and the development of self-regarding attitudes. These behaviors result in neither significant differentiation nor individuation. Although they are often recognized and evaluated in terms of moral indignation, the reactions are not strong enough to set the individual apart and to cause conflict with control agents.

Lemert posed an important issue for this perspective: what conditions are necessary for societal reactions to occur? What factors would lead community-control agents to begin the process of differentiation? Lemert's solution was the *tolerance quotient*.[8] This quotient is a mathematical ratio or fraction with the following numerator and denominator:

$$\text{Tolerance Quotient} = \frac{\text{Amount of some disapproved conduct in a stated locality}}{\text{Degree of tolerance that people in this locality have for the behavior in question}}$$

The societal reaction against or tolerance for a specific social deviation was said to be contingent on its visibility, extensiveness, and the original importance attached to the norms from which the behavior or individual is said to deviate. When the tolerance ratio reaches a 1 to 1 value, members of the community or agents of control will begin the process of differentiating the deviating person.

The difficulty with this "solution" to the problem of when or under what conditions the societal reaction will take place is that it is too objective. It assumes that the societal reaction is contingent on some objective *quantity* of deviation. This is problematic because the distinguishing feature of deviant behavior is that it is most often *secre-*

tive—the actual amount or prevalent numbers of deviations of a given variety are seldom objectively determinable. What is important, on the other hand, are the subjective evaluations of the prevalence of a type of deviation. However, the criteria used by individuals to judge the "seriousness" of homosexuality or prostitution might have little to do with objective or subjective estimations of the prevalence or incidence of these behaviors. In this case, we would need a new "numerator" or perhaps a new set of factors to function as decision-making criteria.

In other words, Lemert's formula for the societal reaction fails to account for the more complex set of decision-making rules and situational factors that are part of the actual differentiating process. It fails to explain the subjective definitions of the situation that allow control agents to decide that an individual is violating a social rule.[9] The application, by community agents, of such criteria for differentiation as the responsibility, guilt, or dangerousness of specific individuals in time, space, and circumstance is an essential component of the societal reaction to deviance.

The objective measurement of local tolerance for a particular behavior is problematic for a similar reason: it assumes that control agents maintain a threshold level—one that does not change from situation to situation. It is also possible that the threshold level actually depends upon such factors as (1) the nature of the individual being evaluated—is he black or white, rich or poor, good-looking or deformed?—and (2) the presence of third-party "witnesses," who might influence the differentiating process either as proponents or opponents of the societal reaction.[10]

Although Lemert's solutions are problematic, the question he raises for analysts of the differentiating process is extremely important. If the societal reaction is as vital in the actualization of deviance as Tannenbaum and Lemert claim, the situational and subjective conditions for its occurrence become important topics for study.

Lemert, because of his focus on secondary deviation (designated deviance that influences the self-regarding attitudes of the alleged rule violator), was interested in the process of individuation. His concept of individuation has a marked resemblance to W. I. Thomas's description of the "individualization of behavior" in *The Unadjusted Girl*.[11] For Thomas, the process of individualization meant the learning of *re*definitions of the situation or of rationalizations for behavior that function as motivations for continued participation. He was not concerned, however, with the impact of a differentiating process on the formation of these important definitions of the situation. For Thomas, these redefinitions were the result of the delinquent girl's needs for security, new experiences, recognition—that is, her basic wishes or desires.[12]

Lemert leans toward a need-fulfillment model of individuation by noting that secondary deviance becomes the most satisfactory solution to problems stemming from the stigmatization process.[13] To compensate for the status loss and self-degradation brought on by differentiation, the prostitute, for example, comes to see the positive or self-rewarding aspects of her recurrent involvement in the profession. Negative societal reactions force her to assume positive self-evaluations, which, in turn, lead to continued participation in the deviant behavior.

Lemert adds that the alleged deviant often considers the societal reaction as unjust, inconsistent, or "spurious."[14] It is deemed out of proportion to the seriousness of the behavior engaged in and complained of. Under these conditions, the deviant feels the need to normalize himself and his behavior, and the reaction-formation strategy becomes a principal means of accomplishing this. In effect, the deviant is faced with a situation of *cognitive dissonance*: two dissonant or inconsistent views of self and a need to resolve the situation by changing either the dissonant or the acceptable self-attitudes. Studies have shown that when confronted with dissonant attitudes or definitions *and the pressure to make a decision,* a person will come to accept the dissonant interpretation as being "not so bad after all."[15]

Lemert's secondary deviation implies that societal reactions bring about identity crises, or situations of identity dissonance. In these situations, the most propitious "way out" is for the individual to accept the differentiating *category,* or the *role* based upon it, but to redefine the meaning of the behavior, role, and identity to suit his needs for positive self-evaluation and group identification. Powerful control agents (e.g., psychiatrists, judges, police, educators, social workers, and clinical psychologists), in addition to their professed, manifest functions, also provide the alleged deviant with dissonant categories of "self." They have the prestige and authority to influence these definitional processes. For this reason, Lemert believes it is necessary for sociologists to study the control agents and agencies that process deviants. In *Social Pathology* he outlines the most significant items for such an analysis.

In this proposed analytic framework, Lemert maintains a skeptical or critical perspective on existing control institutions and their practices:

> Not only do many reform and rehabilitative institutions in our society fail to demonstrate scientifically that their work actually accomplishes what is claimed for it, but their staffs would be hard put to prove that their efforts did not have effects opposite from what was intended.[16]

These comments should be understood in the context of the "self-sustaining" or "amplifying" characteristics of the concept of secondary deviation. Lemert, as well as other contemporary advocates of a societal-reaction perspective, has been criticized for the lack of a value-neutral perspective.[17] Yet Lemert believes that we could not analyze the relationship of control agents to the actualization of deviance if these same agents and agencies were taken only on their own terms and if the official or manifest definitions of their work were accepted as the exclusive definitions of reality.

Lemert's critical stance toward the societal reaction to deviation can best be understood as a strategy for demystifying (revealing the routine, everyday character of) the practices of powerful control agents. In this way, the internal processes of their work with deviants could be assessed. Although it is fundamental to understand the working ideologies and practices of control agents on their own terms —to have a sense of their own constructed realities—to accept them as unanalyzable *givens* prevents us from knowing their influence on the alleged deviants.

As a guide to the analysis of secondary deviation and reaction processes, Lemert offers a 10-point framework that illuminates the empirical examination of these phenomena. Of these 10, the following questions are most noteworthy:

> How many areas of societal participation of the deviant or deviants are controlled? . . .
>
> What is the degree of physical and social isolation produced by control over the deviants? . . .
>
> How does this apply to the agents of control involved: prison guards, ward attendants, police, psychiatrists, social workers, clinicians, physicians, and teachers? . . .
>
> Where clinical therapy is used, what effects does it have in terms of self-definitions, self-help, and dependence? Is communication established? How well are therapeutic facilities correlated with the clients' needs in time?
>
> How much instability and inconsistency are there in the agency functioning which are caused by internal-disruptive and external-intrusive factors?
>
> What opportunity exists for the development of deviant social organization within the framework of the agency organization? What use, if any, is made of it where it exists? . . .
>
> After contacts and interaction with societal-control agencies what opportunities exist for the entrance of deviants into

groups from which they were formerly excluded? What groups
now exclude the deviants as a result of contacts with the control agency?[18]

Through the investigation of these items for specific categories
of deviants, Lemert believes that a systematic theory of social pathology can be tested and reformulated to fit the available empirical
evidence.

In the second part of *Social Pathology,* Lemert applies this analytic scheme to particular varieties of deviant behavior. Initially using
the research reports of other investigators, he analyzes the differentiation and treatment along with primary and secondary representations of such behaviors as blindness, speech defectiveness, radicalism,
prostitution, drunkenness, and mental disorders. Lemert was concerned with the consequent participation in society for "processed"
deviants of these varieties. By analyzing the dramatic curtailment of
participation by deviants in economic, familial, political, and recreational areas of life, Lemert pointed to the linkages between the processes of stigmatization, secondary deviation, and the consequent life
careers of such individuals. To be labeled "radical" or "emotionally
disturbed" influenced the formation of an individual's self-conception
and role performance. The consequences of this often severely altered the life patterns and careers of labeled deviants. Labeled radicals and disturbed individuals, for example, often have difficulty advancing their education.[19]

The research evidence used to make such characterizations was
admittedly unrefined. Lemert calls for a theoretically and methodologically unified study of behavior, individuals, and reaction processes,
so that secondary deviation could be better understood and specific
components of his theoretical framework tested. To this end, Lemert
offers students of deviation certain recommendations for studying the
life histories of deviants.[20]

It is important, he claims, to develop accounts for different steps
of the labeled deviant's behaviors and experiences. First, the investigator should describe the nature of the deviation, the situation and
cultural context in which it occurred, and the social organization associated with it.[21] Second, the societal reaction itself must be examined
and the following specified: the degree of social distance between
deviant and community; the prevalent attitudes, stereotypes, and my-
thology that the community holds for individuals of this type; the
nature, objectives, and methods of control used to handle such individuals; and the consequences of this control for role performance.

A third objective is to specify the natural history of the deviant.
The researcher needs a description of childhood and adult experiences that influenced the formation of self-conceptions; family reac-

tions to the alleged deviant behavior; entrance into deviant social organizations and relationships; and a description of the correspondence between the deviant's present self-conception and the definitions of him maintained by significant others. A final objective is the characterization of the labeled deviant's social participation in economic, family, political, religious, educational, and recreational spheres of life.

Lemert thus offers a unified framework for studying social deviation. It permits the systematic analysis of different types of rule-violating behavior by focusing upon those factors that are supposedly common to each type and essential to its actualization.

After the publication of *Social Pathology,* there was no immediate interest in research based upon its recommendations. Few sociologists other than Lemert and his own students pursued the systematic investigation of reaction processes. Perhaps the liberal, sociopolitical ideology that underlies the societal-reaction perspective was out of step with both the dominant political philosophies and conservative sociological perspectives popular during the 1950s. The attention of sociologists continued to be focused on the deviants themselves and those factors of predisposition that led to deviation. In the decade of the 1960s this changed dramatically with the developing interest in reexamining the *processes* of interaction and definition that led to the stigmatization of rule breakers.

THE NEOSOCIETAL-REACTION PERSPECTIVE

Although the model for a societal-reaction perspective had been established by Lemert, there was a need to clearly define the conceptual apparatus to be used in investigating deviance. The task of Lemert's disciples and of those who had a more direct link to the symbolic-interactionist tradition of the Chicago School[22] became the detailed conceptual clarification of the processes of evaluation, differentiation, and individualization.

The explanations that had been offered for the societal reaction to deviance presented many problems. It was difficult to understand what constituted a societal reaction and what were the conditions under which it was likely to occur. It would be necessary to understand more fully the relationship between institutional policy, practice, and organization and the processing of labeled deviants.

In some instances the concept of secondary deviation seemed to imply a social determinism similar to that found in theories of predisposition. If this were so, it would be difficult for a labeled deviant to leave the deviant role or curtail involvement in deviant activities. Yet we know that some factors mitigate the influence of the negative societal reaction and even permit the deviant, in time, to leave the deviant role. Deviants do not always remain such, and the neutralization of stigma and entrance into normal roles is possible under some conditions. These, then, were the more important questions and issues that confronted proponents of the societal-reaction perspective in the 1960s.

Of those who made important contributions to this developing framework, the work of Kitsuse, Becker, Goffman, Erikson, Garfinkel, and Scheff deserve particular attention. Each of these sociologists explored basic features of the actualization of deviance and established a more elaborate framework for its study. Becker and Erikson proposed definitions of deviance; Kitsuse, Garfinkel, and Erikson explored both the "logics in use" that were inherent in the societal reaction and the conditions that facilitate effective labeling. Goffman and Scheff analyzed the institutional and organizational contingencies related to the processing of deviants; Becker began the integration of the societal-raction perspective with the broader interactionist framework; and Goffman focused attention on the process of stigmatization and its consequences.

A Societal-Reaction Definition of Deviance

The first task of any theoretical perspective is to clearly define its working concepts.[23] Perspectives on deviation differ not only because they explain different aspects of deviation, but also because their initial definitions force them to ignore features that seem essential to other perspectives. Sociologists who viewed deviation as an objective reality were unconcerned with definitional processes, which they considered extraneous to the actual behavior in question. On the other hand, a societal-reaction perspective, which viewed the definitional component of deviance as essential to its very "becoming" or "actualization," needed to clearly define its subject matter so that this "evaluative" reality became prominent.

Howard S. Becker (1963) proposed one of the most widely used definitions of deviation as a category of subjective evaluation. For him, deviance

> is created by society. I do not mean this in the way it is ordinarily understood, in which the causes of deviance are located in the social situation of the deviant or in "social factors" which prompt his action. I mean, rather, that *social groups create deviance by making the rules whose infraction constitutes deviance,* and by applying those rules to particular people and labeling them as outsiders. From this point of view, deviance is

not a quality of the act the person commits, but rather a consequence of the application by others of rules and sanctions to an
"offender." The deviant is one to whom that label has successfully been applied; deviant behavior is behavior that people
so label.[24]

Becker, in a more recent review of this statement, indicates that
this definition says, in essence, that deviance, *whatever else it may be,* is
an evaluation made by an individual about someone else's or his own
behavior or identity.[25] Becker adds that these evaluations are more
commonly the result of the joint actions of individuals engaged in
situated interaction. To most analysts of deviance—even to those who
have criticized the labeling perspective—these qualities of deviance
are immutable. One cannot even talk about behavior as deviant without having made some evaluation or having used someone else's evaluation that something is deviant. In this respect, Becker's definition is
a truism, but one whose significant meaning escaped the attention of
other analysts. If these evaluations are central to one's identity as
deviant, as labeling proponents maintain, then the truism contained
in the definition actually becomes one of its most important aspects.
The task of a labeling approach would be to indicate the precise
nature of the relationship between these definitional or evaluation
processes and the deviance they create. What factors operate to keep
a definition *in force?* Are they characteristics of the actor's own behavior or identity? Or are they, indeed, characteristics of the labelers
and the social situations in which the labeling occurs? In considering
the definition of deviance as an evaluation, it is important to ask what
factors facilitate labeling and make it effective.[26]

The "Logics in Use" Inherent in the Societal Reaction

If deviance is defined as a process of evaluation, the decision
making and the explanatory logic behind the evaluation become important topics for sociological investigation.[27] John I. Kitsuse initiated
this form of analysis with his study of the societal reaction to homosexual behavior. He began with the assumption that those who label
others for "sex-inappropriate" behavior are involved in a process
through which certain behaviors and persons are interpreted and
defined as deviant and therefore are accorded treatment considered
appropriate for such behavior and identity.[28] Deviant labeling thus
involves *interpretation, definition,* and the *action* based upon these. The
question becomes one of how do these interpretations and definitions
come about. What evidence is needed to come to such a decision, and
how precisely is the evidence *invoked* that "explains" the deviance in
question? Kitsuse was attempting to clarify the explanatory logic of

labeling: how do labelers reasonably account for the existence of what they define as homosexuality?

In interviews with 700 college undergraduates, Kitsuse discovered that when respondents were asked "When was the first time you noticed (found out) that this person was homosexual?,"[39] two categories of evidence were invoked:

1. *Indirect evidence* in the form of a rumor, an acquaintance's experiences with the individual in question subsequently communicated to the subject, or general reputational information concerning the individual's behavior, associates, and sex predelictions may be the occasion for suspecting him to be "different". . . .

2. *Direct observation* by the subject of the individual's behavior may be the basis for calling the latter's sexual "normality" into question. The descriptions of behavior which subjects took to be indicative of homosexuality varied widely and were often vague. Most frequently the behaviors cited were those "which everyone knows" are indications of homosexuality.[30]

In the latter category of observations were included "effeminate" mannerisms and appearance; not participating in talk of "sexual conquest," or being concerned with having "girls and high times"; and behaviors interpreted as *overt sexual propositions,* in which the alleged homosexual reportedly said or did something that was interpreted as a direct homsexual overture.[31]

Kitsuse pursued the interview with his respondents to elicit explanations for this evidence of homosexuality. For example, he wanted to know the inferential process by which the subject linked information about the individual to the deviant category homosexuality.[32] He discovered that the imputation of homosexuality was documented by a process of "retrospective interpretation": "a process by which the subject re-interprets the individual's past behavior in the light of the new information concerning his sexual deviance."[33] These subjects, in accounting for the alleged homosexuality of individuals in question, would review their interactions with them and would search out "subtle cues and nuances of behavior" to account for or document the alleged homosexuality. The subjects would search their memories to find the evidence which made the present imputation seem reasonable.

These retrospective interpretations functioned as rationalizations for the insight that deviance had existed and that "I should have known all the while that these pieces of evidence when taken together indicated that the individual was homosexual." One respondent, when asked to account for her present interpretation of the homosexuality of an acquaintance, began to interpret retrospectivly the individual's "questionable" behavior in light of her present doubt:

> I probably wouldn't have thought of it . . . the acquaintance [a girl] holding hands with another girl . . . very much. . . .Well, actually, there were a few things that I questioned later on that I hadn't thought really very much about. . . .

> I can remember her being quite affectionate towards me several times when we were in our rooms together, like putting her arm around my shoulder. Or I remember one time specifically when she asked me for a kiss. I was shocked at the time, but I laughed it off jokingly.[34]

"Retrospective interpretation" is thus the method of explanation used by labelers to account for the definitions of deviance. Kitsuse, like Lemert, indicated that such processes of decision making are found not only in the ordinary spheres of interpersonal contacts, but also—more significantly perhaps—in "the bureaucratically organized activities of agencies of control."[35] The agencies and institutions that formally controlled the behavior of those they deem deviant, explain their processing of deviants and deviant behavior in very similar ways. Kitsuse and Lemert were influential in leading students of deviance to the analysis of the specific labeling practices of the agencies and institutions that processed deviants.

Facilitating Labeling

Other sociologists made significant contributions to the analysis of formal societal reactions to deviance. Erikson suggested that sociologists look carefully at "community screening devices." These instruments of social control, such as clinical dossiers, police records, and court reports, act as depositories for information used to label deviants.

> The screening device which sifts these telling details out of the person's over-all performance, then, is a very important instrument of social control. We know very little about the properties of this screen, but we do know that it takes many factors into account which are not directly related to the deviant act itself . . . . In this respect the community screen may be a more relevant subject for sociological research than the actual behavior which is filtered through it.[36]

Such screening devices usually contain a wealth of negative accountings of an individual's behavior. A person's biography is, in effect, passed through a series of sieves.[37] All that remains behind after the screening are those instances that reveal behavior that community-control agents identify as deviant. These screened pieces of information become the rationalizations needed for the application of the deviant label.

Mental-health practitioners, for example, use clinical dossiers to *retrospectively interpret* information about the past "career" of mental patients to justify their current labeling (Suchar, 1972). The clinical record offers numerous instances in which X was acting in a negative manner: it can be shown that X "had been becoming mentally ill and now is most definitely mentally ill." When these instances are taken as a whole, they serve to "justify" the application of labels like "neuroticism" or "schizophrenia." Erikson and Gilbertson have described the function of such community-screening devices as psychiatric records:

> They supply a package of evidence to support the diagnosis made at admission; they offer background material of obvious relevance in choosing a course of treatment; and they furnish important information about the social environment from which the patient comes. But at the same time they have the effect of making it seem logical, reasonable, maybe even inevitable that the patient in question came to occupy the status in which he finds himself. In the mental hospital, the patient's illness provides the lens through which we look at his past or envision his future, and the life details we are able to see through that screen are very often ones which would seem irrelevant in other kinds of biography. Half-remembered dreams, moments of embarrassment or panic, periods of inactivity or loss of control—these are the materials of the case history.[38]

The community screen becomes, in effect, the depository for the developing "dramatization of evil" associated with the individual's behavior and identity. A major task for sociologists studying the institutional processing of deviants should be the analysis of the construction of such community-screening devices and their use in labeling and decision making.

Another important line of analysis was the investigation of the conditions for *successful* or *effective* labeling. Garfinkel, in his examination of "conditions of successful degradation ceremonies," drew attention to two basic characteristics of the societal reaction to deviant behavior. Labeling essentially involves the status degradation of the alleged deviant, as well as the degradation of the person's total identity. Public shaming or stigmatization is a rather common feature in most societies and is a principal means of societal control. Garfinkel raised the question of how this degradation or shaming was accomplished so that it was maximally "effective" in altering both the social status and personal identity of the alleged deviant. A "successful" denunciation of the individual, as Garfinkel points out, does not so much change the individual's identity as it "reconstitutes" that identity.

> The former [predegradation] identity, at best, receives the accent of mere appearance. In the social calculus of reality representations and test, the former identity stands as accidental; the new identity is the "basic reality." What he is now is what, "after all," he was all along.[39]

Stigmatization or degradation thus often demonstrates that the present deviant identity is the person's "basic reality." Goffman distinguishes between the individual's *actual social identity*—the identity that he can be shown to possess—and the *virtual social identity*—that which the person appears to be. Goffman defined stigma as the difference between virtual and actual social identity.[40] Douglas, in a similar fashion, notes a difference between the *substantial self* and *situated self*. The substantial self is what we consider to be the person's essential self. What we impute to individuals in specific situations (situated self) is largely dependent upon this classification.[41] In general, the process of degradation or stigmatization involves the establishment of the person's "actual social identity," or "substantial self" as being essentially deviant.

Garfinkel indicated that successful denunciation is accomplished under the following conditions:

1. The event (that for which the perpetrator is being blamed) and the perpetrator must be made to appear "out of the ordinary."

2. The character of the event and of the perpetrator must not be made to appear as a passing thing; as unique or not recurrent: "Similarly, any sense of accident, coincidence, indeterminism, chance, or momentary occurrence must not merely be minimized. Ideally, such measures should be inconceivable; at least they should be made false."[42] In addition, the denouncers should underscore the severity of behavior in question by appealing to its "dialectical counterpart": prostitution and the prostitute are denounced by appealing to virginity, "wholesomeness," "modesty," and "human decency."

3. The denouncer should be identified as acting not in his capacity as a private citizen but as a public figure with the interests of the collective and witnesses at heart.

4. The denunciation should be made in the name of the collective and its values, which the denouncer is said to represent and support.

5. Ideally, the denouncer should be socially distant (have higher social status) from the individual being denounced and from the witnesses who will attest to the denunciation. As Becker has indicated, there exists a "hierarchy of credibility" so that the opinions of some individuals and their evaluations of goodness/badness, sickness/health are believed more than others. Thus, the judgments of psychiatrists, judges, and clergy often appear credible because of the high status these individuals have in the eyes of others.[43]

6. "The denounced person must be ritually separated from a place in the legitimate order, i.e., he must be defined as standing at a place opposed to it. He must be placed "outside," he must be made "strange.""[44]

Garfinkel, by his own admission, was able to specify only the major *structural* conditions for successful degradation. A more meaningful analysis of these conditions would have to include the dynamic and interactive conditions representing the means by which degradation was accomplished. Some "strategies" or techniques of degradation were, ostensibly, more effective than others, and their analysis was also needed.[45]

The model of degradation that Garfinkel outlines for us is perhaps best exemplified by the court's processing of criminals. This is a particularly good characterization of the "effective" societal reaction to behavior that is said to evidence clear-cut moral irresponsibility and in which volition can be imputed to the individual being denounced. However, the conditions in this model do not always apply to other forms of deviant behavior, in which stigmatization is accomplished in relative "privacy" and in which the behavior in question is not clearly "volitional."

Some status degradation is "effective" (results in more severe ostracism and stigmatization) by the very nature of the accusation brought against the individual. There are no more highly stigmatizing and status-degrading categories in our culture than "sexual perversion" and "intellectual incapacity." Sexual or intellectual inadequacy can be called *ontological* deviant labels, for they touch upon the culturally defined "essence" of what it means to be human.[46] Ontological labels have greater power to degrade the status of the accused, and when used by "experts" at the top of the hierarchy of credibility, they become extremely effective means of negating "normal" group membership.

Although Garfinkel's model allows us to understand the formal labeling of individuals deemed deviant, it gives little insight into informal ostracism and status degradation. The more ordinary denunciations that occur in everyday life can be equally effective and "successful" in altering the status and personal identity of nonconforming individuals. These less structured degradation ceremonies are often effective because the denouncers are the status *equals* of the denounced. The status degradation by peers and by those who were formerly friendly associates of the alleged nonconformist can be extremely significant in altering self-regarding attitudes. The support of these individuals is usually relied upon as a means of defending one's "self" from attacks by status superiors. When this line of defense itself becomes a source of denunciation, stigmatization can be highly successful.

Weinberg and Williams, in their attitude study of homosexuals, indicate that male homosexuals are significantly influenced by the reactions of both heterosexuals and other homosexuals:

> If a person is negative toward homosexuals and his opinions are held in great esteem by a particular homosexual, he is in a position, by slight and innuendo, to cause great misery. This may also be the case, however, for a person whose opinions the homosexual may not regard as important. This is so because any negative reactions which the homosexual perceives may symbolize the rejection of the homosexual in the larger society. . . . Heterosexual reaction in the main is an important source of insecurity for the homosexual. The reaction from other homosexuals, however, is also tremendously important. . . . Not to feel accepted by other homosexuals can produce an acute sense of isolation, marginality, and psychological strain. . . .[47]

Homosexuality, as a form of nonconforming behavior, also illustrates another problem with Garfinkel's model. Carol Warren has pointed out that behavior like homosexuality rarely results in formal degradation or degradation by *stigmatizing audiences* (specific individuals or sets of individuals who denounce the "deviant" and who influence his behavior and identity.)[48] More commonly, the homosexual is influenced by what Warren calls *symbolic stigma*:

> The very fact of the deep stigma against the homosexual in our society provides him with an environment that symbolically stigmatizes even the secret homosexual who is never directly labeled by a social audience. . . .Symbolic stigma comes from the mass media, from the educational system, and from casual contacts. . . .[49]

Furthermore,

> through many socialization processes, the mass media, and the typically taken for granted understandings of everyday interaction, homosexuals are symbolically labeled as deviant. . . .The process very rarely consists of a dramatic, official stigmatization through arrest and trial; however, the *potential threat* that this, or other equally "serious" troubles could happen, is not to be under-estimated in its symbolic importance.[50]

Stigmatization and consequent identity degradation can apparently be difficult to situate in some "locales" in which the alleged deviant is confronted by a denouncer. If we assume that many individuals define themselves as nonconforming members of society and remain "secret deviants" because of the symbolic stigma they experience, then the analysis of this variety of societal reaction becomes difficult.[51] It is nevertheless important for students of deviance to study both formal degradation ceremonies and these more privatized and less accessible forms of stigmatization. Labeling by stigmatizing audiences and self-labeling through the influence of symbolic stigma can both result in very effective degradation. Critics of the labeling perspective have frequently pointed to the lack of formal labeling in many cases of deviance as a refutation of the labeling approach.[52] Although such criticism points to a weakness in the perspective's orientation (a relative neglect of "symbolic stigma"), it overstates the case against the perspective as a whole.

Becker's early definition of deviance gave the impresion that only stigmatizing audiences were important in its determination. His more recent clarification of this point indicates that the concern of students of deviance ought to be with the defining or labeling process itself, whether a formal audience is present or not. There is adequate room in the perspective for situations of self-labeling and of degradation by "symbolic stigma."[53]

The Formal Processing of Deviants

There are several reasons why an emphasis on official labeling and thus formal degradation ceremonies is advantageous for a sociology of deviance. The official processing of criminals, the maladjusted, the emotionally disturbed, and the mentally ill has, by itself, a profound impact on their lives. Studies have demonstrated that legal stigma and the stigmas of mental illness and emotional disturbance, for example, profoundly influence the opportunities for employment and education and the lifestyle of individuals so labeled and treated. Life chances are often dramatically curtailed by official labeling.[54]

The problem of stigmatization by official "experts" is that few means of *neutralization* exist. "Once a crook, always a crook" can be taken to mean that individuals cannot shake off the categories in which we have placed them. Somehow, the labels "criminal" and "criminal but already punished," as well as "mentally ill" and "mentally ill but treated," have the same status-degrading features. Although the institutions and agencies that process nonconforming members of society have developed intricate procedures and technology for gathering and storing information and for decision making, few have, at the same time, developed techniques of neutralizing the accompanying stigmatization.

Analysts of these labelers have emphasized the formal processing of deviants because they have generally agreed that the consequences of this processing are significant social problems in themselves. For maintaining this position, proponents of the perspective have been both praised and severely criticized. The next chapter will review the many debates created by this stance toward the study of societal-reaction processes.

The study of the official processing of deviants has decided methodological advantages over the analysis of informal labeling and "symbolic stigma." The obvious advantage is accessibility to the interactional scenes through which the social definitions of deviance are constructed. To understand the components of the societal reaction to deviance, we must study the reactions as they occur—as applied in particular situations to specific individuals and their behavior, The study of official processing affords us such an opportunity.

Although there are certainly many difficulties associated with conducting research in these settings, the literature of the past two decades has shown that sociologists have been able to study a vast array of deviant processing systems: courts, police stations, mental hospitals, drug clinics, homes for unwed mothers, juvenile-delinquent detention centers, alcoholic treatment clinics, prisons, physical-therapy centers, institutes for the blind, and so on. In addition to accessibility and the more direct observation of decision making, the study of official processing allows us to observe the influence on the alleged deviant of the societal reaction. It is possible to separate more clearly the complex set of factors related to deviant role-playing and secondary deviation. In some respects, the institutional processing of deviants reflects the attitudes and informal societal reactions of the community. Often, the attitudes of the community and the ideologies and the practices of control agents mutually influence each other. If this is so, the study of official processing can inform our studies of less formal reaction processes.

INSTITUTIONAL AND ORGANIZATIONAL CONTINGENCIES
RELATED TO PROCESSING DEVIANTS

Institutions that process deviants are, from several points of view, unique formal organizations. Some share a combination of characteristics that, together, make them different from other social organizations. No matter what their formal philosophies and purpose—punishment, diagnosis, correction, or rehabilitation—the fact that they must deal with large numbers of labeled or "possible" deviants on a daily basis leads them to structure their programs and practices in very similar ways. Erving Goffman refers to some of these places as *total institutions.*

According to Goffman, there are five principle types of total institutions:

1. institutions for persons who are "incapable" and "harmless"—the blind, aged, orphaned

2. institutions for persons who are incapable and pose an unintended threat to the community—mental hospitals, TB sanitaria

3. institutions for persons who intentionally endanger the community—prisons, jails pow camps, concentration camps

4. institutions established for some instrumental task—army barracks, boarding schools, work camps

5. institutions that are retreats from the secular world: abbeys, monasteries, convents, and cloisters.[55]

These institutions share a number of significant structural and "process" characteristics, most notably:

1. All aspects of life are conducted in the same place and under the same single authority.

2. Each phase of the member's daily activity is carried on in the immediate company of a large batch of others, all of whom are treated alike and required to do the same thing together.

3. All phases of the day's activities are tightly scheduled, . . . the whole sequence of activities being imposed from above by a system of explicit formal rulings and a body of officials.

4. Social mobility between the two strata is grossly restricted; social distance is typically great and often formally prescribed.

5. There exists a work ideology which the institution may define as treatment, rehabilitation, punishment, etc.

6. There exists a system of rewards and punishments which takes in the total life situation of the "inmate."

7. There exists a "mortification" or "stripping" process where "desocialization" or "disculturation" takes place and "resocialization" begins.[56]

Goffman's analysis indicates that institutions organized in this way must concern themselves with establishing and maintaining social control over the inmate population. To successfully "handle" whole blocks of people, the staff must impose itself upon the inmates and their daily regime in such a way that compliance with institutional rules and staff expectations is taken for granted. This is most effectively accomplished by means of the "mortification process." In order for inmates to be resocialized as compliant members of the institution, they must first be desocialized: their personal identities and roles must be transformed from "normal" to "inmate" status.

The mortification process begins with the stripping away of an individual's "identity kit"—those aspects of social "self" that permit a normal self-definition. The intake process, common to many institutions, initiates this stripping: personal possessions are taken away, an institutional wardrobe is given, perhaps an institutional identity tag with the inmate's ID number is issued. During this intake process, the individual's "life history" is recorded; he is asked to divulge information about his past, much of which may be personal or embarrassing. Goffman points out that there is "a violation of one's informational preserve regarding self."[57] The novice inmate loses control of information about himself that in normal life is used to patch together a tolerable self-conception. That information is now used by the staff to help control the behavior of the inmate.[58]

After intake or admission, other rules and practices within the institution continue the mortification process: the restriction to specific geographical areas, periods of forced work or forced leisure, the censoring of mail, lack of heterosexual contact, lack of privacy, the need to request supplies for smoking or shaving, or the need to request permission to go to the toilet. These practices collectively serve to convince inmates and staff that the former no longer have "normal" status as defined outside the institution. Goffman summarizes the mortification process by noting that

> total institutions disrupt or defile precisely those actions that in civil society have the role of attesting to the actor and those in his presence that he has some command over his world—that

he is a person with "adult" self-determination, autonomy, and freedom of action.[59]

The mortification process does not continue indefinitely. The inmate's compliance is also obtained by rewards given out in the "privilege system." Such privileges as increased recreational time and the granting of visitation rights and additional monetary rewards are also used to resocialize the inmate to his new status.[60] In mental hospitals, patients are often rewarded for coming to the realization that they are mentally ill, having insight into their problems, and learning that compliance with the therapeutic regime is good for them. Patients often become "apostles" of their therapists and are rewarded for using the clinical language of the institution to describe their own problems and those of their fellow patients.[61]

The net effect of the mortification process and reward system is entrance into the *inmate role.* The individual is made to play the role of the institutionally acceptable mental patient, prisoner, disabled person, or whatever. Scheff has formulated a theory of mental illness that offers an explanation for the acceptance of this deviant role. Like Goffman, Scheff indicates that mental patients are rewarded for playing the deviant role of the mentally ill and are punished when they attempt to play the normal or conventional role.[62] Scheff adds that

> in the crises occurring when a residual rulebreaker is publicly labeled, the deviant is highly suggestible, and may accept the proffered role of the insane as the only alternative.[63]

The inmate, because of the institutional pressures to conform to staff expectations and the need to resolve the dissonance produced by incompatible definitions of self, may become quite anxious and latch on to the proffered role. Scheff concludes that

> when a residual rule-breaker organizes his behavior within the framework of mental disorder, and when this organization is validated by others, particularly prestigeful others such as physicians, he is "hooked" and will proceed on a career of chronic deviance.[64]

The observations of both Goffman and Scheff concerning the emergence of deviant role-playing fits into Lemert's conception of "secondary deviation." They echo the view that official societal reactions to the alleged deviant often encourage the acceptance of the role status prophesied at the beginning of the institutional career. The "people-work"[65] engaged in by the staffs of these deviant-processing systems becomes unmanageable unless the inmates "know their place" and live up to expectations of the "good" institutionalized deviant.

Under such total institutional conditions, one of the gravest rule violations is the public questioning of one's deviant status.

In his own research on the processing of child deviants, the
author has witnessed several situations in which juvenile mental patients have openly insisted that they were no longer "sick" or had
already solved their "emotional difficulties" and wanted to go home.
Rather than deal with this request on its "face value," the clinical staff
were concerned with "why the child needed to make such statements." To the staff it was "obvious" that the child must really have a
severe disturbance because he has not yet realized that he is sick.[66]
This "Catch-22" reasoning is an example of what Goffman calls
"looping":

> An agency that creates a defensive response on the part of the
> inmate takes this very response as the target of its next attack.
> The individual finds that his protective response to an assault
> upon self is collapsed into the situation; he cannot defend
> himself in the usual way by establishing distance between the
> mortifying situation and himself.[67]

"Looping," as a form of societal reaction, may be the ultimate technique of labeling in a total institution; the failure to play the deviant
role only confirms the belief that the deviant is a deviant.

Many contemporary sociologists and criminologists have criticized the deviant role-playing assertion of the labeling perspective.[68]
They claim that such sociologists as Lemert, Goffman, and Scheff
offer an overly deterministic and simplistic explanation of how individuals become deviant. It appears, they claim, that certain structural
contingencies present within a total institution coerce the person into
a deviant role. Are not some mental patients "really" sick, rather than
playing a role foisted upon them by institutional staff? Is it not true
that some institutionalized deviants do not feel overly stigmatized, can
quite easily reenter normal roles once they leave the institution, and
are not unduly troubled by their previous inmate status? In other
words, are there not exceptions to the secondary deviation that may
be initiated by the institutional reaction to the alleged deviant? Is is
true that most institutional processing of deviants shares, to some
degree, the features described by these sociologists?

As we will see in the next chapter, much research corroborates
the assertions of the labeling perspective, but there are also findings
that make some of these explanations for deviant role-playing and
deviant careers problematic. Some contemporary sociologists feel that
the official processing of deviants does not have the consequences
predicted by the societal-reaction perspective. Others, the author included, believe that there is ample evidence to support the basic tenets

of the labeling perspective and that the analysis of the official processing of deviants contributes to our understanding of the meaning of
deviance in society.

INTEGRATING THE SOCIETAL-REACTION PERSPECTIVE WITH THE BROADER INTERACTIONIST FRAMEWORK

The study of official reaction processes does not, by itself, ex-
haust the possibilities inherent in an interactionist approach to deviant behavior. Neglected, sometimes, in such reaction research
are the very social-psychological dynamics that are central to the
symbolic-interactionist perspective. The focus on the structural characteristics of total institutions and on institutional and agency decision
making take attention away from the processes of learning involved in
"becoming" deviant. The developing interactionist analysis of deviant
behavior needed an example, if not a specific didactic model, to unify
labeling with the other interests of these students of deviance: socialization patterns, the role of deviant subcultures, the development of
deviant careers and patterns of interaction between deviants and
"straights," as well as between the deviants themselves. With the publication of Howard S. Becker's *Outsiders: Studies in the Sociology of
Deviance,* one model for integrating these interests was made
available.

In *Outsiders,* Becker unites the basic social-psychological and sociological themes of the interactionist perspective. The contents of the
book can be divided into four major topical areas:

1. a review of several theories of deviance and the presentation of a labeling definition of deviance, as well as a
model for studying the development or progression of
careers of deviation

2. an analysis of the social and social–psychological factors
influential in the advancement through three principle
career stages of marihuana use

3. an analysis of the role and function of deviant subcultures (specifically the subculture of the dance musician),
as well as an analysis of the career problems of deviant
"professionals"

4. the analysis of the societal reaction to marihuana use
and a general depiction of the role of "moral entrepreneurs" (moral crusaders who create and enforce rules,

the violation of which results in the ascription of deviant status).

We have already briefly depicted Becker's contribution to the definition of deviance; so we turn to what is perhaps the single most significant contribution that Becker makes in *Outsiders:* the establishment of a "career" perspective in the study of deviant behavior.

Careers of Deviation

Becker brings to the interactionist perspective an analysis of deviation within the framework of the sociology of occupations and professions. Here he was influenced by his association, as a student, with Everett Hughes at the University of Chicago. Using professional careers as a model, he indicates that deviant behavior does not come about all of a sudden, but that it develops over time in a "sequential" pattern.[69] Those factors, or "career contingencies," that promote involvement in deviant activities do not operate "simultaneously" but become important during different career "stages."[70] Some factors are important in influencing why a person will be present in situations in which, for example, marihuana or hard drugs are used. Other factors may be important in influencing why, in those situations, a person will begin experimenting with these drugs. Still other factors may be important in determining why, after initial use, the person continues to involve himself in these activities.

Different definitions of the situation may have to be learned, different types of decisions made, and many factors weighed before one stage or a series of these stages of *commitment* and involvement are passed through.

The process of *commitment*—the combining of interests to engage in some line of behavior—usually also shows a sequential patterning. Becker points out that the analysis of commitment to deviant behavior has traditionally searched for predisposing motivations, which scholars have often located in the personality structure of the individual. But, as in the commitment to occupational careers, motivations to deviant behavior have a social character: they are learned in interaction with others.[71] They develop *after* the individual has had certain experiences and has learned certain definitions of the situation and "vocabularies of motives."

A very important "career contingency" is the experience of being discovered and publicly labeled as a deviant. The individual, in these situations, is assigned a "master status trait": homosexual, drug addict, prostitute, juvenile delinquent, or others.[72] These are the master traits around which the identity of the individual will be formed. If one is labeled a juvenile delinquent, this label will dominate all other "characteristics" of the individual; "good athlete," "good conversationalist," "good dancer," and the like are subordinated to or negated by this trait, which is immediately felt to be more central to the "actual" identity of the individual.

In fact, associated with these master status traits are "auxiliary status traits, which are assumed to be "naturally" linked to it. For example, someone labeled a drug user may be seen as "hedonistic," "childlike," "crazy," "criminal," "a social menace," "amoral," and so on. These auxiliary status traits can serve as "explanations" or rationalizations for the master status trait: "The guy's a drug user *because* he's hedonistic, childlike, crazy . . . ," and so forth. Labelers, *as well as those labeled,* can "explain" the deviance by recourse to such stereotypic and readily available characterizations.

As an illustration of this mode of "sequential" analysis, Becker traces the career development of a marihuana user. He divides this career into three stages: (1) the *beginner* stage, at which the individual is using marihuana for the first time; (2) the *occasional* stage, at which there is sporadic use; and (3) the *regular* stage, at which the use of marihuana is a daily routine.[73] At the very beginning of his analysis, Becker tells us that

> marihuana use is an interesting case for theories of deviance, because it illustrates the way deviant motives actually develop in the course of experience with the deviant activity. To put a complex argument in a few words: instead of the deviant motives leading to the deviant behavior, it is the other way around; the deviant behavior in time produces the deviant motivation. Vague impulses and desires—in this case, probably most frequently a curiosity about the kind of experience the drug will produce—are transformed into definite patterns of action through the social interpretation of a physical experience which is in itself ambiguous. Marihuana use is a function of the individual's conception of marihuana and of the uses to which it can be put, and this conception develops as the individual's experience with the drug increases.[74]

The principal conditions for entering a career of marihuana use are not preexisting motivations or personality characteristics, but the learning of a conception about the drug and its use, as well as a conception about oneself as a drug user. Learning to smoke the drug, learning to perceive the subjective effects of the "high," and coming to define the drug use as "pleasurable" are the significant contingencies for entering the *beginner* state of usage.

After learning the proper techniques for smoking the drug, the beginner must learn to define the physical effects of drug smoking as pleasurable and must come to relate these effects to the socially defined expectations for being "high" or "stoned." This is important for drugs like marihuana. Such drugs can produce different effects depending on the person's conceptions of the drug, his expectations for the "high," and his definitions of the situation in which the drug is used. The range of possible subjective experiences obtained by using marihuana for the first time is quite large.

As Becker and others have demonstrated, some experience little or no pleasurable subjective response, while others experience a surprising range of sometimes opposing reactions: feeling hot or cold, feeling time to be of short duration or peculiarly extended, seeing distortions in shapes and objects or seeing them stand out boldly and sharply. The novice user is highly *suggestible* in such situations and is particularly influenced by the prevailing definitions of what one "should" experience. Entrance into a career of marihuana use is contingent upon successfully learning these definitions of the situation.

Socialization into the career role of the marihuana user, however, is dependent on three social controls that are major "career contingencies": *supply* of the drug, *secrecy* in using the drug, and definitions of the drug usage as *immoral*.[75] According to Becker, unless the marihuana smoker has an available supply of the drug, is able to control himself and maintain some level of secrecy about his behavior in the presence of nonusers or control agents, and is able to define the usage as not being immoral, passage from beginner to occasional to regular user is improbable.

At each stage in the career, these social controls take on new meaning and must sometimes be dealt with in different ways. The manner in which the beginner deals with "secrecy" contingencies may be to severely limit drug use and knowledge of it to a few individuals who can be trusted not to reveal this to others. The advanced or regular user simply learns to control the high in the presence of nonusers; as Becker points out, the problem almost ceases to exist if the regular user can join a user group that has substantially cut itself off from nonusers.

The three career contingencies present the user with problems of maintaining a tolerable self-conception, sustaining relations in both the "user" and "straight" world (if the complete integration into the user world cannot be made), and avoiding the control agents who may punish him. This is accomplished by learning new definitions of the situation, "vocabularies of motive" or rationalizations that sustain tolerable self-concepts and behavior, and new strategies of interaction that protect the user from the negative reactions of the society. Becker explains how involvement with marihuana use is influenced by social-psychological factors that make the behavior meaningful to participants and by sociological factors that effect the context of drug usage. Thus, he documents the *actualization* of this variety of deviant behavior.

Implicit in Becker's description of marihuana use is the role and function of fellow users in helping the user structure his behavior. It is, however, in Becker's description of the subculture of the dance musician that we more fully see the influence of group support in sustaining deviant identity and behavior.

The subculture of deviant groups has received wide attention in the study of deviant behavior. Cohen, in his analysis of delinquent subcultures, has indicated that delinquents join subcultures as a reaction to negative evaluations of them and their behavior. Feeling that they have been rejected by the dominant society,

> they not only reject the dominant value system, but do so with a vengeance. They "stand it on its head," they exalt its opposition; they engage in malicious, spiteful, "ornery" behavior of all sorts to demonstrate not only to others, but to themselves as well, their contempt for the game they have rejected. . . .[76]

Cohen adds that "the crucial condition for the emergence of new cultural forms is the existence, in *effective interaction with one another, of a number of actors with similar problems of adjustment.*"[77]

Kitsuse and Dietrick, in a critique of Cohen's theory, indicate that it explains only the *emergence* and not the *maintenance* of a delinquent subculture. A delinquent subculture is maintained by *repeated* negative societal reactions; the delinquents join gangs as a result of rejection by the dominant societal agents. Once participation takes place, however, "the delinquent subculture creates similar problems for all its participants."[78] They reject, and are in turn rejected by, the middle-class or dominant value system, and this reinforces their identity with the subculture. What develops, therefore, is a heightening of deviant behavior and an intensified commitment to the deviant subculture as a result of *mutual* reaction processes of exclusion and rejection.

Becker shares the views of Kitsuse and Dietrick concerning the amplifying effect of continued isolation, segregation, and outsider status as a result of societal reactions and of identification with the "deviant" subculture:

> Musicians are hostile to their audiences, afraid that they must sacrifice their artistic standards to the squares. They exhibit certain patterns of behavior and belief which may be viewed as adjustments to this situation. These patterns of isolation and self-segregation are expressed in the actual playing situation and in participation in the social intercourse of the larger com-

munity. The primary function of this behavior is to protect the musician from the interference of the square audience and, by extension, of the conventional society. Its primary consequence is to intensify the musician's status as an outsider, through the operation of a cycle of increasing deviance. *Difficulties with squares lead to increasing isolation which in turn increases the possibilities of further difficulties.*[79]

Becker goes on to show how musicians isolate themselves socially and psychologically from their audiences and maintain their differences from "squares." Becker believes that these behavioral strategies are common to many deviant subcultures. What varies from one subculture to another are the specific definitions of in-group and out-group differences and the components of self-identification. These help maintain the subculture and, in turn, participation in deviant behavior.

The last section of *Outsiders* discusses *rule enforcement* as a crucial factor in the social creation of deviance. Becker traces the contemporary societal reaction to marihuana use to the creation of the Marihuana Tax Act of 1937. This historical survey is used to illustrate the manner in which rules are created, enforced, and applied by persons whom Becker calls "moral entrepreneurs." The initiative and personal interests of the moral entrepreneur become important in establishing the need for a social rule. With the adequate publicity, power, and prestige that may come from high status within the "hierarchy of credibility," the moral entrepreneur can use commonly held values to establish the need for controlling objectionable behavior.[80] Values contained in such phrases and maxims as "equality," "a crime against the person is a crime against society," "people should be fully in control of themselves," and "people should not be overly hedonistic" are used to establish rules that are said to be in the interest of the entire community.

Once the rule is established, its enforcement is discretionary or subject to the interests of enforcers and the conditions of enforcement. Some rules are never enforced, some only when certain types of individuals are believed to have violated them, some only during certain periods of time when there is pressure exerted for their enforcement by interest groups. According to Becker, we need to study the development of rules from values, the role of moral entrepreneurs, and the discretionary power of enforcers, for they are essential to understanding the social meaning of deviant behavior as objects of social control.

The creation of the Marihuana Tax Act is Becker's case in point. He shows how the Treasury Department's Bureau of Narcotics publicized and characterized the urgency of the "marihuana menace." By grounding their campaign upon values they believed were generally shared by the American public (e.g. people should be completely responsible for their actions; actions solely for purposes of achieving states of ecstasy are disapproved), and by offering carefully selected atrocity tales as evidence of the harm caused by this drug, they succeeded in influencing the passage of the Tax Act. Becker, above all, stresses that such rule creation is a *moral enterprise* that seeks to create new definitions of right and wrong. By doing so it also creates outsiders. Rule enforcement is similarly interested in maintaining the definition of various problems and the belief that something ought to be done about them and, in fact, is being done. Rule enforcers, however, often create their own definitions of the seriousness of rule violations, and these categories of meaning influence actual enforcement efforts. The analysis of the enforcers' categories of meaning is thus a necessary step in investigating the actualization of deviance. Becker concludes that

> once a rule has come into existence, it must be applied to particular people before the abstract class of outsiders created by the rule can be peopled. Offenders must be discovered, identified, apprehended and convicted (or noted as "different" and stigmatized for their non-conformity, as in the case of legal deviant groups such as dance musicians). This job ordinarily falls to the lot of professional enforcers who, by enforcing already existing rules, create the particular deviants society views as outsiders.[81]

Deviant behavior is thus dependent on the self-definitions of actors, on the career contingencies of their involvement in the behavior, and on their membership in supportive deviant subcultures. Deviance is contingent on the discretionary powers of control agents. Through Becker's analyses, we see how these components are intertwined and (although separated in *Outsiders* for analytic and didactic purposes) are implicitly parts of an interrelated *process* of deviance development. Becker's analysis reminds students that although labeling processes ought to be a major subject for interactionist investigation, it is one piece in the larger puzzle of deviation.

The analysis of socialization into roles and careers and of deviant subcultures gives us an understanding of how *behavior* that is deemed to be deviant is learned. The analysis of rule creation and rule enforcement allows us to understand the actualization of community disapproval and repudiation and, therefore, of deviance as an evaluative reality. Official societal reactions do not, however, occur in the vast majority of cases of nonnormative behavior—here the learning of *behavior* is the most significant subject for interactionist analysis. Self-labeling remains an important factor, however, and "secret deviance" a significant category of deviation.

In some cases, the behavior complained of has not actually occurred or it is questionable whether the criteria for the label have been applied adequately or fairly. Here deviance exists as an evaluative reality because control agents have so decided. Some individuals are mislabeled or unjustly labeled, and for them the consequences of the societal reaction (e.g., repudiation, rejection, stigmatization) will be similar to those who may have violated the norm in question. With this category of deviance, interest lies in whether the societal reaction brings on adjustments in the self-regarding attitudes and behavior of indivudals so labeled.

Finally, we have the category of deviation in which both behavior is learned and evaluated as deviance by significant others. Here, a major interest of interactional analysis, in addition to themes mentioned above, is the relationship between the learning of behavior and the societal reaction to it. What influence does one have upon the other? Does the societal reaction reinforce the behavior in question, and if so with what consequences for the participants? It is important to know what attributes of behavior, individuals, and situational conditions are conducive to triggering a reaction and thus establishing a claim of deviance. It is equally important to know whether certain patterns of action–reaction amplification in the behaviors of labelers and those labeled are general to some types of deviation, or whether they differ markedly according to the behavior, the labelers, those labeled, and situational conditions. These are among the more interesting topics for an interactionist analysis of deviant behavior and deviance.

STIGMATIZATION AND ITS CONSEQUENCES

The societal-reaction perspective, as a form of interactionist analysis, is concerned with the symbolic attributes of deviance, as well as the practical *consequences* of assessment for the deviant. Labeling is the symbolic recasting of social role and identity so that the individual's "virtual social identity" is discredited.[82] In its place is substituted a "master status trait"—homosexual, insane, criminal—that orients the reactions of others to the deviant, and establishes for the deviant a need to adjust to these reactions. Stigmatization, as a consequence of the labeling process, is significant because it influences the meaning-laden base of social interaction between deviants and nondeviants, as well as between the deviants themselves.

Erving Goffman, in his book *Stigma,* indicates that two varieties of deviants can be differentiated, based upon the visibility of their stigma symbols. *Discredited* individuals have open, known-about, or visible stigma symbols (e.g., the blind and paraplegic, as well as those labeled deviants who are still under the control of community agents or agencies). *Discreditable* individuals have hidden or concealable stigmas; a negative societal reaction may follow the discovery that the individual is not who he appears to be but, in fact, someone with a stigma.[83] The basic interactional problem for the discredited individual, according to Goffman, is managing tension; and for the discreditable individual, the managing of social information about self. The blind person usually adjusts his behavior with the knowledge that most individuals will notice his blindness and relate to him as a "blind person." The homosexual who is concerned about family and employers finding out about his sexual preferences can conceal this by managing information so that these stigmatizing facts never surface. Thus the interactional strategies used by discredited and discreditable individuals for everyday encounters with nondeviants differ.

According to Goffman, the behavior of "normal" individuals in relation to "deviants" is often contingent on prevailing *stigma theories*.[84] A stigma theory is an ideology that not only explains why an individual has become deviant and *ought* to be reacted to negatively, but also indicates the type of reaction called for. Goffman, as an illustration, points out that sighted individuals often speak to the blind in an overly loud voice, assuming that they must also be hard of hearing. Normal individuals often associate disease or uncleanliness with physical disfigurement, and their immediate reaction is avoidance or an inability to come in physical contact with such persons. Adults labeled as mentally ill are sometimes thought to have low intelligence and are talked to as though they were children. In some neighborhoods and social groups, the display of effeminate characteristics and behavior among males is met with violent reactions by other males.

These and similar attitudes and behaviors on the part of normals imply the existence of a culturally supported stigma theory or ideology that prescribes the social meaning of the behavior and individuals in question and suggests acceptable reactions to them. A major shortcoming of societal-reaction research has been the insufficient exploration of the normative components of stigma theories. Although research has focused on the ideologies of control agents who interact with deviants, the stigma theories of large segments of the lay public have not been sufficiently studied.

Goffman provides an excellent review of strategies that discredited and discreditable individuals employ in attempting to "pass" in daily interaction with the nonstigmatized: from attempts to correct the stigma through plastic surgery to the use of "disidentifiers" (objects or behavior that divert attention from the stigma symbols, such as sunglasses worn by the blind).[85] However, he does not fill out the counter strategies of the nonstigmatized. Such an analysis would give a more rounded understanding of the microprocesses surrounding deviation and its attendant societal reactions.

Stigmatization brings with it more wide-ranging consequences than the requirements for "passing" indicate. The life futures of individuals are often structured by the stigmatization process. The early labeling of children as "slow learners," "maladjusted," or "noncollege material" has significant consequences for their future careers.[86] Stigma theories are also at work in the minds of decision makers who do the hiring and firing and who decide the "value" of the stigmatized for specific niches in the social order. Such interpretations of labeled deviants usually involve low estimations of their intellectual ability, their lack of trustworthiness, their dangerousness, their bad influences on others, their pervasive immorality, or perhaps only the fact that someone of high credibility has labeled them as nonconformists and the feeling, therefore, that "something must be wrong with them."

The specific attributes of stigma theories and reaction processes that influence the life futures, careers, and lifestyles of labeled deviants need to be analyzed more carefully and with greater attention to the normative organization of the decision making involved. For how long does the stigma influence the career-blocking reactions of important gatekeepers in the opportunity structure of society? Do such gatekeepers respond to organizational pressures to block channels of opportunity for the stigmatized? And is rejection of various categories of deviants systematic?

A growing literature in the field of deviance has focused on such issues, but much more research is needed to specify not only the decision-making criteria for initial labeling but also the decision making and evaluations that follow upon and are reactions to that initial labeling. Just as we have primary and secondary deviations, we also have primary and secondary reaction processes to deviant behavior. Careers of deviation may have accompanying "careers" of reaction to them. Emphasis has so far been given to the primary labeling reactions and to more immediate and consequent secondary reactions. We also need to understand the more protracted "career history" of secondary reactions to deviant behavior and stigmatization.

There are significant methodological problems in doing this longitudinal analysis, but such investigations are important if it is true that the "dramatization of evil" is also sequential, historical, and has its own significant contingenices. We need to know how secondary reactions are related to the preceding reactions (e.g., is rejection of the former mental patient from employment opportunities dependent only on the primary reaction—his presence in a mental hospital or in private therapy—or may it also be influenced by the rejections of other employers?).

We also need to know the responses of the stigmatized to such secondary reactions. It is important to know how secondary reactions influence secondary deviation, if they do. In many cases the secondary reactions are completely independent of the individual's behavior but still exercise a strong influence over his conception of self-worth, his relations with others, and his thoughts about his social future.

SUMMARY AND CONCLUSIONS

This chapter has reviewed the basic conceptual framework of the societal-reaction and the broader interactionist perspectives on social deviance. In doing so, it has synthesized the contributions of sociologists writing in the 1950s and 1960s who established the analytic language and the focus of this departure from more traditional conceptions of deviance. This review has been intended to be a guide to this body of literature. The student is urged to consult the various primary sources for a more detailed understanding of these central ideas.

There are two interrelated concerns of the interactionist perspective on deviation: (1) the learning of behavior defined as deviant and (2) the actualization of deviance as an evaluating reality—the evaluation that a breach of the social order has taken place. The proponents of a societal-reaction perspective focused their attention more clearly on the latter. These sociologists were concerned with basic components of the societal reaction, as well as with the influence of that reaction on *careers* of deviation.

Attention was given to the conditions of the societal reaction by attempting to discover *when* it occurs *(tolerance quotient),* and *how* it occurs as a decision-making reality *(retrospective interpretation).* In addition, they explored the structural and interactional factors that facilitated effective degradation and stigmatization (conditions for successful *degradation ceremonies, total institutions,* the *stripping* or *mortification* process, *"looping,"* the *apostolic function).* The analysis of the societal reaction to deviance became primarily interested in official reactions by control agents because of their significant consequences for the alleged deviant, even though some forms of deviance rarely result in degradation by *stigmatizing audiences.* This emphasis on official reactions brought attention to the role of *moral entrepreneurs* and the *hierarchy of credibility* in establishing the need for rule creation, enforcement, and the overall control of rule violators.

While some sociologists emphasized the role of reaction processes in actualizing deviance, others suggested a more unified and integrated investigation of both the learning of deviant behavior and the actualization of deviance as an evaluative reality. It was necessary to study deviant careers and career contingencies other than the admittedly significant contingency of labeling itself. The commitment to deviant behavior and roles and the influence of group or subcultural membership in this regard were also seen as significant topics for interactionist research.

Finally, the interest in labeling was associated with its consequences for those who were stigmatized. The implications of stigmatization for the everyday interaction between deviants and nondeviants were explored. Other investigators studied the effect of stigmatization on limiting the deviant's access to society's opportunity structure. This analysis offers insight into the long-term consequences of societal-reaction processes.

These conceptual elaborations of the societal-reaction school extended the analytical framework initiated by Lemert. They especially provided students of deviation with a working language for investigating the actualization of deviance. The decades of the 1960s and 1970s would see the application of this conceptual framework to the analysis of different forms of deviation. To some observers, the results of these empirical investigations were not always consistent. Severe criticisms were lodged against the "labeling" perspective, and new perspectives emerged that offered alternative approaches.

We turn now to the elements of the many debates that have emerged since the introduction of the labeling perspective. Chapter 7 examines the evidence used to support and criticize it. New perspectives in the analysis of deviation will be examined as reactions to the basic ideas that have been presented in this chapter.

---

[1]The student should not be confused by Lemert's use of the term "sociopathic"—he means deviant behavior. Lemert indicated that "the objective of this work is to study a limited part of deviation in human behavior and a certain range of societal reactions, together with their interactional products, and by the methods of science to arrive at generalizations about the uniformities in these events. The aim is to study sociopathic behavior in the same light as normal behavior and, by implication, with extensions or deviations of general sociological theory." Edwin M. Lemert, *Social Pathology: A Systematic Approach To The Theory of Sociopathic Behavior.* New York: McGraw-Hill, 1951, p. 23. Also see Lemert, "Some Aspects of a General Theory of Sociopathic Behavior," *Proceedings of the Pacific Sociological Society,* Research Studies, State College of Washington, Vol. 16, no. 1 (1948), pp. 24ff.

[2]Lawrence Guy Brown, *Social Pathology: Personal and Social Disorganization.* New York: F. S. Crofts, 1942, preface.

[3]Ibid., pp. 76–77.

[4]Ibid., p. 76.

[5]*Social Pathology,* pp. 22–23.

[6]Ibid., p. 22.

[7]Edwin M. Lemert, *Human Deviance, Social Problems and Social Control.* Englewood Cliffs, N.J.: Prentice-Hall, 1967, pp. 40–41.

[8]Lemert, *Social Pathology,* pp. 57–58.

[9]Some sociologists believed that it would be important to investigate the decision rules used by labelers to decide that deviance existed. See Peter McHugh, "A Common-Sense Conception of Deviance," in Jack D. Douglas, ed., *Deviance and Respectability.* New York: Basic Books, 1970, pp. 61–88.

[10]For example, the discretionary power of police not to make an arrest is limited if there are numerous witnesses to an event who insist on pressing charges against an individual.

[11]See W. I. Thomas, *The Unadjusted Girl.* New York: Harper Torchbooks, 1967; originally published in 1923 by Little, Brown.

[12]See Chapter 5, footnote 31, of this volume.

[13]Lemert, *Human Deviance,* p. 55.

[14]Lemert, *Social Pathology,* pp. 55–56. See also *Human Deviance,* p. 43.

[15]See, for example, J. W. Brehm and A. R. Cohen, *Explorations in Cognitive Dissonance.* New York: Wiley, 1962.

[16]Lemert, *Social Pathology,* p. 68.

[17]This and other criticisms will be discussed in the next chapter.

[18]Lemert, *Social Pathology,* p. 71.

[19]Ibid., pp. 219–22.

[20]Ibid., pp. 445–46.

[21]It was particularly difficult to specify the situations in which deviance occurred because the investigator could not always be present when the behavior was in progress.

[22]Lemert, in a more recent article, has voiced dissatisfaction with the prevalent "symbolic interactionist" approach to the study of deviance. See Lemert, "Beyond Mead: The Societal Reaction to Deviance," *Social Problems,* Vol. 21 (April 1974), pp. 457–68.

[23]These contributions are not analyzed in the chronological order of their publication.

[24]Howard S. Becker, *Outsiders: Studies in the Sociology of Deviance.* New York: Free Press, 1963, pp. 8–9. Emphasis in original.

[25]See next chapter.

[26]By "effective" is meant that it will have consequences for some party to the joint action that is deviance. For another popular definition of deviance, see Kai Erikson, "Notes On The Sociology of Deviance," in Howard S. Becker, ed., *The Other Side.* New York: Free Press, 1964, p. 11.

[27]These are the decision-making criteria or rules used to account for deviance. Sociologists believe that these are often firmly embedded in the folk wisdom of a culture and are learned early in primary socialization.

[28]John I. Kitsuse, "Societal Reaction to Deviant Behavior: Problems of Theory and Method," in Becker, ed., *The Other Side,* 1964. Originally published in *Social Problems,* Vol. 9 (Winter 1962).

[29]Ibid., p. 91.

[30]Ibid., pp. 92–93.

[31]Ibid., p. 94 (a person asking the subject if he could touch his penis or becoming "intimate" in some less direct manner, such as having one's school tennis coach invite you to dinner and then put his arm around you and ask if you want your back rubbed).

[32]Ibid., pp. 95–96.

[33]Kitsuse and Cicourel borrow this term from Karl Mannheim's "documentary method," and this has affinity with Garfinkel's "documentary method" in Harold Garfinkel, *Studies in Ethnomethodology*. Englewood Cliffs, N.J.: Prentice-Hall, 1967.

[34]Kitsuse, "Societal Reaction," pp. 96–97.

[35]Ibid., p. 101.

[36]Erikson, "Sociology of Deviance," pp. 11–12.

[37]"Biography" is the historical image of the deviant held by control agents. It is a pattern of knowledge held by the labeler about the deviant who must be "accounted" for.

[38]Kai T. Erikson and Daniel E. Gilbertson, "Case Records in the Mental Hospital," in Stanton Wheeler, ed., *On Record: Files and Dossiers in American Life*. New York: Russell Sage Foundation, 1969, pp. 389–412, 404.

[39]Harold Garfinkel "Conditions of Successful Degradation Ceremonies," *American Journal of Sociology*, Vol. 61 (March 1956), pp. 421–22.

[40]Erving Goffman, *Stigma: Notes on the Management of Spoiled Identity*. Englewood Cliffs, N.J.: Prentice-Hall, 1963, pp. 2–3.

[41]Jack D. Douglas, *The Social Meaning of Suicide*. Princeton, N.J.: Princeton University Press, 1967.

[42]Garfinkel, "Conditions," pp. 422–42.

[43]See Howard S. Becker, "Whose Side Are We On?" *Social Problems*, Vol. 14 (1967), pp. 239-47.

[44]Garfinkel, "Conditions," p. 423.

[45]A moral objection may be raised concerning sociological attempts to find the most conducive strategies and techniques for degradation ceremonies. Sociologists do not necessarily condone their use. It is however, important to understand those that are used "effectively."

[46]For an explanation of "ontological" labels, see Jack Katz, "Deviance, Charisma, and Rule-Defined Behavior," *Social Problems*, Vol. 20 (1973), pp. 186–202.

[47]Martin S. Weinberg and Colin J. Williams, *Male Homosexuals: Their Problems and Adaptations*. New York: Oxford University Press, 1974, pp. 155–56.

[48]Carol Warren, *Identity and Community in the Gay World*. New York: Wiley, 1974, pp. 146–47. See also Carol Warren and John M. Johnson, "A Critique of Labeling Theory from the Phenomenological Perspective," in Robert A. Scott and Jack D. Douglass, eds., *Theoretical Perspectives on Deviance*. New York: Basic Books, 1972.

[49]Warren, *Identity and Community*, p. 146.

[50]Warren and Johnson, "Critique of Labeling Theory," p. 78. Emphasis in original.

[51]For an explanation of "secret deviant," see Becker, *Outsiders*, p. 20, and also Becker, *Outsiders*, rev. ed., 1973, Ch. 10, "Labeling Theory Reconsidered."

[52]See the next chapter for a discussion of controversy over the secret-deviant category and definitions of "objective deviance."

[53]See again Becker, *Outsiders*, rev. ed., Ch. 10.

[54]See, for example, Richard D. Schwarz and Jerome Skolnick, "Two Studies of Legal Stigma," *Social Problems*, Vol. 10 (Fall 1962), pp. 133–142. See also Derek Phillips, "Rejection: A Possible Consequence of Seeking Help for Mental Disorders," *American Sociological Review*, Vol. 28 (December 1963), pp. 963–72.

[55]Erving Goffman, *Asylums*. Garden City, N.Y.: Anchor Books, Doubleday, 1961, pp. 4–5, 7, 18–20.

[56]The "mortification" or "stripping" refers to the process by which the individual's social self is changed so that a new self-concept and role (one supported by the total institution) can be adopted. Inside the institution there occurs a movement from desocialization to resocialization. Desocialization refers to the tearing down of social self and is synonymous with the stripping process. Resocialization refers to the taking on of a new social role and self-concept.

[57]Goffman, *Asylums*, p. 23.

[58]Ibid.,pp. 155–60.

[59]Ibid., p. 43.

[60]Ibid., pp. 48–60.

[61]For an explanation of "apostolic functions," see M. Balint, *The Doctor, His Patient, and the Illness*. New York: International University Press, 1957. Also Thomas J. Scheff, *Being Mentally Ill: A Sociological Theory*. Chicago: Aldine, 1966, pp. 84–85.

[62]Scheff, *Being Mentally Ill*, pp. 84–87.

[63]Ibid., p. 88.

[64]Ibid.

[65]For an explanation of "people-work," see Goffman, *Asylums*, p. 74.

[66]Charles S. Suchar, *The Social Organization of Child Therapy*, unpublished PhD dissertation, Northwestern University, 1972, pp. 302–5.

[67]Goffman, *Asylums*, pp. 35–36.

[68]We will discuss some of these criticisms in the next chapter.

[69]Becker *Outsiders*, p. 23.

[70]Ibid., p. 24.

[71]Ibid., p. 31.

[72]Ibid., pp. 32–33.

[73]Ibid., p. 61.

[74]Ibid., p. 42.

[75]Ibid., pp. 59–78.

[76]Albert K. Cohen, *Deviance and Social Control*. Englewood Cliffs, N.J.: Prentice-Hall, 1966, p. 66.

[77]Albert K. Cohen, *Delinquent Boys*. New York: Free Press, 1955, p. 59. Emphasis in original.

[78]John I. Kitsuse and David C. Dietrick, "Delinquent Boys: A Critique," *American Sociological Review*, Vol. 24 (April 1959), pp. 213–15.

[79]Becker, *Outsiders*, pp. 95–96. Emphasis my own.

[80]Ibid., Chs. 7 and 8.

[81]Ibid., p. 163.

[82]Goffman, *Asylums*, pp. 2-3.

[83]Ibid., pp. 4, 41–42.

[84]Ibid., p. 5.

[85]Ibid., Chs. 1 and 2.

[86]See, for example, John I. Kitsuse and Aaron V. Cicourel, *Educational Decision-Maker.* Indianapolis: Bobbs-Merrill, 1963.

SELECTED READINGS

1963   Howard Becker, *Outsiders: Studies in the Sociology of Deviance.* New York: Free Press.

1951   Edwin Lemert, *Social Pathology: A Systematic Approach to the Theory of Sociopathic Behavior.* New York: McGraw-Hill.

1962   John I. Kitsuse, "Societal Reaction to Deviant Behavior: Problems and Method," *Social Problems,* Vol. 9 (Winter 1962).

1963   Erving Goffman, *Stigma: Notes on the Management of Spoiled Identity.* Englewood Cliffs, N.J.: Prentice-Hall.

1966   Thomas J. Scheff, *Being Mentally Ill: A Sociological Theory.* Chicago: Aldine.

1961   Erving Goffman, *Asylums,* Garden City, N.Y.: Doubleday Anchor Books.

1971   Edwin M. Schur, *Labeling Deviant Behavior: Its Sociological Implications.* New York: Harper & Row.

SELECTED APPLICATIONS

The following selections illustrate several characteristics of the labeling of deviants and the process of self-labeling. The article by Hawkes demonstrates the precarious nature of the institutional processing of the mentally ill. Sagarin discusses the socialization process and the construction of deviant self-concepts.

THE HIGH PERSONAL COST OF WEARING A LABEL
Edward Sagarin

The little verb "to be" has caused a great deal of pain. I want to alleviate some of that pain by clearing up a terrible confusion.

When we speak about a person who behaves in eccentric ways —who does eccentric things and commits eccentric acts—we tend to say

Reprinted by permission from *Psychology Today* Magazine. Copyright © 1976 by Ziff-Davis Publishing Company.

that he "is" an eccentric. This usage is perfectly harmless because eccentricity doesn't raise many passions these days. It's the same when we say that a person "is" a thief, a cheat, a philanthropist or a jaywalker. "Being" any of these things may mean that the actions are committed once, sporadically, or commonly. But they are still actions, and we wouldn't necessarily say that they concerned a person's identity.

The problems crop up when we start talking about other types of deviant behavior. We say of a person who drinks too much that he "is" an alcoholic, and we say of people who think bizarre thoughts that they "are" schizophrenic. This person is a drug addict and that person is a homosexual. Others are sadomasochists, pedophiliacs, juvenile delinquents. The English language is constructed in such a way that we speak of people *being* certain things when all we know is that they *do* certain things.

The result is an imputed identity, or rather a special kind of mistaken identity. Since a person's sense of his identity can have immense consequences, mistaken identity can be tragic. The tragedy has been particularly acute among people thought "to be" homosexual, and the confusion increases with today's demand by the Gay Liberation movement that thousands of men come out of the closet and identify themselves as homosexuals.

Let me make my point about the verb "to be" as plain as possible. The world's meaning varies depending on its context. "He is a prisoner," for example, need not imply that a person is permanently a prisoner, or that prison is essential to his being. "He is male," on the other hand, does imply a more or less permanent identity. In other cases ("the chicken is a two-legged animal") *is* refers to certain traits or characteristics; and in still other cases *is* refers to a certain kind of behavior, deviant or average. Behavior, however, is not necessarily identity. Behavior can change, but identity cannot change.

Good-Boy Delinquents   Perhaps the confusion started with Freud and the concept of latency, the imagined quality of people who had an identity that had not yet manifested itself. Some years ago, August Aichhorn, Freud's chief disciple in the field of juvenile delinquency, suggested that there were two types of juvenile delinquents: those who committed what he classified as "dissocial" acts, and those who did not. One would think that the two together make up the entire youthful population, but not Aichhorn. For him, there were good-boy delinquents, youths with unresolved internal psychological problems of which they were unaware. One might call them potential delinquents, although that terminology is shunned by many who insist that it can become a self-fulfilling prophecy. For Aichhorn, the term "delinquent" was an identity, existing in an individual regardless of his behavior, desire, knowledge of self, or self-description. Some persons, he said, did not realize that they were delinquents. In the language of homosexuality, they had not yet "come out."

The idea of "coming out" implies that a condition existed before its recognition, that it is there to be discovered, that it will remain even if repudiated. It would be scientifically more accurate, and offer infinitely greater freedom of choice of individuals in their development, if our language implied change, or at least changeability, rather than permanence and immutability. Note, for example, what Wardell Pomeroy, close collaborator of Kinsey, wrote about the early work at the Institute for Sex Research. "In Kinsey's files were the records (as early as 1940) of more than 80 cases of men who had made a satisfactory heterosexual adjustment which either accompanied or largely replaced earlier homosexual experience." People do change, and Kinsey knew it. He had seen enough people who had changed. Pomeroy writes, "to convince him that the psychologists were making matters worse by starting with the assumption that homosexuality was an inherited abnormality which could not be cured simply because it was inherent." The "inherited-abnormality" idea has been long abandoned but in its place there has appeared something equally resistant to change—the idea of identity. This idea presumes that one realizes what one is, that one discovers an identity rather than becoming it through behavior.

Deviants as Victims That kind of identity is a myth. Admittedly, if a person believes the myth, the chances rise that he will assume the appropriate, narrowly defined role. Believing that one is an addict, an alcoholic, a schizophrenic, or a homosexual can result in relinquishing the search for change and becoming imprisoned in the role.

Social scientists, unfortunately, have contributed to such real-life prisons through their work on labeling theory. Labeling theory reached its academic zenith during the 1960s, a period of great social change, and it did a mighty job of turning the world of social respectability upside down. Labeling theorists sympathized with deviants of various sorts, they questioned the norms, labels and stereotypes of middle-class society, and they found it useful to look at deviants more as victims than as victimizers.

Labeling theorists have outlined clearly the stages by which a label becomes a reality. A person takes his first hesitant steps toward deviance; he learns the roles and social expectations; he learns how to navigate within his own role, and so on, until he becomes entrenched in it. A deviant identity emerges. And after being treated by society as if he actually were what he was supposed to be, he eventually becomes just that. But—some writers contend—maybe the person was just that all along. He did not realize it, because the behavior had not yet come to the fore, in other words, it was a matter of latency.

The concept of latency, used in this manner, is scientifically unsound, conceptually useless, and socially pernicious. It is unsound because a potential for developing in a heterosexual or homosexual, sober or alcoholic direction is nothing more than being human. In that sense everyone has latent tendencies. The concept is useless, since it fails to distinguish between those who might more easily or less easily develop in a given direction. And it is pernicious because it supports the belief that one can somehow "be" whatever is under consideration, even though one does not behave in the manner called for by the role, or even have conscious desires or interests. This deviant identity is a sort of presumed being, a little gremlin within the individual.

It is true, of course, that all forms of behavior are preceded by certain developments of character and personality. But this is as true of pre-heterosexuals as it is of pre- or proto- or latent homosexuals. If the idea of latency has any validity, then it should be used for all kinds of behavior. Moreover, it should only be used with full knowledge that a mere potential is quite different from an all-but-born reality. It *can* come to the fore, but it can also be channeled elsewhere. In fact, no behavioral, characterological, or personality type that is not yet in existence within the individual is inevitable.

This distinction can mean the difference between success and failure to anyone looking for therapy, since a belief in the possibility of change, both in therapist and patient, is crucial to the therapeutic process. I suspect that the belief can be created, particularly in the patient, by emphasizing that schizophrenia, depression, alcoholism and homosexuality refer to what a person does rather than to what he is. Unfortunately, the commoner belief is that a person either is or is not a schizophrenic, alcoholic, or homosexual, and the belief carries with it a sense of destiny.

In general, the language we use when we talk about such matters tends to become flesh and blood and behavior. It can reinforce an identity and imprison someone in a role. As C. Wright Mills once put it, "Men discern situations with particular vocabularies," and of course these vocabularies have particular consequences. Thus sociologists and other behaviorial scientists, although intending just the opposite, have helped create a trap for deviants. The liberal minded labeling theorists are the ones who have insisted on the importance of identity, being, discovering, realizing what one is—in a phrase, "coming out."

Part of the problem here may lie in the positive associations of the word "identity." People are urged from all quarters to know who they are and to accept themselves. Erik Erikson, for example, who has written extensively on this theme but who has avoided a definition, uses the expression "ego identity" to describe "a persistent sameness within oneself and a persistent sharing of some kind of essential character with others." But no matter *how* persistent it is, a characteristic of personality or behavior need not be permanent unless it has biological, chemical, or physiological referents—and even then the characteristic would not necessarily be permanent. Moreover, "the sharing of some kind of essential character with others" tends to be self-perpetuating, especially when a person internalizes the notion of identity and says to himself, "That is what I am." He would be freer if he said, "That is what I do." There are choices inherent in doing, in action; the future is open. There is a relative lack of choice in being.

To "come out" and accept any identity is not freedom but a renunciation of freedom. The ultimate freedom of a human being is to become what he chooses and wishes to become, restrained only by forces that are genuinely beyond his control. There is no alcoholic, heterosexual, or homosexual identity. There are only people who behave in a given manner, at various times of their lives, in some cases over an entire lifetime. The behavior is real, but the identity is an invention. It is an invention believed in so thoroughly by some people that they have become what they were improperly tagged as being.

WHO'S CRAZY? WHO ISN'T?
Nigel Hawkes

A bizarre experiment has demonstrated that some psychiatrists cannot distinguish effectively between people who are mentally disturbed and those who are sane.

According to its originators, supervised by Stanford University Prof. D. L. Rosenhan, the experiment demonstrates the fallibility of conventional psychiatric diagnosis. It also lends considerable support to the position taken by radical psychiatrists like R. D. Laing, who argue that diagnoses of mental disease are often no more than convenient labels designed to make life easier for doctors.

Eight perfectly normal people, by shamming symptoms of a mild kind, successfully gained admission to psychiatric wards, where they remained undetected for as long as they could stand it. Once admitted, their behavior was normal in every way. But doctors and nurses continued to treat them as disturbed.

In every case but one, the diagnosis was schizophrenia. Once they were labeled as mentally ill, everything the pseudopatients did tended to confirm the diagnosis in the eyes of the medical staff, though other patients in the hospital were much less easy to convince.

The eight pseudopatients included three psychologists, a pediatrician, a psychiatrist, a painter and a housewife. All eight assumed false names and those connected with the medical profession also invented false occupations, so as not to attract special attention. The hospitals chosen ranged from expensive private units to dingy public institutions.

To gain admission the pseudopatients told the whole truth about their lives, their emotions and their personal relationships—all of which were within the normal range—and lied only about their names, symptoms and, in some cases, their occupations. The symptoms they complained of were hearing disembodied voices saying the words "empty," "hollow" and "thud."

This was sufficient in every case for them to be classified as mentally ill. Once inside, they stopped pretending and behaved as normally as they could. Their stays inside varied from seven to 52 days, and averaged 19 days.

As many as a third of the real patients inside detected that they

From *The Chicago Sun-Times*, February 7, 1973, by Nigel Hawkes. Reprinted by permission of *The Chicago Suns-Times*.

were frauds. "You're not crazy. You're a journalist or a professor. You're checking up on the hospital," was a typical comment from a fellow patient.

The pseudopatients spent much of their time taking extensive notes. But even this did not apparently raise any suspicions in the doctors' minds. "Patient engages in writing behavior," was the daily nursing comment on one patient. But nobody troubled to ask him what he was writing.

The experiment was carried out under the supervision of Prof. Rosenhan, himself one of the eight fake patients. Writing about the experiment in Science magazine, he concludes: "We cannot distinguish the sane from the insane in mental hospitals. . . . How many people, one wonders, are sane but not recognized as such in our psychiatric institutions? . . . How many have been stigmatized by well-intentioned, but nevertheless, erroneous diagnoses?"

In Rosenhan's view, the hospital itself is an environment that distorts judgment. As evidence, he quotes what happened to patients who asked doctors perfectly sensible questions such as: "Pardon me, Dr. X. could you tell me when I will be eligible for ground privileges?" In almost three quarters of the cases, the psychiatrist's response was to walk on, head averted. Only one doctor in 25 stopped and tried to answer the question.

The clinching piece of evidence comes from another experiment in which a hospital was warned that pseudopatients would be presenting themselves. Faced with this threat to their professional reputations, the doctors admitting patients became much more conservative in their diagnosis. Of 193 patients presenting themselves, one doctor was firmly convinced that 41 were frauds, while another doctor suspected 23. In fact, no fake patients had arrived at all.

In the present state of knowledge, there seems little hope of more accurate diagnostics. Doctors should try to err on the side of caution, in Rosenhan's opinion, and "refrain from sending the distressed to insane places." That, and a more benign environment inside institutions, could help to sort out the insane from the merely confused.

CHAPTER 7

THE SOCIOLOGICAL REACTION TO LABELING

From its inception, the interactionist perspective on deviance has met with a variety of reactions from sociologists. Its impact upon the study of deviance and crime can be assessed by the many debates it has stirred and the number of journal articles and books that it has generated. This broad range of literature, published after the majority of these ideas were proposed in the early 1960s, has a number of significant and distinguishing characteristics.

One common and somewhat confusing aspect of this theoretical discussion is the designation of the interactionist perspective as the target of criticism. Both proponents and opponents of the perspective use the terms "interactionist," "labeling," and "societal reaction" interchangeably. As we have seen in the previous chapters, labeling is only one concern of interactionists, albeit a major one. The brunt of criticism, however, has been leveled not at the interactionist perspective as a whole, but primarily at those perspectives concerned with (1) the actualization of deviance as evaluative reality, and (2) the impact of the societal reaction on the later careers of those designated as deviant (secondary deviation). On the other hand, there has been a relative lack of criticism of the interactionist stance concerning the importance of analyzing how one learns to become a prostitute, student radical, drug user, homosexual, or professional thief. There have been few criticisms of the significance of analyzing socialization into a deviant role, the development of self-attitudes, skills, beliefs, motivations, values, or the impact of subcultural participation on deviant role-playing and deviant careers.

A good many criticisms have, however, centered on the predicted negative effect that official or institutional labeling has on the lives and futures of those labeled. Many critics have also questioned the conclusions drawn by labeling sociologists concerning the process of rule creation and enforcement, the tolerance levels of control agents, and the rational bases of official decision making and evaluation that is said to be central to deviance. In fact, a large number of criticisms seem to have been leveled at what is perceived to be a muckraking analysis of the societal reaction to deviants and deviance. Critics have been annoyed at the "more sinned against than sinning" theme that they detect in the empirical research of certain labeling analysts. Concern has also been voiced over a perceived disregard for the legitimate interests of official agents of social control and an overemphasis on the harms done to labeled rule violators.

A more recent set of criticisms have focused on what might be called the well-intended but misguided liberalism of labeling analysts. These sociologists are charged with failure to understand the full scope of the issue. The social-psychological framework of these sociologists, critics insist, are blinders that force them to disregard the structural determinants of the societal-reaction process. Taking a Marxist perspective, such critics maintain that social-control institutions and their practices reflect the conflicts inherent in the class structure of society. The struggle between rule enforcers and labeled deviants over what is acceptable or unacceptable social behavior reveals the class interests of those in power and the plight of the expropriated. Labeling practices, it is charged, preserve the status quo. Rather than study labeling as the essential ingredient in the creation of social problems, sociologists should focus their attention on the broader structural problems of which labeling and stigmatization are only symptoms.

Like their fellow structuralists, Marxist analysts of deviance are concerned that the focus on labeling will avoid what they feel to be more significant *causal* investigations. Although it is acceptable to study the actualization of deviance through the examination of official societal-reaction processes, this is insufficient without the attendant search for structural sources of the societal reaction.

All of these criticisms of the labeling perspective can be differentiated by several themes that are consistently present. This chapter will review the most prominent among them.

One familiar theme is the view that the definition of deviance proffered by labeling analysts is inconsistent, thus producing a problematic understanding of what is and is not deviant. There are also attendant problems of operationalizing the concept of deviance in the way it has been defined. Another theme, quite common in criticism of the perspective, is the perceived disregard for the conventional focus on causality, the structural realities and objective conditions and nature of deviance, and the determinant of the rate of deviance and changes in the rate.

Still another theme is the concern over the consequences of labeling for the alleged deviant. Lemert and others have been challenged on the concept of secondary deviance—labeling that leads to continued role playing and career involvement in deviance. The political implications of the perspective and its ramifications for the policy and practice of institutions that process deviants have also been criticized. Finally, some sociologists have questioned the explanatory value of the labeling perspective with regard to particular kinds of deviation. Some varieties of deviance, they contend, are not subject to the practices described by these analysts, and such rule violators do not mirror the role-playing models constructed by the theorists.

CRITICIZING THE LABELING DEFINITION OF DEVIANCE

> The deviant is one to whom that label has successfully been applied; deviant behavior is behavior that people so label.
>
> Deviance is not a property inherent in certain forms of behavior. It is a property conferred upon these forms by the audiences which directly or indirectly witness them.
>
> Forms of behavior per se do not differentiate deviants from non-deviants; it is the responses of the conventional and conforming members of the society who identify and interpret behavior as deviant which sociologically transform persons into deviants.[1]

These basic definitions of deviance underscore the importance of the evaluative reaction of significant others. They have been criticized on several grounds. Jack P. Gibbs initially maintained that such conceptions of deviance compromised the accepted sociological understanding that deviant acts are essentially behaviors contrary to norms or rules.[2] The identification of deviant behavior as contingent on reactions to it implies that the violation of a rule is not a *necessary* feature of deviance. Becker's designation of the "falsely accused" and "secret deviant" as categories of deviation has led critics like Gibbs to insist that the perspective was explaining reaction processes rather than deviant behavior per se.

According to Gibbs, a sociology of rule violations would necessarily have to offer an explanation for rule violations outside of the framework of reactions to the violations. Otherwise, the sociologist would have to limit himself to forms of "discovered" deviation. Gibbs's concern was that an "undiscovered" (unlabeled) case of deviation, such as adultery or rape, would be denied "sociological relevancy" according to the definitions of labeling analysts. Labeling explanations, by calling into question the "reality" or objective status of deviance as violations of rules, were "relativistic in the extreme" and thus lacked the conceptual clarity and stability upon which empirical investigation could be based. Gibbs also saw a danger in identifying *deviant behavior* exclusively in terms of reactions to it.

Edwin Schur, commenting on Gibbs's critique, noted that such views fail to understand the essential attribute of the labeling perspective:

> Nobody argues that the behavior that we call "homicide," "mental illness," "homosexuality," and "theft" would not occur if it were not defined as "deviant." Rather, it seems simply meaningless to try to understand and "explain" such deviation without taking into account the fact that in a given social order they are inevitably defined and reacted to in various specific ways. Such reaction processes affect the nature, distribution, social meaning, and implications of the behavior, *whatever* other factors may help to account for the initial acts of such deviation, by particular individuals. The focus, then, is on *what is made of an act socially.* . . .[3]

Gibbs, in fact, confuses the orientation of labeling theorists with those of other interactionists. Labeling theorists are not identifying *deviant behavior* exclusively in terms of societal reactions, but are instead identifying *deviance* primarily in terms of the subjective evaluation of social-control agents. Labeling analysts *do not* intend their explanations to cover the initial precipitants of deviant acts. Gibbs, commenting on the definitions of deviance proposed by Becker and Kitsuse, states:

> Becker is pursuing a theory about deviant behavior or a theory about reactions to deviation. If it is the latter, then his focus on deviants rather than reactors is puzzling. Kitsuse is concerned with reaction to deviant behavior as a process, but he views reaction not only as a criterion of deviant behavior but also (evidently) as the decisive factor in relation to incidence. As such, he is apparently seeking a theory about deviant behavior and not reactions to it.[4]

If Gibbs is referring to Becker's discussion of marijuana users or dance musicians as his "focus on deviants," then he is mistaken about Becker's supposed inconsistent analysis based upon his initial definition of deviance. As Chapter 6 indicated, *Outsiders* integrates the two interactionist themes—the learning of deviant behavior and the actualization of deviance as an evaluative reality (labeling). Becker illustrates the latter theme quite adequately through his discussion of rule creation and the role of the moral entrepreneur.[5] Gibbs is also mistaken about the principle concern of Kitsuse's investigation. Kitsuse is quite explicit about his interest in investigating reaction processes to *perceived* deviant behavior. His analysis of the decision-making and explanatory logic behind the *evaluation* of deviance seeks to develop a theory of reactions to deviant behavior (deviance) and *not* a theory of the precipitates of deviant behavior.[6]

Gibbs also argues that the labeling definitions of deviance are extremely vague about what constitutes a societal reaction, the conditions under which societal reactions occur, and the precise relationship between these reactions and the deviance that is actualized. If societal-reaction processes are as central to deviance as labeling proponents claim, then they themselves ought to be clearly defined.

This criticism is quite valid. Labeling theorists do not clearly specify the essential characteristics of a societal reaction. Is a societal reaction limited to negative verbal statements about an alleged deviant? Do denigrating gestures qualify as societal reaction? Do *official* societal reactions produce the same kind of "deviance" as less formal or unofficial degradation ceremonies? By not clearly defining the characteristics of a societal reaction, labeling theorists have also left themselves open to attack on how readily the societal-reaction concept can be operationalized. Without a clear statement of what constitutes a societal reaction, critics maintain, it is difficult to find empirical indicators that can be used across forms of deviation.

Some labeling proponents have offered what they feel to be better working definitions of deviance in response to such criticisms. Schur, for example, proposes the following as a labeling definition of deviance:

> Human behavior is deviant *to the extent that* it comes to be viewed as involving a *personally discreditable* departure from a group's normative expectations, *and* it *elicits* interpersonal or collective reactions that serve to "isolate," "treat," "correct," or "punish" *individuals* engaged in such behavior.[7]

Schur assumes that it is not important for a definition of deviance to specify what these interpersonal or collective reactions might be as long as they have the consequences of isolation, treatment, correction, or punishment. Societal reactions might thus be seen as *any* interpersonal or collective response that eventuates in one of these.

Schur fully realizes that such a definition of deviance offers numerous methodological problems for the deviance analyst.[8] It avoids a description of the very contingency factor on which deviance is said to depend for its existence. A thorough definition of deviance would need to tell us more about the characteristics of societal reactions.

The essential difference between labeling definitions of deviance and those that have come before it is very accurately depicted by Gibbs, who also rejects them.

Labeling definitions of deviance insist that it is essentially an evaluative reality, and Gibbs insists that it is the violation of a social norm. Kitsuse (1975) adds that

> the new conception of deviance [labeling] requires that members of the society perceive, define, and treat acts and persons as deviant *before* the sociologist can claim them as subject matter for study. Gibbs rejects this requirement, stating his preference for a definition of deviance as a violation of norms. His preference, however, raises the question of how those norms are to be determined. A consideration of this question reveals the ambiguities of the concept on which the conventional formulations of deviance rely so heavily.[9]

Labeling analysts like Kitsuse believe that the problem with the type of definition that Gibbs and others propose is the inability of the sociologist to clearly identify the social norms from which acts of deviation are said to be departures. How does the sociologist know what norms are related to what behaviors? He can ask the members of the society or social group in question what they feel the behavior "ought" to be for a particular person under specified conditions.[10] What the investigator discovers, however, are the "ideal" conceptions of how members "ought" to behave. This is meaningless if we cannot also provide a definition of the sanctions that would be applied for violations of those norms *when particular acts occur.*

Kitsuse indicates that we could also observe the behavior of members of society and infer from these observations what rules they are using to designate acceptable and unacceptable behavior. Here it is likely that the sociologist's own conceptions of what the "norms" are get confused with those of the group members he is observing.

> Indeed, sociologists may perceive norms where members see nothing at all. This being so, it would not be unusual or surprising if the sociologist's definition and characterization of norms differ from, even conflict with, those of the members whose conduct is asserted to be governed by those norms.[11]

The essential problem here is whether it is possible to determine "objectively" what norms exist or operate and hence when departures from these norms occur. Also, can such determinations be made outside of particular situations in which normative or nonnormative behavior is perceived to exist?

IS DEVIANCE AN OBJECTIVE REALITY?

When deviance is defined in terms of the violation of norms, the underlying assumptions seem to be that (1) the norms can be objectively determined and that (2) norm violations also have objective status—they are "real" regardless of who (whether it be the sociologist, the deviant, an agent of social control, or some bystander) is perceiving the *behavior* in question. Critics of the labeling perspective have frequently asked the following types of questions: "Wouldn't a' given example of rape behavior always be deviant regardless of who is reacting to it?" or, "Do you deny that deviant behavior *really* exists outside of the subjective reactions to it?"

Very clearly, labeling analysts do *not* deny the reality of any *behavior* that is observable, especially any behavior that several observers can agree exits. What critics maintain is an objective case of deviant behavior implies a high degree of *intersubjective* or interobserver agreement. A handful of us at a party might very easily agree that it is *undeniable* that Joe over there in the corner is drinking a can of beer. However, we might have problems agreeing whether Joe is undeniably *drunk* or evidences drunk behavior. In this instance, it is the extent of intersubjective agreement that determines whether Joe is "undeniably" or "really" drunk. Now, if we wished to pursue the question of whether this behavior was good or bad, acceptable or nonacceptable, rule-conforming or rule-deviating, this would call for some *valuation* or *evaluation* on our part; for we cannot directly *observe* a norm being violated—we can only *infer* that it has been or has not been violated. It is conceivable that we might strongly disagree or agree that, in fact, a norm violation has really occurred. It might be that Joe is up to his old tricks of acting drunk in hopes of becoming the life of the party.

It should be clear that the reality of deviant behavior, as well as the reality of deviance, is contingent on degrees of subjective evaluation and intersubjective agreement. As we move from the evaluation of directly observable behavior to inferences concerning less observable conditions like norm violation or deviance, the reality of the *attributions* are open to subjective interpretation. Again, *deviance* is an *ascription,* an *inference,* an *evaluative* reality. Norm violation as a social reality is not independent of subjective evaluation, it is clearly contingent upon it.

As stated before, the real problem with the basic definitions of deviance and deviant behavior proffered by the labeling analysts is that they fail to clearly tell us what constitutes a societal reaction; how societal reactions differ and with what consequences; and what is necessary for a societal reaction to eventuate in deviance. We return to these themes in the course of our discussion.

CONCERN OVER CAUSATION AND RATES OF DEVIATION

Gibbs (1966, 1972) has indicated that labeling conceptions of deviance suggest that the analysis of the rates of deviation and the investigation of the reasons for the variance in rates are not significant. Since the days of Quetelet, Guerry, van Oettingen—the early social statisticians—as well as the tradition of research established by Durkheim and his disciples, the investigation of the rates of deviation was considered vital to the study of society. In hopes of determining the causes of deviant behavior, social scientists have long been trying to explain those factors that account for the variance in rates. Critics of the labeling perspective maintain that the acausal analysis of labeling scholars ignores questions that are central to the discipline. In Gibbs's terms, these perspectives do not provide answers for the basic question "Why does the incidence of a particular act vary from one population to the next?"[12]

The investigation of the rates of deviant behavior as a means of determining its causes has indeed been denigrated primarily because of labeling analysts' focus on the *rate-producing function* of social-control institutions. Through the analysis of the societal reaction, labeling analysts have studied the manner in which the institutional processing of deviants generates rates of deviance (Kitsuse & Cicourel, 1963). The rates of deviant behavior have traditionally been viewed as "facts" about objective behaviors and social actors and as unquestioned "givens" about the reality, prevalence, or incidence of these behaviors and individuals. Rarely have analysts treated the production of rates of deviance as *dependent variables*. However, rates of deviation are *products* of the organizations responsible for documenting the existence of such categories of events. Kitsuse and Cicourel indicate that

> the rates of deviant behavior are produced by the actions taken by persons in the social system which define, classify, and record certain behaviors as deviant. If a given form of behavior is not interpreted as deviant by such persons, it would not

appear as a unit in whatever set of rates we may attempt to explain. . . . From this point of view, *deviant behavior* is behavior which is organizationally defined, processed, and treated as "strange," "abnormal," "theft," "delinquent," etc. by the personnel in the social system which has produced the rule.[13]

Labeling analysts argue that the *social meaning* of rates of deviation cannot be understood unless we examine the variety of organizational and situational contingencies that influence the process by which deviants are differentiated from nondeviants, since each differentiation accounts for one unit of frequency within the rates. Since the various behaviors that are classified under one deviant category, such as "suicide," are not necessarily similar and are subject to the *subjective interpretations* of personnel who do the differentiating (e.g., personnel within the coroner's office who decide whether the death was a suicide), the decision-making and organizational procedures that generate rates are themselves likely focii for sociological analyses. The social meaning of the rates of deviant behavior can be known only if we understand the criteria for decision making and the definitions used by personnel as they apply the deviant categories to the events or individuals in question.

Jack D. Douglas has indicated that the use of rates to explain suicide has severe limitations. Analyses of decision making that generates suicide rates reveal that it is unclear what criteria decision makers use to designate a death as a suicide. Also, the determination of suicide is initially contingent on evaluating the "facts" of a death. But suicide analysts have known that there are ways of successfully concealing the suicide of an individual—or ways of avoiding categorization of the death as a suicide.[14] Some research indicates that concealment of suicide might vary by religious and class distinction:

As a general proposition, it seems most plausible to hypothesize that the rate of attempted concealment of suicide will vary directly with the degree of (self-estimated) potential loss to the suicide's social self (and to the suicide's significant others) involved in having the death categorized as a suicide. This leads to the hypothesis that the rate of attempted concealment will vary directly with the degree of negative moral judgment associated with the act of suicide and with the degree of negative sanctions *believed* to be imposed for violations of the moral judgments. This hypothesis then leads us to expect that there will be certain systematic biases in the official statistics on suicide.[15]

Although this hypothesis has not been fully tested, there seems to be some indication that middle-class status and Catholicism are characteristics that are positively related to concealment of suicide.[16] The

Catholic Church condemns suicide and has refused to sanction burials of those whose death was attributed to suicide; thus, there is reason to avoid the categorization of suicide.

Douglas also indicates that a principal means used by coroners in deciding whether a death was a suicide is the discovery and imputation of a motive. The imputation of a motive is contingent on the interpretation of a person's past life, his character, what events led up to the death, the meaning of communication to others, and interpretation of numerous internal states of the individual—emotions, beliefs, attitudes, and so on.[17] These interpretations can hardly be "value-free" or objective. Therefore, what appears to be an objective unit of measurement of suicide is actually contingent on numerous (and as-yet-unspecifiable) imputations that are made by decision makers in the differentiating process.

Douglas thus indicates that behind the rates of suicide lies the unanalyzed or taken-for-granted reality of organizational processing and human decision-making that is inextricably linked to the social reality of suicide. Analyses that ignore the operational definitions of deviance lying behind the rates do not understand the meaningful context in which these "facts" are generated. For these reasons, studies that abstract rates of deviation from the context of their production and then use them for causal analysis or even as indices for the incidence or prevalence of deviation are severely limited.

This is not to say that the investigation of rates of deviation is an entirely useless enterprise or that the question that Gibbs posed— "Why does the incidence of a particular act vary from one population to the next?"—is sociologically unimportant.

Sociologists ought to be interested in observing that different cities have different rates of deviant behavior and that the distribution of deviation may vary from time to time in one locale and between locales, or may be influenced by various sociocultural conditions. The point remains, however, that to understand what these rates *mean* requires extensive empirical investigations of organizational personnel responsible for applying categories of deviance to behavior and individuals. The investigation of the societal reaction to deviance thus becomes a necessary preliminary to an analysis of changes in the incidence of deviation. To maintain, therefore, that the societal-reaction perspective is inadequate because it fails to explain changes in the rate of deviation misses the point, for changes in the rate may have a great deal to do with the variable nature of societal reactions.

CAUSAL ANALYSIS

The discussion of deviance and deviant behavior has been concerned with three varieties of causal explanations. The first two are more traditional: what determines deviant behavior and what causes membership in deviant groups, such as delinquent gangs. The third type of explanation—which can rightfully be described as "causal" even though it emerges from a "labeling" analyses of deviance—is what determines commitment to a deviant role or career. Lemert's concept of secondary deviation incorporates just such an explanation of career commitment and has been *extremely* controversial. We will devote special attention to this third form of causal explanation later in this chapter.

The labeling perspective does not offer any explanation for the precipitates of deviant behavior. It is not at all concerned with causal explanations of predisposition that attempt to isolate factors ultimately responsible for rule-violating behavior. Nor does the perspective attempt to explain the ultimate causes of deviant group formations (although some have attempted to explain how deviant groups, once formed, are *maintained*). The labeling perspective is not *by itself* intended as a comprehensive explanation of what we call social deviations. It does not pretend to raise, let alone answer, all of the significant questions that relate to these social phenomena. Even if we add the learning of deviant behavior to the analysis of the actualization of deviance as an evaluative reality, we still have not exhausted the many important questions that analysts of deviation have asked.

Interactionists do not concern themselves with the ultimate precipitates of deviance, but this does not mean that it is therefore an invalid perspective on deviance. Rather than deny the possibility of understanding the ultimate precipitates of deviant behavior, most interactionists believe that it is more important to examine those *processes* that make deviation the socially meaningful reality that it is. Attempts to look for the ultimate precipitates have generally led to inconclusive results. The inability of analysts to link factors of predisposition with components of actualization have severely undermined the usefulness of such causal analyses.

James Q. Wilson, in a discussion of causal theories of crime, maintains that causal analysis is a worthwhile sociological enterprise but one that does not greatly inform us about criminals, criminal behavior, and how society reacts to them.[18] If its goal is the gathering of facts to be used in eradicating a "social problem," Wilson claims that it has generally failed to live up to expectations. He distinguishes between *causal analysis* and *policy analysis* and maintains that we need not understand the root causes of crime to establish social policy toward criminals:

> But ultimate causes cannot be the object of policy effort, precisely because, being ultimate, they cannot be changed. For example, criminologists have shown beyond doubt that men commit more crimes than women and younger men more (of

> certain kinds) than older ones. It is a theoretically important
> and scientifically correct observation. Yet it means little for
> policy makers concerned with crime prevention, since men
> cannot be changed into women or made to skip over adoles-
> cent years.
>
> It is the failure to understand this point that leads statesmen
> and citizen alike to commit the causal fallacy—to assume that
> no problem is adequately addressed unless its causes are elim-
> inated. . . . If we regard any crime-prevention or crime-reduc-
> tion program as defective because it does not address the
> "root causes" of crime, then we shall commit ourselves to
> futile acts that frustrate the citizen while they ignore the
> criminal.[19]

Causal analyses of the precipitates of deviant behavior suffer
similar dilemmas. Underlying many of the empirical attempts to un-
cover these "ultimate" determinants are theoretical/methodological
difficulties of knowing the incidence, prevalence, or "reality" of generally secretive behavior. If official rates of deviance were equated with
deviant behavior, then an analysis of rates would be sociologically
more relevant if we had a more developed understanding of the
rate-producing process that is a vital component of labeling research.
Otherwise we lose sight of the social meaning of deviation rates and
deviant behavior.

Even assuming that these difficulties are surmountable, we are
faced with problems intrinsic to causal analysis in the behavioral
sciences. The ultimate causal factors related to deviance are usually
found to be only "intervening variables" related to hard-to-specify
ways to deviant behavior. Occasionally, for particular deviation (like
pecuniary criminal acts), we are able to single out motivational and
structural factors (the desire for money or status, the impoverishment
of the "deviant") that seem logically responsible for the behavior in
question; but it is difficult to see how social deviation can more generally be influenced by these factors. Nor is it possible to understand
exactly how these factors, whether "ultimate" or "intervening," relate
to the actualization of behavior. If "ultimate" variables turn out to be
"intervening" variables in the development of deviant behavior, it is
dubious why they deserve analyses before an investigation of the
learning of behavior. If the focus of investigation is the deviant *behavior,* the most significant "intervening" variable or proximate factor
relating to becoming deviant may be the modes of learning. If it is
deviance that we wish to explain, then the evaluative component of
the societal reaction should be the target of our analysis.

Some critics, however, maintain that the focus on labeling ignores the precipitates of the societal reaction itself. While agreeing in
part that traditional causal analyses have been inconclusive or inade-

quate, these sociologists believe that labeling analysts have particularly ignored the *structural determinants of social control and its relationship to individual human action.*

STRUCTURAL DETERMINATION: THE "NEW-CRIMINOLOGY" PERSPECTIVE

In their book *The New Criminology: For a Social Theory of Deviance* (1973), Ian Taylor, Paul Walton, and Jock Young offer an essentially Neo-Marxist critique of existant perspectives on deviance, including the labeling perspective. The authors maintain that a truly comprehensive *social* theory of deviance must begin with the role of the social structure in influencing the social arrangements within which deviance processes occur. Such a theory would particularly need to explain the role of power and the material conditions of social life in the development of deviant behavior and of deviance. They hold that crime and other forms of deviation are ultimately due to inequalities of wealth and power, property, and life chances. The "social arrangements" within a particular society determine the separate components of the social reality of deviance.

Taylor and colleagues propose that a social theory of deviance must explain seven major components of deviance:

1. the wider origins of the deviant act
2. immediate origins of the deviant act
3. the actual act
4. immediate origins of social reaction
5. wider origins of deviant reaction
6. the outcome of the social reaction on the deviant's further action
7. the nature of the deviant process as a whole.[20]

The authors maintain that each component calls for a different explanation. The immediate origins of the deviant act and the immediate origins of the social reaction (proximate causality) calls for a social-psychological explanation; the wider origins of the deviant act and the wider origins of the social reactions call for a "political economy" of deviance—that is a structural/causal theory of predisposition. The analysis of the deviant act requires an account of the "social dynamics" surrounding the acts. The authors thus indicate that a theory of deviance must include a variety of explanations for these several components.

When the authors criticize the labeling perspective, they claim that it is "one-sided" or "incomplete" in that it gives no attention to structural determinants. They claim that it "lapses into a relativistic idealism" that cannot cope with the broader *social* context in which deviant behavior and deviance are lodged. They are also convinced that the "guts" of the theory—the essential characteristic—has not been substantiated; that those who are labeled deviant continue to be deviant (secondary deviation).

There are multiple misunderstandings in the position of the "new criminologists." Essentially, they add very little that is new to existing sociological paradigms for investigating deviation. What is new is the theoretical/ideological base for the causal theories of predisposition that they propose for the origins of deviation and deviance. The integrative model they propose for a social theory of deviance unites a Marxist/structuralist analysis with a social-psychological analysis of the actualization of deviant behavior and deviance. As we will see in Chapter 8, an integrative model is needed—no one perspective can allow us to understand all the significant features of social deviation. However, the problems with theories of predisposition and with a structuralist analysis are equally significant for a politicoeconomic perspective on the broader origins of deviation. This perspective assumes that deviant acts will depend on "rapidly changing economic and political contingencies of advanced industrial society."[21] Although some forms of deviant behavior might well be influenced by politicoeconomic factors—just as some delinquency might be influenced by the differential-opportunity structure—it is very difficult, as we have seen, to unite these structural factors with the genesis of social deviation. The new criminologists offer us little additional insight into how these analyses might proceed.

The new-criminological perspective, insofar as it attempts to reveal the "wider origins of deviant reaction," adds an interesting dimension to the study of societal-reaction processes. The basic assumption is that political and economic imperatives undergird reaction policies and *determine* labeling outcomes. Although it seems plausible that an investigation of the politicoeconomic context of societal reaction would inform our investigation of labeling practices, this does not mean that such an analysis is necessary.

Labeling analysts have long been interested in the impact of social organization and institutional/bureaucratic structure on labeling practices. Numerous studies from a labeling perspective have focused on precisely these social-organizational factors. It is not evident why we would need to go beyond the social-organizational features of deviant-processing systems to larger structural determinants to understand how deviance as a social problem is actualized. Becker has already indicated that the analysis of rule creation and role enforcement ought to be a fundamental feature of deviance analysis. To insist that we need to know the politicoeconomic forces that account for reaction policies, control-agent ideology, or institutional social organization may only add to what Becker has called the "mystification" of deviance:

> We ignore what we see because it is not abstract and chase after the invisible "forces" and "conditions" we have learned to think sociology is all about. . . . We see that people who engage in acts conventionally thought deviant are not motivated by mysterious, unknowable forces. They do what they do for much the same reasons that justify more ordinary activities. We see that social rules, far from being fixed and unstable, are continuously constructed anew in every situation to suit the convenience, will and power position of various participants.[22]

To demystify deviance, we must study the social construction of deviant realities in the particular situations in which these constructions take place. The analyses of the wider origins of the societal reaction attempt to tell us why reactions come about. We would need to step outside the interactive social realm in which the evaluations of deviance take place and search for these predisposing factors in the politicoeconomic structure of society. Such an enterprise is *not* necessary for an understanding of the actualization of deviance, as a number of theorists have already demonstrated. The societal reaction can best be understood in the natural situations in which judgments concerning deviants are made and policies, reactions, and procedures are carried out. As processes, societal reactions must initially be assessed for how they come about.

The preference for investigating "how" questions over "why" questions might seem arbitrary, but as we have demonstrated, there are very good reasons for focusing on those social factors that have a more direct bearing on "how" deviance comes about. This does not mean that a Neo-Marxist investigation of the origins of societal-reaction processes is without merit. Such analyses might well inform us about the deviance-constructing behavior of agents or agencies of social control. As students of *social behavior,* however, it would be more advantageous for us to focus on the collective or joint actions that have a more proximate bearing on the construction of moral meaning in everyday social life.

The new criminologists should be commended for seeking an integrative "social" theory of deviance. The benefit of a politicoeconomic approach to deviance can be validly assessed only after proponents have actually carried out research into the wider origins of deviant behavior and societal reactions. By underscoring the importance of social-psychological analyses of the immediate origins of deviance and behavior, the new criminologists have essentially agreed with labeling analysts on the importance of understanding the actualization of deviance.

SECONDARY DEVIATION: THEORETICAL PROBLEMS

No single concept in the labeling framework has provoked as much criticism as Lemert's secondary deviation. In fact, most critics have interpreted the concept as central to labeling and to the broader interactionist stance toward social deviance. The feeling among many critics seems to be that if one can find fault in this concept, the entire "theory" of labeling must be seriously questioned. Is this concept as pivotal as the critics maintain? What evidence is offered by both opponents and proponents? What is the relationship of this concept to the broader interactionist framework? Is the concept out of place in an explanation of the development of deviant behavior? These questions have permeated much theoretical discussion of social deviance in the past several years.

Lemert, it will be recalled, defined secondary deviation as behavior that is a reaction to societal responses to deviance. The labeled deviant experiences problems because of the differentiation made by control agents. The problems produced by the differentiation effect changes in the self-regarding attitude of the individual and produce a specialized organization of the labeled deviant's social role. Secondary deviation thus implies a socialization process that either crystallizes the deviant role for the individual or in some way leads to the *normalization* of deviation and immersion into a deviant role. Lemert uses the term "stabilization of deviance" to describe the condition that results from the differentiating reactions of social-control agents.[23]

Lemert clearly uses societal reaction as an independent variable related to the stabilization of deviant roles and behavior and to concommitant changes in "self-regarding attitudes." It would not be wrong to assert that Lemert is drawing a *causal* link between societal reactions, the socialization process, deviant roles, and behavior. Secondary deviation as a type of *deviant behavior* is to some degree an artifact of its social control and is thus a derivative of a self-fulfilling prophecy.

There are two vital questions, the answers to which will help us through the flood of criticisms that will be discussed in this section.

1. Are *all* the cases of deviance that labeling analysts study in their investigation of societal reaction examples of secondary deviation?

Figure 7-1

	Stabilized Deviant Role or Behavior	No further Deviant Behavior
Accept Proffered Label	"Pure" secondary deviation.	"Reformed deviant."
Reject Proffered Label	Belligerent deviation. "Reaction formation."	"Maturation effect."

2. For cases of deviance that are termed "secondary deviation," is the role or behavior produced by the differentiating process irreversible?

The answer to both questions is No!

Lemert's "secondary deviation" does not include all the forms of deviance that are of interest to labeling analysts. Essentially, Lemert's secondary deviant results from either (1) an acceptance of the proffered deviant label, identity, and the role based upon it, or (2) the labeled deviant's rejection of the proffered role, but his continuation, in defiance of the labelers, of the behavior as a form of retaliation for stigmatization.

Type one is Lemert's "pure" secondary deviant. Type two does not necessarily evidence the changes in self-regarding attitudes that secondary deviation would call for. It is possible that the labeled deviant *rejects* the proffered label, but continues to engage in deviant behavior for other reasons—he finds it a rewarding or pleasurable experience. Obviously some people who accept the proffered label of deviant will not continue to engage in deviant behavior and might be termed the "reformed deviant." Some reject the proffered-label and control-agent definitions of deviance, but for other reasons (the maturation phenomenon noted for labeled juvenile delinquents) cease to engage in deviant behavior. The typology shown in Figure 7-1 illustrates these basic variants.

All four of these ideal-typical "deviants" encounter the societal reaction to perceived deviation. Their interpretation of the meaning of the reaction and their subsequent behavior varies. Some critics (e.g., Gove, 1975) would have us believe that labeling analysts are concerned only with "pure" secondary deviation. This view, it would appear, is based on an examination of the labeling literature of the mid- and late 1960s that was influenced by the work of Thomas Scheff (1966) and Erving Goffman (1961) on the sociology of mental illness and mental institutions.

Scheff's theory of mental illness, or "residual deviance," claims that the *social role* of the mentally ill is *primarily* (but not exclusively) *caused* by the societal reaction.[24] The role of the mentally ill is crystallized as a result of the rewards and punishments used by significant others (most probably the staff of the mental institution and members of the individual's family) to coerce the individual into the deviant role:

> In the crisis occurring when a residual rulebreaker is publicly labeled, the deviant is highly suggestible, and may accept the proffered role of the insane as the only alternative. . . .
>
> Among residual rule-breakers, [primary deviants] labeling is the single most important cause of careers of residual deviance.[25]

Goffman's (1961) analysis of total institutions indicates that the peculiar organizational characteristics of these institutions—and particularly the mortification or stripping processes of desocialization—function to "put the inmate in his place" and force him into the role of the mental patient in order to best serve the social-control interests of the institutional staff.

Gove is probably correct in asserting that such societal-reaction notions have implications primarily for what happens *inside the mental hospital*.[26] Scheff's and Goffman's analyses have less to do with the determinants of "pure" secondary deviation than with (perhaps) temporary adjustments to contingencies of the mental institution. Whether these adjustments to the hospital sick role have consequences for the behavior of the individual *outside* the institution has been a major point of contention between some labeling analysts and a host of critics.

SECONDARY DEVIATION: EMPIRICAL PROBLEMS

Scheff (1974), in a response to Gove (1970), Gibbs (1972), and Davis (1972), has reasserted that societal reaction is significant in fostering commitment to the role of the mentally ill. Scheff cites research by Denzin (1968), Denzin and Spitzer (1966), Greenley (1972), Haney and Michielutte (1968), Haney, Miller, and Michielutte (1969), Linsky

(1970a, b), Rosenhan (1973), Rushing (1971), Scheff (1964), Temerlin (1968), Wilde (1968), and Wenger and Fletcher (1969) that are consistent with the labeling theory of mental illness.

On inspection, however, most of these studies are primarily concerned with showing that labeling practices or evaluations of patients in mental facilities are contingent on factors that lie outside the patient and his behavior. Labeling practices are studied as *dependent variables,* and analysts have discovered an array of factors that influence labeling outcomes: for example, the willingness of parents or family to have the patient at home influences the length of stay in the hospital and psychiatric diagnosis; the imputed responsiblity of the parents in fostering the child's pathology is important in determining the diagnosis of the child's "mental problems" and the prognosis for rehabilitation; the training of the therapists influence the diagnostic categories in which patients are placed. This line of analysis is assuredly in keeping with the interests of the labeling perspective, *but it fails to examine the societal reaction as an independent variable—precisely what the concept of secondary deviation would call for.*

Gove (1975) maintains that few studies support the secondary-deviation contention for mental illness. They fail to demonstrate clearly that continued mental illness or some other unacceptable behavior is the result of the societal reaction. The societal reaction's link to changes in self-regarding attitudes and, in turn, to sustained or amplified deviant behavior or role playing is also questioned. Scheff (1975), in his defense of the labeling theory of mental illness, does *not* in fact cite a single study that would confirm the proposition that

> among residual rule-breakers, labeling is the single most important cause of careers of residual deviance.[27]

It is indeed very difficult to understand what would constitute a confirmation of secondary deviation. Would relabeling or rehospitalization suffice as a measurement; or perhaps some evaluation by the labeled deviant of changes in self-attitude? Rehospitalization or *secondary* labeling might have little to do with primary labeling. In any case, secondary deviation is concerned with the learning of *deviant behavior,* while rehospitalization might be indicative only of the reactualization of an *evaluation* (it *might* be unrelated to the behavior or role playing of the alleged deviant). Rehospitalization is thus an inappropriate measure of behavior per se. It might more clearly inform us of the contamination effect of initial labeling on further considerations of an individual's moral status.

This lack of empirical confirmation of secondary deviation is not confined to mental illness. The impact of the "dramatization of evil" on continued deviant behavior has not been clearly demonstrated for other forms of deviant, criminal, or delinquent behavior. What has been demonstrated is that the *reassessment of deviance* may be an artifact of its initial control.

Lemert, the principal proponent of secondary deviation, has given few empirically tested examples of the variety of deviance amplification in which *behavior* is reinforced through the reactions of significant others or community control agents. In "Paranoia and the Dynamics of Exclusion" (1962), he shows that exclusionary reactions on the part of friends, work associates, and family sometimes do follow situations in which the individual has experienced a loss of status: the loss of a job, failure to be promoted, changes in family relationships, the loss of respect, and so on. The loss of status brings with it the status traits of "unreliable," "untrustworthy," or the feeling among some that they do not wish to be involved with such an individual.[28] The exclusionary reactions of significant others leads to attempts on the part of the individual to "appeal" the sensed injustice of the exclusion. This, in turn, may lead to "spurious interaction" between the individual and significant others, which only serves to impede the communication flow, enhance the exclusionary reactions, and heighten the individual's sense of conspiratorial behavior directed against him.[29] When these informal reactions lead to *formal* exclusion, the suspicions of conspiracy appear to be confirmed, and the resultant protests of the individual serve to convince significant others of the extent to which the paranoic patterning of the individual's behavior has been developed.

Lemert's discussion of the social bases of paranoia is perhaps his best empirically verified example of secondary deviation, *but it is not an example of pure secondary deviation.* The individual who is excluded does not accept the proffered label of "paranoid," but in effect rejects it. It is through this rejective behavior and the "tragedy of errors" that the amplification of deviation and societal reactions occur. This type of deviance amplification appears to be one variant of the reaction-formation behavior described by some analysts of juvenile delinquency: a case in which the condemned condemn the condemners and in which the deviant behavior that follows springs from a sense of injustice (Cohen, 1955). When attempts to neutralize stigma lead to behavior that flaunts authority or significant others (Sykes & Matza, 1957), we have a situation in which the societal reaction leads to sustained deviant behavior or role playing. But even proponents of this point of view hold that this amplification process is not all that common. Matza, it will be recalled, maintained that motivation toward deviation was more directly related to the definitions of the activity as enjoyable, fun, thrilling, or something to do, rather than due to structural constraints, the oppositional behavior of youth, or value-conflict predispositions toward sustained deviant behavior (Matza, 1964).

If the evidence for pure secondary deviation is as difficult to gather as it appears, it is not surprising that opponents have been able to point to research findings that question the extent to which it is a significant social reality.

Hirshci (1975), in a review of the empirical literature, claims that research on the treatment or rehabilitation of delinquents generally reveals that the treatment reaction has no effect, one way or the other, on sustained delinquent behavior. McAuliffe (1975), in a similar review of the empirical evidence on heroin addiction, indicates that labeling does not appear to lead to amplified secondary drug use. Tittle (1975) indicates that the secondary-deviation concept has not been given a rigorous test, principally because of the inability of proponents to formulate a precise hypothesis and the inadequacy of available data. However, after a review of available literature on the effect of the societal reaction on crime and criminal behavior, Tittle concludes:

> Of the three studies most nearly fulfilling necessary methodological criteria, one favors the labeling argument while two are contrary to it. General studies of recidivisim do not confirm labeling expectations that more than half will be recidivists, and case materials provide many exceptions to labeling predictions. The weight of the evidence, then, is contrary to the idea that labeling leads to crime in the general case or that it is the most important variable in the production of criminal careers. Nevertheless the data do not justify dismissal of the idea that labeling may have some effect on criminal behavior.[30]

Despite Tittle's caveat at the end of this quote, he along with many others is clear in his rejection of the purported extensive effect of the societal reaction on deviant behavior and role playing.

Finally, Sagarin and Kelley (1975), in a review of sexual deviance and secondary deviation, also conclude that the implied causal relationship between the societal reaction and homosexuality must be seriously questioned. Examining the work of Williams and Weinberg (1971, 1974) on the problems and adaptations of male homosexuals, they perceive ample evidence that *officially* labeled homosexuals, in comparison with those whose deviation remained secretive, did not experience greater problems of self-acceptance and that their participation in homosexual behavior was not overly stimulated by the official labeling. Weinberg and Williams, themselves proponents of an interactionist perspective, conclude that

> among the homosexual's problems, perhaps societal rejection is *not directly* the most important, and the effect of societal

reaction on psychological problems may be small compared
with the effect of other factors. . . .[31]

Rather than being influenced by the denouncements of control
agents, homosexuals appear to be influenced by what Warren calls
"symbolic stigma." "Stigmatizing audiences," according to Warren,
rarely effect the self-regarding attitudes of the homosexual. Thus,
pure secondary deviation is questionable for this form sexual
deviation.[32]

What, then, are the implications of these findings and evaluations for the labeling and interactionist perspectives? It would seem
that the claims of proponents of secondary deviation are highly questionable. Does this undermine the foundation of a labeling or societal-
reaction focus on deviance? Certainly not, since secondary deviation is
not an essential part of a labeling approach to *deviance*. It suffers from
the same problems as afflict theories of predisposition that have been
discussed earlier. Its claim to be a causal explanation of deviant role-
playing and careers has simply not been well substantiated. As Tittle
indicates, only with more precisely formulated hypotheses and adequate data will we ever know how extensive a phenomena it is for
particular kinds of deviant behavior.

Secondary deviation, in any case, is not essential to a labeling
perspective because labeling is primarily concerned with the actualization of *deviance* and not the development of deviant behavior. Labeling analysts are concerned with the *construction of moral meaning* and
the interpretations of social-control agents that designate acceptable
and nonacceptable behavior. It studies deviance as an *evaluative reality*. The focii of the labeling perspective are the social and social-
psychological dynamics that influence definitions of the social worth
of individuals and groups. To be sure, we are interested in the social
and social-psychological *outcomes* of interpretations of deviance, but
these outcomes are not as confining as the concept of secondary deviation implies. As evidenced by the simple typology in Figure 7–1,
labeling analysts are equally interested in situations in which no further deviant behavior is claimed as in situations in which deviant
behavior or role playing continues. There is a greater concern for
outcomes of secondary *deviance* than for secondary *deviation*. But if
careers of institutionalization or reinstitutionalization do not occur,
this does not invalidate the labeling approach.

The focus on labeling practices was not intended to be a *causal*
analysis of deviant behavior, but an examination of the *evaluation* of
deviant behavior. Through the study of the joint actions, interactive
patterns, and constructed definitions of the situation involved in social arenas where deviance is evaluated, the analyst arrives at an un-

derstanding of the social meanings, roles, and functions of deviance for particular sets of social actors.

Some critics have seen the centrality of secondary deviation in its role as a theoretical link between the interactionist's concern with socialization into deviant roles and careers, and the labeling analyst's concern with determinations of *deviance*. There is a tendency to equate the *integration* of these aspects of an interactionist analysis with a need to establish a causal relationship between the two objects of study—the actualization of deviance and the learning of deviant behavior. Some labeling analysts, as we have seen (Scheff & Lemert), have done just this. Becker is a good deal more cautious on this point. In *Outsiders* he does not maintain that the enforcement of the Marihuana Tax Act and the moral entrepreneurship of control agents led directly to career involvement in marihuana use. Through his examination of deviant subcultures, he shows that the amplification of deviation is far more complicated. The reactions of straights and the problems they pose for the deviant may lead to intensified ties with the deviant subculture. Subcultural involvement and increased isolation from straights may lead to commitment to certain self-regarding attitudes and lifestyles that amplify deviant role-playing. Yet faced with the same reactions from "straights" or "squares," other deviants decide that it is best not to flaunt the expectations of the straight world; societal reactions may lead them to shift self-regarding attitudes *away* from the ideals of the subculture.

Becker's somewhat oblique analysis of the amplification or intensification of deviant status is best considered a description of factors that lead to the maintenance of some deviant subcultures.[33] In this respect, it is similar to Kitsuse and Dietrick's clarification of the influence of the societal reaction in maintaining delinquent subcultures.[34] Obviously only some varieties of deviant behavior are subcultural, and only some subcultures show this pattern of amplification. Such analyses of subcultural maintenance do not necessarily confirm the presence of secondary deviation, nor was this the analysts' intention.

The examination of careers in deviance will hopefully reveal the relationship between deviant behavior and deviance, or the lack of it. We need longitudinal analyses of involvement in behaviors that are labeled "deviant" and of particular patterns of involvement with social-control agents. We need to know the extent of the interpenetration of deviance and deviation. Aside from this, the interactionist's concern with the learning of deviant behavior and the labeling analyst's concern with the actualization of deviance stand as distinct subjects for empirical study. *The investigation of one without knowledge of the other, however, leaves our understanding of the social meaning of these phenomena incomplete.*

The worth of a labeling analysis of deviance has been amply illustrated by studies showing that deviance ascription is not solely contingent on the behavior of the alleged deviant. But even if the evaluations were based entirely on the perceived behavior of the individual, an examination of the evaluative process would still be sociologically and social-psychologically relevant. There would still be a need to know how agents of social control document or account for perceived violations of social norms. The social meaning of deviance can be fully understood only by an examination of the process of deviance construction. The labeling perspective is grounded in the understanding that social evaluation and deviance construction, in particular, are contingent on situated joint or collective actions. This, rather than the study of secondary deviation, is the focus of labeling.

PHENOMENOLOGY AS AN INTEGRATIVE MECHANISM

The social construction of moral meaning, as the focus of labeling, has a direct affinity with the phenomenological analysis of deviation. Sociological phenomenologists, influenced by the philosophers Husserl, Scheler, and Schutz, attempt to understand social realities as they are directly experienced by members of society. For them, social reality is continually constructed in the minds of human actors. This perspective shares many of the same subjectivist orientations as symbolic interaction.[35] It, too, is concerned with examining shared definitions of meaning, situated interactions, and the development of social "consciousness" and "intersubjectivity," or "intersubjective understanding." Sociological phenomenologists are concerned with the analysis of "everyday life"; with the methods (ethnomethods) used by human actors to account for their social experiences and participation in social action; and with the means by which social actors frame social realities (the process of "typification") and thereby assign meaning to it.[36]

Dreitzel (1970) has commented on the role of typification in the work of phenomenological sociologists:

> Interaction in this case is seen as a process of interpretation and of *mutual typification* by and of the actors involved in a given situation. Typification means an abstraction from the unstructured mass of given sensual data under the guidance of previously acquired typification schemes. Every typification, then, has the character of a rule or guideline for the behavior of the actors, since it contains the relevant features in a given situation. Thus out of a mutual process of defining and redefin-

ing the relevant or "meaningful" elements of situations, something like a social structure, however unstable, gradually
emerges. The precarious nature of such social structures lies
in the fact that they are subject to constant revision in accord-
ance with the changing interpretations of the involved actors.
The social construction of reality of which Berger and Luck-
mann speak is, then, an ongoing process of interpretation.
This process becomes a reciprocal typification of the actors
involved that is referred to as negotiation.[37]

The learning of deviant behavior and the actualization of deviance as evaluative realities evidence these typifications, reality constructions, and negotiated orders. Sociological phenomenologists
have been interested in the essential characteristics of these typifications, both for the labelers of deviance and for those who engage in
behaviors that are typified in this way.

McHugh (1970) argues that commonsensical ascriptions of deviance are essentially based on two decision rules, both of which, in
turn, are grounded in commonsensical notions of responsibility: (1)
conventionality—about the particular behavior, typifiers must be able
to say, "It might have been otherwise"; and (2) *theoreticity*—labelers
must be able to say, "He knows what he's doing." If an affirmative
reply to these considerations is in order, the behavior in question,
according to McHugh, can be labeled deviant. It need not *necessarily*
be labeled deviant, but ascriptions of deviance are *minimally* contingent on these decision rules.

McHugh's attempt to locate these decision rules is commendable
—it is an important way in which we can specify the essential attributes of societal reactions and labeling.[38] It is questionable, however,
whether these are, in fact, the commonsensical rules used to ascribe
deviant labels. The application of these decision rules eliminates mental illness, types of drug use, alcoholism, and individual disabilities
from being commonsensibly considered deviant (e.g., for mental illness it can be argued that "it could *not* have been otherwise" and that
"the person did *not* know what he was doing"). Yet we know that these
kinds of people are stigmatized and *are,* according to common sense,
thought of as departing from conventional behavior. What is important for us here is that phenomenologically oriented sociologists are
also concerned with detailing the components of social responses to
deviance so that we can better understand the construction of moral
meanings.

Interestingly Jack D. Douglas and Alan Blum, principal proponents of a phenomenological perspective on social deviation, claim
that a basic problem with the labeling perspective is that it never
explores the meaningful bases of categorization or labeling, but only
affirms that the process exists and uses this as a way attacking con-

tending perspectives on deviance.[39] Numerous "labeling" studies have explored the meaningful bases of categorization and have attempted to account for "the methods and procedures which members employ to make [deviance] describable."[40] Symbolic interactionists and phenomenologists, as exemplified by Denzin and Douglas, share a number of concerns with the construction of moral meanings and typifications. Sociologists have explored the process of deviance typification and self-typification long before the phenomenological analysis of deviance was initiated in the late 1960s and early 1970s.[41]

Douglas claims that labeling analysts have avoided "the microscopic analysis of the social uses of the categories to determine the general properties of such uses."[42] He also admits that few phenomenologists have done this type of research. Blum's analysis of mental illness is noted as an example of such work. But Blum merely outlines one way in which sociologists can study the social contingencies that lead to the production of deviance typifications: a quasi-linguistic analysis of conversations about the "cultural competence" of particular people, in therapeutic interviews.[43] There is little question that the analysis of the evaluations of competency by psychiatrists will allow us to understand the construction of mental illness. But has this line of analysis not already been initiated? It is certainly at the heart of the labeling perspective. Scheff's (1966) work on typifications of mental illness, Daniels and Clausen's (1966) and Daniels's (1970) research on military psychiatrists explore the social bases of the construction of moral meanings as they relate to individual competencies.

For years labeling analysts have been concerned with the decision-making basis for typifications of deviance. The analyses of the logic of labeling, the development of professional and lay rationalizations for deviance ascription, the organizational constraints on typification practices, and the processes of deviant self-typification have generally attempted to understand the construction of moral meaning.

However, there has been a reluctance among labeling analysts to go outside official arenas of deviance ascription to less formal, everyday occasions in which moral meaning is constructed. The discovery of the general properties of typifications of deviance might necessitate going beyond the official institutions that normally label deviants. This is the implication of some phenomenological work in the area of deviance (e.g., McHugh, 1970; Scott & Lyman, (1970).

McHugh's search for the decision rules behind ascriptions of deviance tacitly assumes that professional conceptions of deviance are grounded in the same commonsensical understanding as found in lay conceptions. The social meaning of particular deviance ascriptions can thus be found outside the mental hospital, the court, and the police station. It has simply been methodologically much easier for analysts to study official labeling practices—to study "kept" populations of deviants. Phenomenologists correctly point to the narrowness of this approach. Moral meanings and constructions of deviance—typifications of others and of self—are everyday realities and are found in the ordinary or "normal" life experiences of individuals in society. Our commonsensical notions of responsibility, good and bad character, intellectual ability, and moral integrity are applied in everyday life and it is in these natural arenas of interaction that research is needed.

By stressing the significance of typification (Douglas), accounts (Scott & Lyman), ethnomethods (Garfinkel), and moral justifications (Jacobs), phenomenologists have more clearly demarcated the attributes that are common to the actualization of deviance as an evaluative reality and to the learning of deviant behavior.

Jacobs (1970), for example, examines the construction of moral justifications for suicide. Through the analysis of suicide notes, diary materials, and autobiographical sources, he traces the ways in which religious beliefs are used to rationalize the suicide attempt:

> The expectation is that one's problems will be resolved in death. This discussion of the way in which death is viewed as the only respite to life's problems leads us to the specific way in which religious dogma may work to encourage suicide. There would be little point in resolving one's problems in this life, only to incur a new set as bad or worse in the hereafter. The suicide's ability to convince himself that death will reduce or eliminate his problems is the final ingredient for the previously described peace and calm found among suicides immediately preceding their act. It is in his search for a means of achieving this outlook that religion holds a promise. The suicide is able to acquire this optimistic outlook toward the hereafter by adopting one of several situated interpretations toward existing religious dogma.[44]

The implication of Jacobs's analysis is that, for the "typifier" or "self-typifier," constructions of moral meaning are tied to the vocabularies of motive, redefinitions of the situation, and reconstructions of self that help *account for* the behavior in question. This is quite similar to the basic line of analysis in W. I. Thomas's *The Unadjusted Girl,* discussed in Chapter 5.

TYPIFICATION AND SOCIALIZATION

Phenomenological analyses of moral justifications for deviant behavior bring to mind other possible models for studying the relationship between typification and deviant behavior. There are, no doubt, several different typification processes involved in the development of deviant behavior. The socialization process includes a number of seemingly important typifications that facilitate involvement in deviant activities. The socialization model described below is only suggestive of the kinds of typifications that the sociologist might explore to document the learning of deviant behavior.

Socialization into the deviant career can be considered as a series of resolutions of life issues and moral dilemmas encountered by an individual. In a general sense these issues are not vastly different from the career contingencies that Becker originally discovered in his analysis of marihuana users. Assume that we are analyzing socialization into homosexuality or the "coming-out process." The available literature indicates that homosexual socialization can be seen as a process of resolving certain dilemmas that are really a consequence of growing up and functioning in a heterosexual world and of having to make sexual role and behavior choices that are out of keeping with that heterosexual world. Coming out of the closet entails contending with at least some of the following dilemmas and resolving them with appropriate self-enhancing typifications:

1. *Contending with homosexual self-images.* The questions behind our analyses become: what experiences, redefinitions of the situation, or moral constructions might convince a person that either being a homosexual or engaging in homosexual activities is not something objectionable and that such an identity and behavior are (respectively) *acceptable* and *pleasurable?*

2. *Contending with issues of the availability and quality of opportunity.* The investigation would be concerned with the typifications made by the individual regarding the accessibility to other homosexuals and to locales where they can be encountered. If one can only have access to "tea-room trade" (quick, impersonal sex in public washrooms), the individual might define this as insufficient: "Is this what sex really is—no tenderness, no caring for each other?" Such definitions might limit commitment to a homosexual career.

3. *Contending with problems of secrecy.* The individual is confronted with the following problems: How long can one stay a closet queen? Can I hide this behavior and identity from family, coworkers, and straight friends, or is it possible for me to "pass" in the straight world while being a homosexual?

4. *Contending with thoughts about one's personal and social future.* How does the individual resolve doubts about the

implication of his homosexual identity and behavior for the future stability of the love–sex relationship and for other considerations, such as having children.

Although some contingencies may be insignificant in some situations, research findings indicate that such issue resolutions do underlie the commitment to homosexual careers.[45] These decisions are not necessarily made in the order listed above, nor are they made as formally as this model appears to imply. We know so little about how these life problems are worked out, and about how socialization into deviant roles proceeds as a result both of self-oriented constructions of personal commitment, social identity, and moral meaning and of other-oriented definitions of the situation.

To some sociologists and psychologists, this model of socialization may appear to be too "rational," or the actors may appear to be motivated at too conscious a level. Yet actors do develop very involved explanatory models of their participation in what others perceive to be deviant activities. These social-moral constructions of reality, situated in the interactive context of everyday life, are the key subject matter of a subjectivist analysis of deviance and deviant behavior.

In summary, the integration of the interactionist perspective on the learning of deviant behavior and the labeling perspective on the actualization of deviance can be accomplished in ways other than *causal* analysis of secondary deviation. The focus on typification, the use of accounts, and the construction of moral meaning joins together the research on the social meaning of deviation, the agents of social control, and those who are engaged in deviant behavior.

"LABELING" AND POLITICAL–IDEOLOGICAL CRITIQUES

In the revised edition of *Outsiders* (1973), Becker has addressed himself to the "moral problems" of deviance theory.

> Moral problems arise in all sociological research but are specially provocatively posed by interactionist theories of deviance. Moral criticism has come from the political center and beyond; from the political left, and from left field. Interactionist theories have been accused of giving aid and comfort to the enemy, be the enemy those who would upset the stability of the existing order or the Establishment. They have been accused of openly espousing unconventional norms, of refusing to support anti-Establishment positions, and (the left-field position) of appearing to support anti-Establishment causes while subtly favoring the *status quo*.[46]

When the arguments from the left and right are distilled, we can detect the various claims of "biased perspective."

The Conservative View

Those who take a more conservative view of social control systems and their policies see labeling as an attack on conventional wisdom on the responsibility for social deviation. Several reactions seem quite common. Some, taking the secondary-deviation notion to heart, feel that labeling analysts unjustly accuse control agents and agencies for causing deviant behavior. The effect of this is (1) the undermining of public confidence and trust in established authority and (2) the absolution of responsibility and blame for the deviant's actions. In other words, some perceive labeling as a somewhat anarchistic, politically motivated ideology—an apologia for the deviant and an attack on the institutions that "protect us."[47]

It is certainly true that interactionist analyses have frequently perceived deviant behavior from the perspective of the deviant. No major labeling analyst claims a value-neutral position (Becker, 1967), but such analysts generally indicate the unavoidability of seeing the reality of social deviation through the eyes of participants in the *behavior*. However, it is quite inaccurate to claim that labeling analysis has avoided looking at the control-agent's perceptions of *deviance*, for that is exactly what it has done.

From our discussion of secondary deviation, it is apparent that there is a problem in the claims of some labeling analysts that control-agent reactions are responsible for *deviant behavior*. There is still insufficient evidence to this effect. However, it is quite clear that control-agency constructions of categories of moral meaning are responsible for determinations of *deviance*. By defining the universe of moral condemnation that is of relevance to their work, control agencies:

> become responsible for drawing clearer lines than in fact exist either in everyday life or in the processes by which people were originally led into their services, and agencies may come to define people as deviant who would not ordinarily have been so defined. Both professionalism and bureaucratization objectify deviance and verify diagnostic categories. In this sense, while such agencies may not actually *create* deviant roles, they do by the nature of their activities refine and clarify their boundaries and, by assuming responsibility for their control, add elements to the roles that may have not have existed previously, and so encourage pulling new people into them.[48]

This is in no way meant to be an apologia for deviant behavior, nor is it *necessarily* meant to say that control agents "don't know what they're doing" or "are screwing over the people they process." Labeling analysts have indeed found numerous occasions on which the determinations of deviance have had nothing to do with the behavior of the alleged deviants and have spoken out on the human problems this produces. But it is not our exclusive mission to discover those occasions and to castigate the "evildoers" who mislabel people.

Our primary concern is with discovering how these constructions of moral meaning come about and their behavioral implications for the several parties to these collective enterprises. The social meaning of deviance is ascertainable only if we analyze the decision-making work of those responsible for its construction. Perhaps a muckraking posture gets in the way of a sound examination of the evaluative process and the highly complex social and social-psychological contingencies upon which it is based.

The study of control-agent decision making is understandably threatening. When sociologists question the rational bases of various bureaucratic organizations and their work, cries of "political motivation" have been heard. What is rational and irrational, sensible or not, is hard to prove, and there will be endless battle if sociologists insist on their own definitions. On the other hand, the sociologist is in an advantageous position, through the examination of labeling practices, to comment on the consistent or inconsistent application of labeler-avowed criteria to situated determinations of deviance. A thorough examination of decision-making rules and the organizational and social-psychological contingencies that influence their application should allow us to see the degree of internal coherence of labeling practices and procedures.

The View from the Left

While one set of critics see labeling as subversive, those on the other end of the political-ideological continuum, according to Becker, see labeling as establishmentarian—as an apologia for the status quo, the "system."[49] Their claim, generally, is that labeling theorists are lukewarm liberals at best, and "don't really tell it like it is." Either they do not "recognize that class oppression, racial discrimination and imperialism are *really* deviant, or that poverty and injustice are *really* social problems, however people define them";[50] or they refuse to look at the causes of the problems in the larger social system that fosters these conditions (Taylor, Walton, & Young, 1973). Becker points out that such critics "want to see their ethical preconceptions built into scientific work in the form of unsuspected factual assertions. . . ."[51] They fail to realize that such conditions or behaviors may not be universally defined as deviance. They merely want their definitions of reality accepted over that of others.

Perhaps extensive agreement *can* be reached on the deviance of particular acts of discrimination and injustice, but it is in the nature of these things that disagreement about them is *possible*. And, if so, the moral/ethical judgments need to be examined empirically to understand how the social meaning of the deviance or social problem in question is defined in light of these differences. For the labeling analyst to accept one definition of deviance over any other would mean the predetermination of exactly what ought to be the focus of study.

Other critics from the political left—especially the New Criminologists and Neo-Marxists—are particularly annoyed that labeling analysts have not concerned themselves with the structural origins of labeling. Again, although this may indeed prove to be a rewarding enterprise, it is not necessary for an understanding of the actualization of deviance. It is initially important to concentrate on the social construction of deviance in the particular situations in which they take place. The analysis of the politico-economic and the reaction origins of deviance may be able to discover the broader societal ramifications of moral constructions and control policies; this is an area of research that deserves a great deal more attention than has been shown it until now.

In conclusion, the political/ideological criticisms of labeling have not adequately shown the misguidedness of its primary focus: the construction of moral meaning. The critiques from both the left and right, however, have struck valid notes of caution over how labeling analysts treat the preconditions, consequences, and implications of labeling. Perhaps labeling analysts, on some issues, ought to take greater care in their examinations and, on others, simply extend their focus of attention.

----

[1]These three major labeling definitions of deviance are to be found, respectively, in Howard S. Becker, *Outsiders*. New York: Free Press, 1963; Kai Erikson, "Notes on the Sociology of Deviance," *Social Problems*, Vol. 9 (Spring 1962), p. 308; John I. Kitsuse, "Societal Reaction to Deviance," *Social Problems*, Vol. 9 (Winter 1962), p. 253.

[2]Jack P. Gibbs, "Conceptions of Deviant Behavior: The Old and the New," *Pacific Sociological Review*, Vol. 9 (Spring 1966), pp. 9–14.

[3]Edwin M. Schur, *Labeling Deviant Behavior: Its Sociological Implications*. New York: Harper & Row, 1971, p. 16. Emphasis in original.

[4]Gibbs, "Deviant Behavior," pp. 9–14.

[5]Becker, *Outsiders*, Chs. 7, 8.

[6]Kitsuse's examination of the logic of labeling behind ascriptions of homosexuality demonstrates the need for a theory of reactions to homosexuality and *not* the precipitates of homosexuality.

[7]Schur, *Labelling Deviant Behavior*, p. 24. Emphasis in original.

[8]Ibid. p. 25.

[9]John I. Kitsuse "The 'New Conception of Deviance' and Its Critics," in Walter R. Gove, ed., *The Labelling of Deviance: Evaluating a Perspective.* New York: Halsted Press, 1975, pp. 273–84. Quotation on p. 276.

[10]Ibid. p. 277.

[11]Ibid. p. 278.

[12]Gibbs, "Deviant Behavior," pp. 9–14.

[13]John I. Kitsuse and Aaron V. Cicourel, "A Note on the Use of Official Statistics," *Social Problems,* Vol. 11 (Fall 1963), pp. 131–39. Emphasis in original.

[14]Jack D. Douglas, *The Social Meaning of Suicide.* Princeton, N.J.: Princeton University Press, 1967, pp. 205–16.

[15]Ibid. p. 208. Emphasis in original.

[16]Ibid., pp. 206, 210–11.

[17]Ibid., pp. 216–23.

[18]James Q. Wilson, *Thinking about Crime.* New York: Random House, 1975, pp. 45–63, 50.

[19]Ibid., p. 50–51

[20]Ian Taylor, Paul Walton, and Jock Young, *The New Criminology: For a Social Theory of Deviance.* London: Routledge & Kegan Paul, 1973, pp. 165, 270–78.

[21]Ibid., p. 270.

[22]Becker, *Outsiders,* p. 190.

[23]Edwin M. Lemert, *Human Deviance, Social Problems, and Social Control,* 2nd ed. Englewood Cliffs, N.J.: Prentice-Hall, 1972, p. 69.

[24]Thomas Scheff, *Being Mentally Ill: A Sociological Theory.* Chicago: Aldine, 1966, p. 54.

[25]Ibid., pp. 88, 92–93.

[26]Gove, ed. *Labelling of Deviance,* p. 57.

[27]Sheff, *Being Mentally Ill,* pp. 92–93.

[28]Lemert, *Human Deviance,* p. 253.

[29]Ibid., pp. 253–54.

[30]Charles R. Tittle "Labeling and Crime: An Empirical Evaluation," in Gove, ed. *Labelling of Deviance,* p. 174.

[31]Martin S. Weinberg and Colin J. Williams, *Male Homosexuals: Their Problems and Adaptations.* New York: Oxford University Press, 1974, pp. 268–69.

[32]Cf. footnotes 48, 49, and 50 in Chapter 6 in this book.

[33]Becker, *Outsiders,* p. 96.

[34]John I. Kitsuse and David C. Dietrick, "Delinquent Boys: A Critique," *American Sociological Review,* Vol. 24 (April 1959), pp. 213–15.

[35]See, for example, Norman K. Denzin, "Symbolic Interactionism and Ethnomethodology: A Proposed Synthesis," *American Sociological Review,* Vol. 34, no. 6 (December 1969) pp. 815–31.

[36]See Jack D. Douglas, ed., *Deviance and Respectability.* New York: Basic Books, 1970, pp. 3–30.

[37]Hans Peter Dreitzel, ed, *Recent Sociology No. 2,* New York: Macmillan, 1970 p. xi.

[38]Peter McHugh, "A Common-Sense Conception of Deviance," in Douglas, ed., *Deviance and Respectability,* pp. 61–88.

[39]Douglas, ed., *Deviance and Respectability,* p. 12.

[40]Alan F. Blum, "The Sociology of Mental Illness," in Douglas, ed., *Deviance and Respectability.* pp. 31–60.

[41]For example, see the following authors on mental illness: Thomas J. Scheff, "Typification in the Diagnostic Practices of Rehabilitation Agencies," in Marvin B. Sussman, ed., *Sociology and Rehabilitation.* Washington, D.C.: American Sociological Association, 1966, pp. 139–44; Arlene Daniels, "Normal Mental Illness and Understandable Excuses: The Philosophy of Combat Psychiatry," *American Behavioral Scientist,* Vol. 14, no. 2 (November/December 1970), pp. 167–84. On skid-row alcoholism, see Jacqueline P. Wiseman, *Stations of the Lost: The Treatment of Skid Row Alcoholics.* Englewood Cliffs, N.J.: Prentice-Hall, 1970. On criminal behavior see David Sudnow, "Normal Crimes: Sociological Features of the Penal Code," *Social Problems,* Vol. 12 (Winter 1965), pp. 255–70. On unwed mothers, see Prudence Rains, *Becoming an Unwed Mother.* Chicago: Aldine, 1971.

[42]Douglas, *Deviance and Respectability,* p. 12.

[43]Blum, "Sociology of Mental Illness," in Douglas, ed., *Deviance and Respectability.*

[44]Jerry Jacobs, "The Use of Religion in Constructing the Moral Justification of Suicide," in Douglas, ed. *Deviance and Respectability,* p. 237.

[45]See, for example, Weinberg and Williams, *Male Homosexuals.*

[46]Becker, *Outsiders,* rev. ed., p. 194. Chapter 10, "Labeling Theory Reconsidered," was originally a paper presented to the annual meeting of the British Sociological Association, April 1971.

[47]See, for example, David Bordua "Recent Trends: Deviant Behavior and Social Control," *The Annals,* Vol. 369 (Janaury 1967), pp. 149–63.

[48]Eliot Freidson, "Disability as Social Deviance," in Sussman, ed., *Sociology and Rehabilitation,* p. 83.

[49]See, for example, Milton Mankoff, "On Alienation, Structural Strain, and Deviance," *Social Problems,* Vol. 16 (Summer 1968), pp. 114–16; Alvin Gouldner, "The Sociologist as Partisan: Sociology and the Welfare State," *The American Sociologist,* Vol. 3 (May 1968), pp. 103–16; Milton Mankoff, "Power in Advanced Capitalist Society," *Social Problems,* Vol. 17 (Winter 1970), pp. 418-30.

[50]Becker, *Outsiders,* pp. 201–2.

[51]Ibid., p. 202.

SELECTED READINGS

1966   Jack P. Gibbs, "Conceptions of Deviant Behavior: The Old and the New," *Pacific Sociological Review* (Spring 1966), pp. 9–14.

1973   Ian Taylor, Paul Walton, and Jock Young, *The New Criminology: For a Social Theory of Deviance.* London: Routledge & Kegan Paul.

1974   Howard S. Becker, *Outsiders,* rev. ed. New York: Free Press, Chapter 10.

1970   Jack Douglas, ed. *Deviance and Respectability.* New York: Basic Books.

1975   Walter R. Gove, ed., *The Labelling of Deviance: Evaluating a Perspective.* New York: Halsted Press.

CHAPTER 8

THE ACTUALIZATION OF DEVIANT BEHAVIOR AND DEVIANCE: Where Do We Go from Here?

A NOTE ON CONCEPTUAL FRAMEWORKS

The choice of the most advantageous approach to the study of social deviation will not be made soon. There is no one resolution to the analytic problems that we have reviewed in the previous chapters. The sociological perspectives developed in the past half-century are all in need of empirical examination and conceptual/theoretical reformulation based on such examination. To claim major loopholes in the structural-functional, ecological, interactionist, labeling, phenomenological, Neo-Marxist, or conflict perspectives does not relegate these conceptual frameworks to the refuse heap of sociological ideas. Each has penetrated to some understanding of the properties of particular forms of social deviation; each has sensitized sociologists to the importance of examining various characteristics of social deviation.

The critical condition for theoretical growth in any discipline is the determined effort to reformulate analytic frameworks in light of empirical findings and scholarly discourse. All too often, conceptual frameworks provoke hostile reactions because their authors are content to rest with original statements and research efforts, decades old, which therefore have not taken into account more recent developments in the field. A running dialogue between proponents of opposing views is sometimes difficult to achieve, but without it, cries of "misunderstanding" and "misstatement" continue and prevent theoretical rapprochement.

The subjectivist perspectives that have focused attention on the learning of deviant behavior and the actualization of deviance have been particularly beset by a host of problems: misinterpretations of the basic conceptual definitions, goals, and research orientations; overemphasis on the questionable causal relationships of secondary deviation; and a general lack of research momentum to explore the essential social and social-psychological components of the learning of behavior and the evaluative phenomenon of deviance. But these perspectives are a long way from sociological obsolescence. Despite the problems posed in the conduct of subjectivist inquiries into social deviation, they remain significant models of sociological analysis. This does not mean that they are suggested as the *only* feasible mode of studying social deviation. The subjectivist perspectives do, however, offer analytic advantages at the micro level of social behavior that are not found in other perspectives.

Conceptual frameworks can be differentially evaluated on some general criteria. Unlike theories, postulates, and hypotheses, conceptual frameworks are not readily "disproven." The efficacy of a conceptual framework is usually judged by how readily it suggests new and important topics for research; how intensively it penetrates to those critical components of a given reality that establish its order or disorder, unity or disunity; how insightful it is in characterizing the basic principles behind relationships central to the reality under study; and whether it offers a sufficiently intricate and explicit analytic vocabulary to characterize its area of interest. On these criteria, the subjectivist perspectives—interactionist and phenomenological—must rank as major advancements. Their departure from a causal analysis of predisposition, their concern with the processes of learning that lead to deviant role playing and behavior, and their investigation of deviance as an evaluative reality and as the construction of moral meaning have secured for the subjectivist approaches a major role in the analysis of social deviation. *But this role carries with it a responsibility that, until now, has not been fully met by its proponents and disciples.* It is incumbent upon subjectivist analysts of social deviation to pursue the detailed empirical examination of processes of actualization. It is time to respond to the critics, not merely with claims of misinterpretation, but with empirical evidence that substantiates the theoretical contributions. In science there is no explicit statute of limitations that governs the time in which theoretical claims must be substantiated. But the time has assuredly arrived to initiate an intensive examination of deviation actualization and of the construction of moral meaning.

There is one other advantage to the subjectivist approaches to deviation—perhaps the most significant—and one that critics rarely confront. A theory of deviation should begin with those properties of deviation that are most general to its subcategories. Unless we determine that no theory of social deviation is possible—because the separate subcategories of deviation are in need of completely different explanatory frameworks—we must begin our analysis with the characteristics of the phenomena that are *shared* by the subcategories. The question that should continually be asked by theorists of deviation is what do such behaviors as prostitution, drug use, burglary, and mental illness have in *common* that allow us to talk about them as "social deviation"?

The principle of analytic induction, which guided the sociological work of Thomas, Sutherland, Lindesmith, and Becker, and which is tacitly accepted as a standard for theory construction by other subjectivists, remains a respectable guide to theory construction in social deviation. What the separate subcategories of deviation appear to share are processes of learning that lead to role playing and behavior, and *evaluations* of the moral nature of behavior and individuals (or, conditions of self-evaluation).

Perhaps these forms of deviation share another feature, as suggested by the Neo-Marxists—namely, structural origins for both deviant behavior and deviance. We should initiate studies that explore how systematically these factors influence the development of deviation. It is the decided advantage of the subjectivist perspectives, however, that they begin with the examination of events, phenomena, and situations, which are more readily accessible. The structural sources of deviation that are of interest to Neo-Marxists are relatively more difficult to ascertain, and they sometimes appear quite unanalyzable without prior knowledge.

It is initially difficult to examine the structural sources of professional decision making (the origins of the societal reaction) without examining what that decision making consists of. Where does one look for the structural sources of reactions to homosexuals or, indeed, for the structural sources of being a homosexual without some prior knowledge of the learning of homosexuality as behavior and as a moral construction of meaning? Sociological research on social deviation will no doubt continue to proceed at both a micro- and macro-level, but macro-level analyses uninformed by micro-level investigations appear to lack the theoretical closure necessary for a full understanding of the phenomenon. At the same time, subjectivist analyses with no sensitivity to the structural implications of actualization processes are equally lacking not only in theoretical meaning but also in application to practical policy issues. We will return to the latter point in the last section of this chapter.

What, then, are the more significant issues that a subjectivist orientation to social deviation needs to explore? What characteristics of actualization processes do we need to focus our attention on so that we come to terms with the social role and meaning of deviation? We now turn to an examination of some suggested topics for future research.

LEARNING DEVIANT BEHAVIOR

The shift away from an objectivist/structuralist perspective on deviation and toward a sociological perspective on the learning of deviant behavior was the most significant development in the post-Durkheimian consideration of deviation. Taking their direction from early proponents like Thomas and Sutherland and from more recent advocates who propose a "behavior systems" approach to the study of crime and deviation, analysts have examined the learning of deviant behavior. The principal interests of these sociologists with regard to deviant behavior are *what is learned and when, from what sources, and with what consequences for behavior, self-concept, associational ties, lifestyle, and deviant and nondeviant relationships.*

The most advantageous framework for coming to terms with these issues on the learning of deviant behavior is the long-standing tradition of examining the development of ideational-value supports (i.e., motive factors) to involvement in deviant behavior and role playing. The combined conceptualizations of Mills's vocabulary of motive, the use of neutralization techniques, Thomas's redefinition of the moral and self-implications of deviant behavior, as well as basic principles of learning that explain the acquisition of behavior skills, offer the sociologist the analytic tools to explore the details of this mode of actualization. Two basic sets of explanations are called for, which speak to the sequential nature of the commitment to identity and role: one that examines initial socialization into deviant roles and activities or the beginning stages of commitment, and one that specifies the factors that help *sustain* involvement and commitment. In addition, because we know that careers of deviant behavior are *not* irreversible, we need to know what factors are influential in reversing, neutralizing, or obliterating the impact of what has been learned. The interactionist/phenomenological perspectives ask us to give particular attention to the modes of self-typification that order the identification with role and behavior, as well as those that lead away from such identification and participation.

Issues of Socialization

In Chapter 7, we presented an analytic model for examining socialization into deviant roles. This model attempted to isolate some of the major self-enhancing typifications found in the process of commitment to homosexuality. Socialization into deviant roles, we indicated, might be considered as a series of resolutions of life issues and moral dilemmas that confront an individual. These function as career contingencies that control movement along the initial path into a career. The successful resolution of problems with the quality of lifestyle and experience associated with the behavior, and issues of morality, secrecy, family relationships, and future role involvement are important motive factors that enhance the global (i.e., general) acceptability of role and behavior to the individual. Regardless of predisposing factors that might be present for particular forms of deviation, this model indicates that the development of deviant behavior is contingent on these self-enhancing typifications.

There are, however, important subprocesses in this socialization model to which analysts need to give special attention. Special theoretical issues also need to be examined. First, which neutralization techniques, if any, permit a reduction of perceived immorality and which serve to enhance self-concept? (We may, of course, discover that for particular forms of deviation, such as crimes of passion, no distinct neutralization techniques operate, although it is apparent that many convicted criminals, among others, develop obviously self-serving rationalizations for their behavior).

Assuming that we can locate these techniques of neutralization and redefined self-typifications, we also need to know the qualitative sources of these redefinitions of behavior. Do they stem from various personal experiences, from religious beliefs, subcultural ideology, social-class values, or economic or political deprivation or repression?

We must also have a more detailed description of the specific vocabularies of motive that are used in the acquisition of behavior and role. The careful compilation of lexicons of vocabularies of motive used by various individuals to rationalize or give meaning to their activities would be a significant contribution to the field. An ethnolinguistic analysis of the substructures of vocabularies of motive, as well as an analysis of their situated meanings-in-use, would finally allow us to compare across types of deviation for the basic components of learning. We may discover that some forms of deviation, such as illegal-drug use, have totally different vocabularies of motive, techniques of neutralization, and career contingencies than we will find for homosexuality; or they may be surprisingly similar. We may find that our culture supplies us with limited numbers of neutralization techniques and a highly limited vocabulary of motive for engaging in deviant activities. There may be considerable commonality of constructions of moral meaning across types of deviant behavior.

The point remains, however, that little research has been conducted that documents these significant characteristics of deviant behavior. We have a few imaginative examples of such inquiries—for example, suicide victims and survivors (Henslin, 1970; Jacobs, 1970); criminal behavior (the most interesting work has been done by Cressey on embezzlers, pyromaniacs, and kleptomaniacs [1953, 1964]); juvenile delinquency (Sykes & Matza, 1957; Matza, 1964). Yet there has been no coordinated effort to systematically study these details of the development of deviant behavior.

The comparative analysis of neutralization techniques shows particular promise. Juvenile delinquents may neutralize the stigma of their behavior by defining their acts as accidents, as events due to bad luck; they may claim that their behavior is not wrong in light of circumstances and that the "victim" or situation provoked the behavior; they may also deny that any immoral act has been perpetrated and maintain that the behavior in question has its "moral," or "just" side (Sykes & Matza, 1957; Matza, 1964).

Those who engage in other varieties of deviant behavior have also used similar techniques of neutralization. Whether they seek to eradicate responsibility, blame, stigma, or guilt, the various neutralization technique may have many common features across such forms of deviation as alcoholism, drug use, "excessive" gambling, prostitution, and even mental illness. Again, if there are significantly specialized techniques of neutralization used in different forms of deviation, they would need careful documentation.

Henslin (1970), in his study of the guilt-neutralization techniques used by relatives and close friends of suicide victims, has itemized the particular techniques of neutralization that can, in this author's opinion, be applied to many varieties of deviation. Some of the more common are the following:

1. *defining others as being responsible for the act of behavior*—as when a youth holds gang coercion responsible for his involvement in delinquent activities

2. *viewing impersonal or nonhuman factors, situations, or circumstances as promoting the behavior*—the constant drinker who neutralizes the label of alcoholism by claim-

ing that social events and the rigor of the job have led to the particular pattern of drinking; or the labeled alcoholic who explains his behavior as a disease over which he has no control

3. *altogether denying the behavior as being deviant or immoral*—the marijuana smoker who likens the use of pot to alcohol and claims that it merely functions as a youth-culture version of an effective social lubricant

4. *emphasizing the unevitability of the act*—the homosexual who, when asked how he thought he became a homosexual, claims that "it was in me all the while. . . .I just had it in me and then I learned to accept this tendency for what it was and not fight the real me. It was a strong side of my personality and sooner or later it had to come out."

5. *minimizing the behavior*—here the individual looks for ways in which the act could have been worse. Henslin indicates that by emphasizing the "possible worse aspects," their behavior is seen as relatively not too bad; for example, the prostitute who claims that "at least I give them something they want for their money. Believe me, there are far more dishonest ways of making a buck."

6. *conceptualizing the act as good*—the bisexual who defines her sexuality as "more open," and herself a more "totally sexual being . . . open to many sexual possibilities and not "shackled" to one variety of sexual responsiveness"

7. *the use of "guilt neutralizers"*—Henslin defines guilt neutralizers as professionals and nonprofessionals whom individuals use to reduce guilt (psychiatrists, clergy, close friends or associates, etc.). The individual can use the search for and receipt of helping services as a technique for reducing stigma; or stigma can be reduced by the ego-supportive techniques used by some neutralizers.

These neutralization techniques become part of the vocabularies of motive and self-explanatory logics of many different varieties of rule-violating individuals. They form the postbehavioral attitudinal set that is conducive to rationalizing *initial* and *continued* participation in deviant activities. A systematic cross-behavioral comparison of the development and uses of neutralization techniques and comparative analyses of other components of vocabularies of motives would be a significant contribution. Ethnographic studies describing the precise relationship of those vocabularies of motive to situated, contextually bound deviant behavior and patterns of identity formation would greatly advance our sociological understanding of deviation. Proponents of a subjectivist perspective have simply not made much of an advancement in the rigorous examination of these issues.

In the event that our investigations indicate that the acquisition of vocabularies of motive and neutralization techniques are not sufficient explanations for the learning of deviant behavior (perhaps they do not exist at all for some varieties of deviants), then a reformulation of theory will be necessary. If redefinitions of the situation are not significant motivational factors leading to deviant behavior or role playing, then perhaps there is a need to reconsider the influence of structural factors or to consider the impact of *other* situational factors. If all fails, then a theory of deviant behavior—as a generic explanation for a category of behavior—is in strong doubt. Certainly, if we discover that situated factors of interaction or joint actions and constructions of moral meaning are not sufficient or necessary characteristics of the learning of behavior, a subjectivist perspective has not fulfilled its promise. The empirical tests, however, have yet to be made.

Issues of Resocialization, Recommitment, and Career Changes

Labeling analysts, as we have seen, have been criticized for claiming that once stigma has been ascribed and self-attitudes changed, the commitment to deviant role is irreversible. This critique is particularly misplaced and unfair because, as students of deviation, labeling analysts (like other interactionists) understand very well that individuals who commit themselves to deviant roles and behavior often become recommitted to normal ones. Public identity or the evaluative stigma of *deviance* may, in fact, change far more slowly than the behavior of the individual. In any case, individuals move in and out of deviant roles, and the process of commitment is a far more complex issue than typical sequential models of career involvement indicate.

Careers of deviation are not as unilinear as the sequential model of Becker's analysis of marijuana users implies. They are more likely to be characterized by movement from deviant behavior to normal behavior, whether interrupted by societal reactions or not; and by movement back to the same or different deviant behaviors at advanced levels or reduced levels of participation. There is indeed a sequence to these life experiences, but it is not unilinear.

As the Kinsey report initially showed, few homosexuals are exlusively homosexual throughout their lives; prostitutes do not always remain such, and drug users do not follow any single career line toward regular drug use. For example, the sequential career phases of a marijuana smoker as described by Becker are:

Figure 8-1   Becker's Career Model of Drug Use

A more common and specific career might look like the following:

Figure 8-2

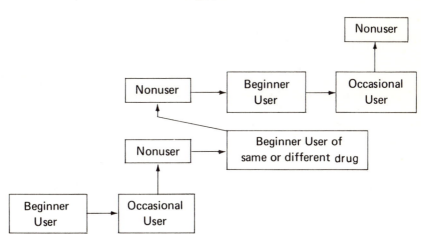

Obviously, numerous varieties of sequential models are possible, and we may find that the back-and-forth movement from participation in deviant behavior to noninvolvement and in different levels of involvement at any one phase, is far more common for most forms of deviation and deviants. This raises numerous theoretical questions for students of deviant behavior.

If individuals are not always deviant and do not always maintain a unilinear pattern of ever greater commitment to deviant roles and behavior, what factors of self-typification, experience, interaction, or joint action account for the changes that occur? Does self-concept change with every movement in and out of a deviant role and with greater or lesser participation in deviant behavior? What is the pattern of self-typification as the individual moves into different kinds of deviant activities or as he emerges from several reentries into normal roles? Are there major differences in the use of neutralization techniques, and do vocabularies of motive change or remain the same? Are the meanings of the behavior to the individual altered by the repeated alternating movement between participation and nonparticipation? At what point in the career do various types of significant others have more or less influence on the individual? Are they important only at the beginning of the career? Are formal societal reactions more effective at certain points than at others? Finally, what factors are influential in fostering a complete return to conventional patterns of behavior and which factors prevent a return to deviant behavior?

It appears that the solutions to these issues of career socialization and resocialization depend on a more thorough specification of the very complex nature of career contingencies. This elaboration is, in turn, dependent on rigorous field work and on the empirical examination of the process of becoming deviant as well as normal.

THE ACTUALIZATION OF DEVIANCE

The previous three chapters have already reviewed the major issues in the study of deviance as an evaluative reality. The ascription of deviance to individuals and their behavior was depicted as the prime focal point of labeling analyses. Sociologists who take this perspective are concerned with the micro- as well as macro- level issues related to the construction of moral meanings.

Micro-Level Concerns

At the micro level of analysis, our interest is in the bases and sources of decision making that eventuates in deviance ascription. We are also concerned with the extent of negotiation among labelers over moral meanings, and with those labeled as well as other joint or collective actions that lead to ascriptions of deviance. Of particular interest are the similarities and differences in such processes for different agents and agencies of social control for different or similar types of perceived deviance. A theoretical examination of deviance necessitates our fleshing out the consistencies in systems of deviance ascription, as well as their unique attributes. As students of deviation, we are also concerned with the impact of such ascriptions on the alleged deviants—both inside and outside the deviant-processing system. At the micro level of analysis our interest is particularly in the implications of the societal reaction for self-regarding attitudes and patterns of behavior and interaction.

A major problem with the societal-reaction approach was the difficulty in specifying the essential attributes of the reaction. Early proponents studied the "logics in use" that facilitated labeling, but few analysts went beyond the description of a few patterns of decision making (e.g., "retrospective interpretation" and the use of community screening devices). In the late 1960s, largely through the efforts of phenomenologically oriented analysts of deviance, an assault was initiated on the bases and sources of the decision making behind labeling practices.

McHugh (1970), for example, analyzed the taken-for-granted decision rules (or, criteria) for what was and was not deviant. *Conventionality* ("Could it have been otherwise?") and *theoreticity* ("Did the person know what he was doing?")—both referring to commonsensical notions of "responsibility"—were said to be the major decision-making criteria for ascriptions of deviance. The problem with McHugh's formulation, however, is that it is doubtful whether these are the sole decision rules in use. They do not seem applicable to categories of stigmatization that many people define as deviant (e.g., the mentally ill, the disabled, narcotic users).

Yet McHugh's assumption that such commonsensical notions exist seems well taken. "Responsibility" may be one criterion for constructions of moral meaning. The perceived harm done to someone else and the perceived direct threat to self may be additional factors. But the more salient criteria for labeling may be the perceptions of the extensiveness of the individual's deviant biography and the "hopelessness" of the social environment in which he lives. Situational circumstances surrounding the behavior or the labeling event itself may be perceived as equally important in the attribution of deviance. The perceived deviation or codeviation of a relative may be an additional factor (Suchar, 1972).

In any case, a considerable amount of research is needed to examine these commonsensical criteria for deviance ascription. The basic empirical question is, what characteristics of the behavior, the person, his background, the labeling event, or other factors are commonsensibly perceived as significant criteria for deviance? If such commonsensical conceptions are shared by large numbers of individuals, how are they organized? How do they relate to the professional conceptions of deviance in which control agents are schooled? Are they consistent or inconsistent? Does one take precedence over the other? Are there forms of deviation around which commonsensical constructions of moral meaning are crystallized, made explicit, and refined? Research must examine whether or not commonsensical conceptions of deviance are organized in lay typologies that are ordered by the "stigma theories" that people learn both as children and as adults. The analysis of children's developing understanding of who is and who is not deviant should be particularly promising.

It is particularly important that the labeling analyst attempt to study the application of these lay typologies and stigma theories in their natural setting. A subjectivist analysis of deviance must be concerned with deviance evaluations "in use," thereby preserving what Douglas has termed the "contextual determination of meaning." Unusually creative fieldwork techniques are required for studying lay ascriptions of deviance for which no formal organizational structure is present. The task is difficult, but hardly insurmountable.

The main effort of our analysis of labeling will continue to be aimed at the decision-making staff of formal deviant-processing systems, public and private, whose function is to make determinations of deviance. Our primary interest in the labeling practices of control agents will remain the typification schemes and explanatory logics used in the decision-making process. What is the nature of the information or "facts" used by decision makers to evaluate the severity of the problem or to determine whether a problem exists in the first place? How are deviant biographies constructed to give evidence to the problem, and how do decision makers interpret the "evidence" or interpretations of control agents in other agencies or institutions, within the "referral system"? More specifically, for treatment, rehabilitation, or punitive institutions, what observations and interpretations lead to *differentiated* control-agent reactions? Why do some labeled deviants, in the view of decision makers, need more extreme institutional reactions than others? A major focus for labeling research in such settings ought to be the criteria for determinations of success or failure, progress or lack of progress, which are major interests of institutional decision-makers. How do such determinations influence the nature of final evaluations when the individual is released from the institution or from the purview of the control agent?

The nature of labeling as a negotiated reality is brought home to the analyst when he observes institutional staff deliberations. The author recalls his three years of observing weekly psychiatric "staffings," during which the clinical team in a children's unit of a state mental-health facility "negotiated" the status of their young charges. The interactive dynamics of child-care workers, psychiatric social workers, special educators, psychologists, program administrators, and psychiatrists were highly complex and instrumental in influencing the evaluations of major decision makers. The members of the clinical team would often begin a meeting with one evaluation of the child's status, but by the end of their deliberations, construct a very different one. Such joint actions should be of particular interest to labeling analysts. What are the respective interests of contributors to such deliberations? Does the negotiation of moral meaning have systematic properties across forms of deviation? Professional ideologies play a role in structuring the evaluative processes and the interactive dynamics of labeling, but how significant a role? Quite frequently the discussion at a psychiatric staffing for a child would change dramatically from such statements as "the ego-destructive relationship between mother and child and the nature of the dependency relationship" to "the mother's just a jerk; she simply doesn't know what's good for her kid; she wouldn't even let him go on field trips with the other kids at school or go to that summer camp." Again, the relationship between professional ideology and commonsensical, lay conceptions of deviance needs to be looked at more carefully. Are they complementary, so that one reinforces the other, or are there occasions in which they are contradictory and thus productive of potential decision-making problems? What factors influence the resolution of such problems?

These are the more significant empirical issues with which labeling analysts need to grapple. As research is conducted, more specific questions will no doubt be raised for each of these topics. The analysis of the situated construction of moral meaning still shows promise as a means to understanding the role of deviance in society.

Macro-Level Concerns

Analysts of formal labeling and stigmatization have long been interested in those structural, organizational, and social-system contingencies that facilitate the work of deviant-processing institutions. Perhaps the most influential conceptual contribution to sociological discussions of these issues was Goffman's *Asylums* (1961), particularly his analysis of the characteristics of "total institutions" and conditions for "mortification." Contrary to critics' claims that interactionists do not care to look at the structural conditions conducive to labeling, Goffman and others (e.g., Strauss et al., 1964) have done just that. Rather than search for the broader social-structural predeterminants of labeling (as Neo-Marxists suggest) these sociologists have examined the structural characteristics of the very institutions, organizations, and processing systems in which labeling occurs.

In such organizations, hierarchical arrangements between staff and inmates and between levels of staff have implications for the nature of deviance ascriptions. The bureaucratic practice of maintaining files and dossiers and the organization's need to record, in writing, the details of the inmates' behavior and the staff's evaluations of it can also have a bearing on the types of deviance ascriptions that are made and the patterning of ascriptions.[1] The bureaucratic constraints of red tape, following schedules, meeting quotas, checking qualification

[1]See, for example, Stanton Wheeler, ed., *On Record: Files and Dossiers in American Life*. New York: Russell Sage Foundation, 1969.

and eligibility requirements, maintaining a good public and media image, and maintaining community acceptance can all affect the construction of deviance typifications. Other factors, such as the presence of untrained staff, frequent staff turnover, and the presence of in-service training programs, can be equally influential. There are, however, very few empirical studies that carefully explore these factors and their specific relationships to labeling outcomes. There is a great need for such research.

Of particular interest to this author is the impact of professional and paraprofessional decision-making territoriality conflicts on labeling. As in medicine, where several new paraprofessions have been created and older medical roles have been redefined and are ascendant in the hierarchy, there is a similar trend in deviant-processing systems. To an increasing extent in the treatment of drug addicts, criminals, the mentally ill, the socially maladjusted, juvenile delinquents, and those with learning difficulties, there has been a trend toward the professionalization of roles for those who work with labeled deviants. These professionals and paraprofessionals do not always share the same perspectives on the nature of the problems and what should be done about them. They each vie for the opportunity to have their respective definitions of reality accepted.

The decision-making territoriality disputes are especially marked in institutions that maintain a wide variety of people-work or people-helping professionals—psychologists, social workers, staff workers, special educators, psychiatrists, occupational therapists, probation workers, psychotherapists, guidance counselors, and so on. Usually one profession—psychiatry for example—will take the dominant role and will structure the final decision-making work. But this is not always so. In some institutions, a degree of democracy might prevail, and each professional group's definitions of reality may be given equal weight in final evaluations of the deviant. In other organizations, the expected hierarchy of credibility and power may be usurped by one or another professional or group of professionals.

For example, in 1976 the author conducted research on the decision-making process in a state diagnostic center for juvenile delinquents in Holland. The institution contained the full array of specialists to diagnose and recommend treatment for labeled juvenile delinquents. Included were psychiatrists, psychologists, educators, youth-team workers, counselors, administrators, and others. Through her seniority and personal influence in the organization, the social worker exercised the greatest control over definitions of the boy's problems and the ultimate disposition and referral of the case. If her evaluations of the family indicated that it was "not the right kind of family for the boy," the probability would be high that this boy would be sent to a custodial institution. If the family were judged to be "good," it was likely that he would be sent home to the custody of his parents. This was true in most cases regardless of the evaluations by other members of the clinical or diagnostic team. To this social worker, the major cause of "serious" delinquency was a bad or disorganized home life. The most significant criterion for diagnostic evaluation of the boy became the evaluation of his family and its "social history."

In other organizations, daily decision-making territoriality disputes may occur among professionals over definitions of client problems and what should be done about them. The negotiative process might produce evaluations of the "clientele" or inmates that are an amalgam of views of different professionals; or different views may come to the fore at different times. The important issues for labeling analysts is how these organizational and professional characteristics implicate the nature of the labels constructed by decision makers, and with what consequences for those who are labeled.

Another level of organizational reality also implicates the societal reaction of deviance ascription. Deviant-processing institutions do not exist in a social vacuum, but are connected in several ways to other community institutions. Quite frequently, any one institution is part of a group of institutions that can be termed a *referral system.* The organizational members of a referral system will typically recommend or order clients to other members of the system for specialized services. As an individual moves from one institution to the next, different evaluations are made and usually are dutifully recorded in the "case record."

Many careers of childhood mental illness, for example, begin in the classroom. For various reasons a teacher may decide to recommend a student to the school psychologist for diagnostic testing. The psychologist may, in turn, recommend the child to the social-psychiatric clinic, which, after appropriate deliberation and service, decides to refer the child to the district mental-health facility. This institution may, in turn, recommend the child to other members of the referral network. Some children, by the age of 12, have been referred to dozens of agencies and professionals.

At each step in a deviance referral system, constructions of moral meaning are being made or facilitated. Although we know very little about the impact of such sequential processing, it seems obvious that, like sequential careers of deviant behavior, sequential careers of *deviance ascription* also exist. Yet we have little information about the "career contingencies" that promote a person through the system. What factors will remove an individual from the referral network? How do these institutions interact to influence the outcomes of deviance ascription? Lemert (1974) has called for an analysis of "group interaction" to explore similar types of bureaucratic influences on the societal reaction to deviance. We need to know whether basic deviance-typification schemes are shared by these institutions. What might be the nature of negotiation over deviance ascriptions among the personnel of these various agencies? Are evaluations transformed from one organization to the next; and, if so, is there some underlying regularity to these transformations? These are only a few of the many questions that might be asked about this institutional-systems level of deviance ascription.

We hope that a concerted micro- and macro-level analysis of these issues will allow us to examine the efficacy of the original insights about the evaluative nature of deviance. There are indications that the study of deviance ascription has not only contributed to our sociological/theoretical understanding of social deviation, but also may offer recommendations for policy issues.

POLICY AND DEVIANCE ACTUALIZATION: AIMING TOWARD PRAXIS

Sociologists who have studied the societal reaction to deviance have most often, *in their written accounts,* been unconcerned with the policy implications of their research. This is somewhat surprising, however, because as Becker (1967) has so well shown, sociologists find themselves unable *not* to take sides between labelers and those labeled. When the topic of debate is concerned with moral issues that influence people's lives, the analyst finds it difficult to be *unbiased.* One would think that students of deviance who are committed to the under dog, as well as those who are strongly committed to the side of the control agents, would have strong feelings about the adequacy or inadequacy of the societal reaction and want to communicate to others their impressions for changing or maintaining existing practices. Most sociologists, in fact, probably hold private opinions about what changes could or should be made. They may, however, feel that their solutions will appear too radical or will appear so biased in favor of those labeled that they would never be heard or headed by the powers that be—those who actually make policy decisions (or so conservative that their more liberal colleagues would be highly enraged).

As students of social problems, however, we ought to know that social-policy issues can never really be approached in a value-neutral way. *All* social problems (and social-policy issues are social problems) are sets of claims made by various parties about some social condition or situation that they are interested in and biased about. If our work as sociologists cannot help but be value-committed, and if the parties to social-problems deliberations cannot but be biased in their claims about such issues as the treatment of criminals or the insane, does this therefore mean that the sociologist has no role in the debate over public policy toward deviants and deviance? On the contrary, it means we have a vital role.

The benefit of viewing the societal reaction to deviance through the interests and the definitions of the situation of one or the other of the parties to the construction of moral meaning is that we are able to express a reasoned systematic and empirically grounded analysis of the *perceived* impact of the evaluative process. Our analyses can be used to clarify and make explicit a set of claims to the policy-issue deliberations. Whether we can offer conclusive evidence that portrays the process of deviance ascription in some "undeniable" way is contingent on the policy decision makers, on their interests, and on whether they can be persuaded. There is no objective "undeniable" solution to *social* problems. There are only solutions that enhance the interests of some individuals, occasionally the interest of most of us, but seldom the interests of all of us.

A CASE IN POINT: THE INSTITUTIONAL REACTION TO THE MENTALLY ILL

The sociological analysis of the institutional treatment of mental patients has produced numerous characterizations of the patient–therapist relationship, the problems of social control in managing groups of patients, the processes of desocialization and resocialization, and the influence of various organizational characteristics on the careers of patients inside the institution. Most significantly, much research has revealed what the reality of mental-health processing looks like to patients and institutional workers.

To the patient, the world of mental hospitalization is often confusing and occasionally highly oppressive. During the initial commitment hearing, the patient does not always know his rights and responsibilities. He sometimes does not know why he is in a mental institution; what it means to be in need of mental treatment; whether he is entitled to a trial, how soon, and whether it can be a jury trial; what it means to sign a request for voluntary admission; or what criteria are used at the hearing to establish mental incompetency. In some mental-health systems, it is clear even at the preadmission stage of the patient's career that there are due process issues that policy decision-makers need to address. Sociological research can help (and in some instances has already helped) to clarify these issues by systematically examining the bases of these perceived difficulties and their consequences.

As a result of having experienced mental hospitalization, many mental patients have come to feel that they have not been given sufficient information about their rights inside the institution; that they have not been given what they perceive to be decent living conditions; that they have not been allowed to retain their personal property; that they have not been given sufficient protection from other inmates and staff; that their communication with the outside world is unjustly censored; that they are not given a right to refuse medication; that they have not been given access to the nature of institutional evaluations of them; that they have not been told the criteria for release from treatment; and that they have been coerced into divulging information about themselves that they would rather have kept personal.

These inmate perceptions, which have surfaced in sociological studies, suggest several changes in the societal reaction to those defined as mentally ill. There is a need for *accountability* in systems of mental-health care. Are institutional practices established for purposes of treatment or merely for social control? If they are proclaimed "therapeutic," then sufficient evidence of success must be offered; if not, these practices or procedures should be eliminated. One issue, of course, is to whom the evidence should be offered. It would be desirable to have extrainstitutional evaluators, who, as in the adversary system of legal representation, clearly represent the interests of the patient.

A patient should have open access to the staff evaluations of him. The criteria for evaluations ought to be made clear, and evaluations that cannot be supported by empirical data ought to be removed from the record. There are some good reasons for *eliminating* clinical dossiers and their deviance ascriptions at the end of the institutional career—one of the few effective means of neutralizing stigmatization. It becomes increasingly clear that the protection of the mentally ill can be assured only by mandatory compliance with regulations that serve as checks and balances in a system in which the exercise of evaluative power has been known, in some instances, to harm those it evaluates.

There are, of course, sociologists who would recommend that few changes are needed in most systems of mental-health care; that the treatment of mental patients is, for the most part, effective and does not "victimize" the patient or unduly jeopardize his social status (e.g., Gove, 1975). These sociologists also bring evidence to bear on their claims. All that we as sociologists can do—both those who have taken the perspective of the labelers and those who are labeled deviant—is to present our data and interpretations to those in positions of policy decision-making, who decide the fate of such matters.

There is no moral imperative that dictates that sociologists *must* be concerned with the policy implications of their research. However, as students of social deviation, we are often closer to the issues than most members of society. Policy makers are often highly dependent on "informed sources" for their decisions, and if we do not contribute to the solution of problems of praxis, others, perhaps less informed, will.

The sociology of deviant behavior and deviance will remain an exciting and demanding area of investigation. There will be no substitute for painstaking, theoretically informed, and methodologically rigorous research on the many issues that have been discussed in this book. Students will have to take each of the available theoretical/conceptual frameworks to task and discover which of their components allow us to increase our knowledge of deviation. No one framework will "win out," but some will be more suggestive and insightful than others. Each framework, we will find, speaks to different characteristics of deviation, and the development of a comprehensive theory will depend on the concerted efforts of many sociologists exploring these different characteristics.

SELECTED APPLICATIONS

The following selection by Zimbardo illustrates the policy stance of one social scientist as a result of his research on guard–inmate relationships. The reader should carefully examine the correspondence between the results of Zimbardo's experiments and his plea for prison reform.

PATHOLOGY OF IMPRISONMENT
Philip G. Zimbardo

I was recently released from solitary confinement after being held therein for 37 months (months!). A silent system was imposed upon me and to even whisper to the man in the next cell resulted in being beaten by guards, sprayed with chemical mace, blackjacked, stomped and thrown into a strip-cell naked to sleep on a concrete floor without bedding, covering, wash basin or even a toilet. The floor served as toilet and bed, and even there the silent system was enforced. To let a moan escape your lips because of the pain and discomfort . . . resulted in another beating. I spent not days, but months there during my 37 months in solitary. . . . I have filed every writ possible against the administrative acts of brutality. The state courts have all denied the petitions. Because of my refusal to let the things die down and forget all that happened during my 37 months in solitary . . . I am the most hated prisoner in [this] penitentiary, and called a "hard-core incorrigible."

Maybe I am an incorrigible, but if true, it's because I would rather die than to accept being treated as less than a human being. I have

Reprinted by permission of Transaction, Inc. from *Society*, Vol. 9, no. 6. © 1972 by Transaction, Inc.

*never complained of my prison sentence as being unjustified except
through legal means of appeals. I have never put a knife on a guard's
throat·and demanded my release. I know that thieves must be punished
and I don't justify stealing, even though I am a thief myself. But now I don't
think I will be a thief when I am released. No, I'm not rehabilitated. It's just
that I no longer think of becoming wealthy by stealing. I now only think of
killing—killing those who have beaten me and treated me as if I were a
dog. I hope and pray for the sake of my own soul and future life of freedom
that I am able to overcome the bitterness and hatred which eats daily at my
soul, but I know to overcome it will not be easy.*

This eloquent plea for prison reform—for humane treatment of
human beings, for the basic dignity that is the right of every American—
came to me secretly in a letter from a prisoner who cannot be identified
because he is still in a state correctional institution. He sent it to me
because he read of an experiment I recently conducted at Stanford University. In an attempt to understand just what it means psychologically to be a
prisoner or a prison guard, Craig Haney, Curt Banks, Dave Jaffe and I
created our own prison. We carefully screened over 70 volunteers who
answered an ad in a Palo Alto city newspaper and ended up with about two
dozen young men who were selected to be part of this study. They were
mature, emotionally stable, normal, intelligent college students from middle-class homes throughout the United States and Canada. They appeared
to represent the cream of the crop of this generation. None had any criminal record and all were relatively homogeneous on many dimensions
initially.

Half were arbitrarily designated as prisoners by a flip of a coin,
the others as guards. These were the roles they were to play in our simulated prison. The guards were made aware of the potential seriousness
and danger of the situation and their own vulnerability. They made up their
own formal rules for maintaining law, order and respect, and were generally free to improvise new ones during their eight-hour, three-man shifts.
The prisoners were unexpectedly picked up at their homes by a city policeman in a squad car, searched, handcuffed, fingerprinted, booked at
the Palo Alto station house and taken blindfolded to our jail. There they
were stripped, deloused, put into a cell with two other prisoners where
they expected to live for the next two weeks. The pay was good ($15 a day)
and their motivation was to make money.

We observed and recorded on videotape the events that occurred in the prison, and we interviewed and tested the prisoners and
guards at various points throughout the study. Some of the videotapes of
the actual encounters between the prisoners and guards were seen on the
NBC News feature "Chronolog" on November 26, 1971.

At the end of only six days we had to close down our mock
prison because what we saw was frightening. It was no longer apparent to
most of the subjects (or to us) where reality ended and their roles began.
The majority had indeed become prisoners or guards, no longer able to
clearly differentiate between role playing and self. There were dramatic
changes in virtually every aspect of their behavior, thinking and feeling. In

less than a week the experience of imprisonment undid (temporarily) a lifteime of learning; human values were suspended, self-concepts were challenged and the ugliest, most base, pathological side of human nature surfaced. We were horrified because we saw some boys (guards) treat others as if they were despicable animals, taking pleasure in cruelty, while other boys (prisoners) became servile, dehumanized robots who thought only of escape, of their own individual survival and of their mounting hatred for the guards.

We had to release three prisoners in the first four days because they had such acute situational traumatic reactions as hysterical crying, confusion in thinking and severe depression. Others begged to be paroled, and all but three were willing to forfeit all the money they had earned if they could be paroled. By then (the fifth day) they had been so programmed to think of themselves as prisoners that when their request for parole was denied, they returned docilely to their cells. Now, had they been thinking as college students acting in an oppressive experiment, they would have quit once they no longer wanted the $15 a day we used as our only incentive. However, the reality was not quitting an experiment but "being paroled by the parole board from the Stanford County Jail." By the last days, the earlier solidarity among the prisoners (systematically broken by the guards) dissolved into "each man for himself." Finally, when one of their fellows was put in solitary confinement (a small closet) for refusing to eat, the prisoners were given a choice by one of the guards: give up their blankets and the incorrigible prisoner would be let out, or keep their blankets and he would be kept in all night. They voted to keep their blankets and to abandon their brother.

About a third of the guards became tyrannical in their arbitrary use of power, in enjoying their control over other people. They were corrupted by the power of their roles and became quite inventive in their techniques of breaking the spirit of the prisoners and making them feel they were worthless. Some of the guards merely did their jobs as tough but fair correctional officers, and several were good guards from the prisoners' point of view since they did them small favors and were friendly. However, no good guard ever interfered with a command by any of the bad guards; they never intervened on the side of the prisoners, they never told the others to ease off because it was only an experiment, and they never even came to me as prison superintendent or experimenter in charge to complain. In part, they were good because the others were bad; they needed the others to help establish their own egos in a positive light. In a sense, the good guards perpetuated the prison more than the other guards because their own needs to be liked prevented them from disobeying or violating the implicit guards' code. At the same time, the act of befriending the prisoners created a social reality which made the prisoners less likely to rebel.

By the end of the week the experiment had become a reality, as if it were a Pirandello play directed by Kafka that just keeps going after the audience has left. The consultant for our prison, Carlo Prescott, an ex-convict with 16 years of imprisonment in California's jails, would get so depressed and furious each time he visited our prison, because of its psychological similarity to his experiences, that he would have to leave. A Catholic priest who was a former prison chaplain in Washington, D. C. talked to our prisoners after four days and said they were just like the other first-timers he had seen.

But in the end, I called off the experiment not because of the horror I saw out there in the prison yard, but because of the horror of realizing that *I* could have easily traded places with the most brutal guard or become the weakest prisoner full of hatred at being so powerless that I could not eat, sleep or go to the toilet without permission of the authorities. *I* could have become Calley at My Lai, George Jackson at San Quentin, one of the men at Attica or the prisoner quoted at the beginning of this article.

Individual behavior is largely under the control of social forces and environmental contingencies rather than personality traits, character, will power or other empirically unvalidated constructs. Thus we create an illusion of freedom by attributing more internal control to ourselves, to the individual, than actually exists. We thus underestimate the power and pervasiveness of situational controls over behavior because: a) they are often non-obvious and subtle, b) we can often avoid entering situations where we might be so controlled, c) we label as "weak" or "deviant" people in those situations who do behave differently from how we believe we would.

Each of us carries around in our heads a favorable self-image in which we are essentially just, fair, humane and understanding. For example, we could not imagine inflicting pain on others without much provocation or hurting people who had done nothing to us, who in fact were even liked by us. However, there is a growing body of social psychological research which underscores the conclusion derived from this prison study. Many people, perhaps the majority, can be made to do almost anything when put into psychologically compelling situations—regardless of their morals, ethics, values, attitudes, beliefs or personal convictions. My colleague, Stanley Milgram, has shown that more than 60 percent of the population will deliver what they think is a series of painful electric shocks to another person even after the victim cries for mercy, begs them to stop and then apparently passes out. The subjects complained that they did not want to inflict more pain but blindly obeyed the command of the authority figure (the experimenter) who said that they must go on. In my own research on violence, I have seen mild-mannered co-eds repeatedly give shocks (which they thought were causing pain) to another girl, a stranger whom they had rated very favorably, simply by being made to feel anonymous and put in a situation where they were expected to engage in this activity.

Observers of these and similar experimental situations never predict their outcomes and estimate that it is unlikely that they themselves would behave similarly. They can be so confident only when they were outside the situation. However, since the majority of people in these studies do act in non-rational, non-obvious ways, it follows that the majority of observers would also succumb to the social psychological forces in the situation.

With regard to prisons, we can state that the mere act of assigning labels to people and putting them into a situation where those labels acquire validity and meaning is sufficient to elicit pathological behavior. This pathology is not predictable from any available diagnostic indicators we have in the social sciences, and is extreme enough to modify in very significant ways fundamental attitudes and behavior. The prison situation, as presently arranged, is guaranteed to generate severe enough pathological reactions in both guards and prisoners as to debase their humanity, lower their feelings of self-worth and make it difficult for them to be part of a society outside of their prison.

For years our national leaders have been pointing to the enemies of freedom, to the fascist or communist threat to the American way of life. In so doing they have overlooked the threat of social anarchy that is building within our own country without any outside agitation. As soon as a person comes to the realization that he is being imprisoned by his society or individuals in it, then, in the best American tradition, he demands liberty and rebels, accepting death as an alternative. The third alternative, however, is to allow oneself to become a good prisoner—docile, cooperative, uncomplaining, conforming in thought and complying in deed.

Our prison authorities now point to the militant agitators who are still vaguely referred to as part of some communist plot, as the irresponsible, incorrigible troublemakers. They imply that there would be no trouble, riots, hostages or deaths if it weren't for this small band of bad prisoners. In other words, then, everything would return to "normal" again in the life of our nation's prisons if they could break these men.

The riots in prison are coming from within—from within every man and woman who refuses to let the system turn them into an object, a number, a thing or a no-thing. It is not communist inspired, but inspired by the spirit of American freedom. No man wants to be enslaved. To be powerless, to be subject to the arbitrary exercise of power, to not be recognized as a human being is to be a slave.

To be a militant prisoner is to become aware that the physical jails are but more blatant extensions of the forms of social and psychological oppression experienced daily in the nation's ghettos. They are trying to awaken the conscience of the nation to the ways in which the American ideals are being perverted, apparently in the name of justice but actually under the banner of apathy, fear and hatred. If we do not listen to the pleas of the prisoners at Attica to be treated like human beings, then we have all become brutalized by our priorities for property rights over human rights. The consequence will not only be more prison riots but a loss of all those ideals on which this country was founded.

The public should be aware that they own the prisons and that their business is failing. The 70 percent recidivism rate and the escalation in severity of crimes committed by graduates of our prisons are evidence that current prisons fail to rehabilitate the inmates in any positive way. Rather, they are breeding grounds for hatred of the establishment, a hatred that makes every citizen a target of violent assault. Prisons are a bad investment for us taxpayers. Until now we have not cared, we have turned over to wardens and prison authorities the unpleasant job of keeping people who threaten us out of our sight. Now we are shocked to learn that their management practices have failed to improve the product and instead turn petty thieves into murderers. We must insist upon new management or improved operating procedures.

The cloak of secrecy should be removed from the prisons. Prisoners claim they are brutalized by the guards, guards say it is a lie. Where is the impartial test of the truth in such a situation? Prison officials have forgotten that they work for us, that they are only public servants whose salaries are paid by our taxes. They act as if it is their prison, like a child with a toy he won't share. Neither lawyers, judges, the legislature nor the public is allowed into prisons to ascertain the truth unless the visit is sanctioned by authorities and until all is prepared for their visit. I was shocked to learn that my request to join a congressional investigating committee's tour of San Quentin and Soledad was refused, as was that of the news media.

There should be an ombudsman in every prison, not under the pay or control of the prison authority, and responsible only to the courts, state legislature and the public. Such a person could report on violations of constitutional and human rights.

Guards must be given better training than they now receive for the difficult job society imposes upon them. To be a prison guard as now constituted is to be put in a situation of constant threat from within the prison, with no social recognition from the society at large. As was shown graphically at Attica, prison guards are also prisoners of the system who can be sacrificed to the demands of the public to be punitive and the needs of politicians to preserve an image. Social scientists and business administrators should be called upon to design and help carry out this training.

The relationship between the individual (who is sentenced by the courts to a prison term) and his community must be maintained. How can a prisoner return to a dynamically changing society that most of us cannot cope with after being out of it for a number of years? There should be more community involvement in these rehabilitation centers, more ties encouraged and promoted between the trainees and family and friends, more educational opportunities to prepare them for returning to their communities as more valuable members of it than they were before they left.

Finally, the main ingredient necessary to effect any change at all in prison reform, in the rehabilitation of a single prisoner or even in the optimal development of a child is caring. Reform must start with people—especially people with power—caring about the well-being of others. Underneath the toughest, society-hating convict, rebel or anarchist is a human being who wants his existence to be recognized by his fellows and who wants someone else to care about whether he lives or dies and to grieve if he lives imprisoned rather than lives free.

BIBLIOGRAPHY

Amir, Menachem and Yitzchak Berman
1970   "Chromosomal Deviation and Crime." Federal Probation (June):55–62.
Anderson, Nels
1923   The Hobo. Chicago: University of Chicago Press.
Aquinas, St. Thomas
1912   Summa Theologica. Literally translated by Fathers of the English Domini-
        can Province. London: Third Number (194).
Balint, M.
1957   The Doctor, His Patient and the Illness. New York: International University
        Press.
Becker, Howard S.
1963   Outsiders: Studies in the Sociology of Deviance. New York: Free Press.
1967   "Whose Side Are We On?" Social Problems 14:239–47.
Bell, Robert R.
1971   Social Deviance. Homewood, Ill.: Dorsey Press.
Blum, Alan F.
1970   "The Sociology of Mental Illness," in Jack Douglas, ed., Deviance and
        Respectability. New York: Basic Books.
Blumer, Herbert
1966   "Sociological Implications of the Thought of George Herbert Mead." The
        American Journal of Sociology 71 (March):537.
Bonger, Wilhelm
        Criminality and Economic Conditions. Bloomington: Indiana University
        Press.
Bordua, David
1967   "Recent Trends: Deviant Behavior and Social Control." The Annals 369
        (January):149–63.
Brehm, J. W. and A. R. Cohen
1962   Explorations in Cognitive Dissonance. New York: Wiley.
Brown, Lawrence Guy
1942   Social Pathology: Personal and Social Disorganization. New York: F. S.
        Crofts.
Cameron, Mary Owen
1964   The Booster and the Snitch. New York: Free Press.
Cavan, Ruth S.
1928   Suicide: A Study of Personal Disorganization. Chicago: University of Chi-
        cago Press.
Chambliss, Rollin
1954   Social Thought. New York: Holt, Rinehart and Winston.
Churchill, Wainwright
1967   Homosexual Behavior among Males. New York: Hawthorne Books.

Cicourel, Aaron V. and John I. Kitsuse
1963   The Educational Decision-Makers. Indianpolis: Bobbs-Merrill.
Clinard, Marshall
1957   Sociology of Deviant Behavior. New York: Rinehart and Company.
Clinard, Marshall and Richard Quinney
1967   Criminal Behavior Systems: A Typology. New York: Holt, Rinehart and Winston.
Cloward, Richard A.
1959   "Illegitimate Means, Anomie, and Deviant Behavior." American Sociological Review 24 (April):164–76.
Cloward, Richard A. and Lloyd E. Ohlin
1960   Delinquency and Opportunity: A Theory of Delinquent Gangs. New York: Free Press.
Cohen, Albert K.
1955   Delinquent Boys: The Culture of the Gang. New York: Free Press.
1966   Deviance and Social Control. Englewood Cliff, N.J.: Prentice-Hall.
Cooley, Charles Horton
1909   Human Nature and the Social Order. Glencoe, Ill.: Free Press.
1962   Social Organization. New York: Scribner's; Schocken.
Cortes, Juan B. with Florence M. Gatti
1972   Delinquency and Crime: A BiopsychoSocial Approach. New York: Seminar Press.
Cressey, Donald R.
1953   Other People's Money: A Study in the Social Psychology of Embezzlement. Glencoe, Ill.: Free Press.
1964   "Some Popular Criticisms of Differential Association," in Donald R. Cressey, ed., Delinquency, Crime and Differential Association. The Hague: Martinus Nijhoff.
Dahrendorf, Ralf
1958   "Toward a Theory of Social Conflict." Journal of Conflict Resolution 2 (June):170–83.
Daniels, A. K. and R. E. Clausen
1966   "Role Conflicts and Their Ideological Resolution in Military Psychiatric Practice." American Journal of Psychiatry 123 (September):280–87.
Daniels, Arlene
1970   "Normal Mental Illness and Understandable Excuses: The Philosophy of Combat Psychiatry." American Behavioral Scientist 14 (November/December):167–87.
Davis, Nanette J.
1972   "Labelling Theory in Deviance Research: A Critique and Reconsideration." Sociological Quarterly 13 (Autumn):447–74.
Davis, Kingsley
1937   "The Sociology of Prostitution." American Sociological Review 2:744–55.
1966   "Sexual Behavior," in Robert K. Merton and Robert A. Nisbet, eds., Contemporary Social Problems. New York: Harcourt, Brace and World.
Denzin, Norman K.
1968   "The Self-Fulfilling Prophecy and Patient-Therapist Interaction," in Stephen P. Spitzer and Norman K. Denzin, eds., The Mental Patient. New York: McGraw Hill.

1969   "Symbolic Interactionism and Ethnomethodology: A Proposed Synthesis."
American Sociological Review 34 (December):815–31.

Denzin, Norman K. and Stephen P. Spitzer
1966   "Paths to the Mental Hospital and Staff Predictions of Patient Role Behavior." Journal of Health and Human Behavior 7(Winter):265–71.

De Quiros, C. Bernaldo
1912   Modern Theories of Criminality. Boston: Little, Brown.

Dewey, John
1922   Human Nature and Conduct. New York: Henry Holt.

Douglas, Jack D.
1967   The Social Meaning of Suicide. Princeton: Princeton University Press.

Douglas, Jack, ed.
1970   Deviance and Respectability. New York: Basic Books.

Dreitzel, Hans Peter, ed.
1970   Recent Sociology No. 2. New York: Macmillan.

Durkheim, Emile
1895   The Rules of Sociological Method. Translated by Sarah A. Solovay and
John H. Mueller, edited by George E. G. Catlin, 1964. New York: Free'
Press.
1897   Suicide. Translated by John A. Spaulding and George Simpson, edited by
George Simpson, 1951. Glencoe, Ill.: Free Press.

Encyclopedia Brittanica. Volume 16, p. 853.

Erikson, Kai
1964   "Notes on the Sociology of Deviance," in Howard S. Becker, ed., The
Other Side. New York: Free Press.

Erikson, Kai T. and Daniel E. Gilbertson
1969   "Case Records in the Mental Hospital," in Stanton Wheeler, ed., On Record: Files and Dossiers in American Life. New York: Russell Sage.

Faris, Robert E. L. and H. Warren Dunham
1939   Mental Disorders in Urban Areas: An Ecological Study of Schizophrenia
and Other Psychoses. Chicago: University of Chicago Press.

Ferri, Enrico
1897   Criminal Sociology. New York: D. Appleton.

Fink, Arthur E.
1938   Causes of Crime: Biological Theories in the United States: 1800–1915.
Philadelphia: University of Pennsylvania Press.

Foucault, Michel
1965   Madness in Civilization. Translated by Richard Howard. New York:
Pantheon.

Fox, Richard G.
1971   "The XYY Offender: Modern Myth?" Journal of Criminal Law, Criminology
and Police Science (March):62.

Frazier, E. Franklin
1931   The Negro Family in Chicago. Chicago: University of Chicago Press.

Freedman, Ronald
1950   Recent Migration to Chicago. Chicago: University of Chicago Press.

Freidson, Eliot
1966   "Disability as Social Deviance," in Marvin Sussman, ed., Sociology and
Rehabilitation. Washington, D.C.: American Sociological Association.

Galen
1916   On the Natural Faculties. Translated by Arthur John Brock. London: William Heinemann.

Gall, Franz Joseph
1807   Craniologie, ou Decouvertes Nouvelles, Concernant le Cerveau, Le Crane et les Organes. Paris: Nicolla.

Galle, Omer R., Walter R. Gove, and J. Miller McPherson
1972   "Population Density and Pathology: What Are the Relations for Man?" Science 176 (April):23–30.

Garfinkel, Harold
1956   "Conditions of Successful Degradation Ceremonies." American Journal of Sociology 61 (March), pp. 420–24.

1967   Studies in Ethnomethodology. Englewood Cliffs, N.J.: Prentice-Hall.

Garofalo, Baron Raffaele
1914   Criminology. Translated by Robert Wyness Millar. Boston: Little, Brown.

Gibbs, Jack P.
1972   "Issues in Defining Deviant Behavior," in Robert A. Scott and Jack D. Douglas, eds., Theoretical Perspectives on Deviance. New York: Basic Books.

Gibbs, Jack P.
1966   "Conceptions of Deviant Behavior: The Old and the New." Pacific Sociological Review (Spring):9–14.

Glueck, Sheldon and Eleanor Glueck
1956   Physique and Delinquency. New York: Harper & Bros.

Goddard, Henry Herbert
1912   The Kallikak Family: A Study in the Heredity of Feeble-Mindness. New York: Macmillan.

1914   Feeble-Mindedness Its Causes and Consequences. New York: Macmillan Company.

Goffman, Erving
1961   Asylums. Garden City, N.Y.: Doubleday Anchor.

1963   Stigma: Notes on the Management of Spoiled Identity. Englewood Cliffs, N.J.: Prentice-Hall.

Gouldner, Alvin
1968   "The Sociologist as Partisan: Sociology and the Welfare State." The American Sociologist 3 (May):103–16.

Gove, Walter
1970   "Societal Reaction as an Explanation of Mental Illness: An Evaluation." American Sociological Review 35 (October):873–84.

Gove, Walter R., ed.
1975   The Labelling of Deviance: Evaluating a Perspective. New York: Sage Publications.

Greenley, James R.
1972   "The Psychiatric Patient's Family and Length of Hospitalization." Journal of Health and Social Behavior 13 (March):25–37.

Haney, C. Allen and Robert Michielutte
1968   "Selective Factors Operating in the Adjudication of Incompetency." Journal of Health and Social Behavior 9 (September):233–42.

Haney, C. Allen, Kent S. Miller, and Robert Michielutte
1969   "The Interaction of Petitioner and Deviant Social Characteristics in the Adjudication of Incompetency." Sociometry 32 (June):182–93.

Henslin, James M.
1970   "Guilt and Guilt Neutralization: Reponse and Adjustment to Suicide," in Jack D. Douglas, ed. Deviance and Respectability. New York: Basic Books, pp. 192–228.

Hirschi, Travis
1975   "Labelling Theory and Juvenile Delinquency: An Assessment of the Evidence," in Walter R. Gove, ed., The Labelling of Deviance: Evaluating a Perspective. New York: Sage Publications, pp. 181–203.

Hollingshead, August, B. and Frederick C. Redlich
1958   Social Class and Mental Illness: A Community Study. New York: Wiley.

Hooker, Evelyn
1967   "The Homosexual Community," in John H. Gagnon and William Simon, eds. Sexual Deviance. New York: Harper & Row.

Hughes, Everett C.
1971   The Sociological Eye: Selected Papers. Chicago: Aldine–Atherton.

Hughes, H. Stuart
1958   Consciousness and Society: The Reorientation of European Social Thought, 1890–1930. New York: Knopf.

Humphreys, Laud
1972   Out of the Closets: The Sociology of Homosexual Liberation. Englewood Cliffs, N.J.: Prentice-Hall.

Jacobs, Jerry
1970   "The Use of Religion in Constructing the Moral Justification of Suicide," in Jack Douglas, ed., Deviance and Respectability. New York: Basic Books.

James, William
1901   The Principles of Psychology. London: Macmillan.

Katz, Jack
1973   "Deviance, Charisma, and Rule-Defined Behavior." Social Problems 20:186–202.

Kinsey, A. C., Wardell B. Pomeroy, C. E. Martin, and Paul Gebhard
1953   Sexual Behavior in the Human Female. Philadelphia: Saunders.

Kitsuse, John I.
1962   "Societal Reaction to Deviance." Social Problems 9 (Winter):253.
1964   "Societal Reaction to Deviant Behavior: Problems of Theory and Method," in Howard S. Becker, ed., The Other Side. New York: Free Press.
1975   "The 'New Conception of Deviance' and Its Critics," in Walter R. Gove, ed., The Labelling of Deviance: Evaluating a Perspective. New York: Sage Publications.

Kitsuse, John I. and Aaron V. Cicourel
1963   "A Note on the Uses of Official Statistics." Social Problems 12:131–39.

Kitsuse, John I. and David C. Dietrick
1959   "Delinquent Boys: A Critique." American Sociological Review 24 (April): 213–15.

Kittrie, Nicholas N.
1971   "Will the XYY Syndrome Abolish Guilt?" Federal Probation 35 (June): 26–31.
Kors, Alan C. and Edward Peters, eds.
1972   Witchcraft in Europe, 1100–1700. Philadelphia: University of Pennsylvania Press.
Kretschmer, Ernst
1951   Physique and Character. New York: Humanities Press.
Kuhn, Thomas S.
1962   The Structure of Scientific Revolutions. Chicago: University of Chicago Press.
Lavater, Johan Casper
1789   Essays on Physiognomy. Translated by Thomas Holcraft. London: G. G. J. & J. Robinson.
Lemert, Edwin M.
1948   "Some Aspects of a General Theory of Sociopathic Behavior." Proceedings of the Pacific Sociological Society. Research Studies: State College of Washington 16:24.
1951   Social Pathology: A Systematic Approach to the Theory of Sociopathic Behavior. New York: McGraw-Hill.
1962   "Paranoia and the Dynamics of Exclusion." Sociometry 25 (March):2–25.
1967a   "The Concept of Secondary Deviation," in Edwin Lemert, Human Deviance, Social Problems, and Social Control. Englewood Cliffs, N.J.: Prentice-Hall.
1967b   Human Deviance, Social Problems, and Social Control. Englewood Cliffs,N.J.: Prentice-Hall.
1974   "Beyond Mead: The Societal Reaction to Deviance." Social Problems 21 (April):457–68.
Letkemann, Peter
1973   Crime as Work. Englewood Cliffs, N.J.: Prentice-Hall.
Leviticus 18:22
Leviticus 20:13
Lindesmith, Alfred and John H. Gagnon
1964   "Anomie and Drug Addiction," in Marshall Clinard, ed., Anomie and Deviant Behavior. New York: Free Press.
Linsky, Arnold S.
1970a   "Community Homogeneity and Exclusion of the Mentally Ill: Rejection vs. Consensus about Deviance." Journal of Health and Social Behavior 11 (December):304–11.
1970b   "Who Shall Be Excluded: The Influence of Personal Attributes in Community Reaction to the Mentally Ill." Social Psychiatry 5 (July):166–71.
Lombroso, Cesare
1918   Crime, Its Causes and Remedies. Boston: Little, Brown.
MacIver, Robert M.
1942,
1968   Social Causation. New York: Harper Torchbooks.
Mankoff, Milton
1968   "On Alienation, Structural Strain, and Deviance." Social Problems 16 (Summer):114–16.

1970   "Power in Advanced Capitalist Society." Social Problems 17 (Winter): 418–30.

Maruyama, Magorah
1968   "The Second Cybernetics: Deviation-Amplifying-Mutual Causal Processes," in Walter Buckley, ed., Modern Systems Research for the Behavioral Scientist. Chicago: Aldine.

Mathison, Richard R.
1958   The Eternal Search. New York: Putnam's.

Matza, David
1964   Delinquency and Drift. New York: Wiley.
1969   Becoming Deviant. Englewood Cliffs, N.J.: Prentice-Hall.

Maurer, David
1939   "Prostitutes and Criminal Argot." American Journal of Sociology 44 (January):546–50.
1940   The Big Con. Indianapolis: Bobbs-Merrill.
1964   Whiz Mob. New Haven: New Haven College and University Press.

McAuliffe, William E.
1975   "Beyond Secondary Deviance: Negative Labelling and Its Effects on the Heroin Addict," in Walter R. Gove, ed., The Labelling of Deviance: Evaluating a Perspective. New York: Sage Publications, pp. 205–42.

McHugh, Peter
1970   "A Common-Sense Conception of Deviance," in Jack D. Douglas, ed., Deviance and Respectability. New York: Basic Books.

Merton, Robert K.
1938   "Social Structure and Anomie." American Sociological Review 3 (October):672–82.
1966   "Social Problems and Sociological Theory," in Robert K. Merton and Robert A. Nisbet, eds., Contemporary Social Problems. New York: Harcourt, Brace and World.
1967   "On Sociological Theories of the Middle Range," in Robert K. Merton, On Theoretical Sociology. New York: Free Press.
1968   "Social Structure and Anomie," in Robert K.Merton, Social Theory and Social Structure, enlarged ed. New York: Free Press.

Miller, Walter B.
1958   "Lower Class Culture as a Generating Milieu of Gang Delinquency." Journal of Social Issues 14 (Summer):5–19.

Mitchell, Robert Edward
1971   "Some Social Implications of High Density Housing." American Sociological Review 36:18–29.

Myers, Jerome K. and Bertram H. Roberts
1959   Family and Class Dynamics in Mental Illness. New York: Wiley.

Norbeck, Edward
1961   Religion in Primitive Society. New York: Harper & Bros.

Parenti, Michael
1967   "Introduction," in W. I. Thomas, The Unadjusted Girl. New York: Harper Torchbooks.

Park, Robert E. and Ernest W. Burgess
1925   The City. Chicago: University of Chicago Press.

Parsons, Talcott
1949   The Structure of Social Action. New York: McGraw-Hill.
Phillips, Derek
1963   "Rejection: A Possible Consequence of Seeking Help for Mental Disorders." American Sociological Review 28 (December):963–72.
Plato
926a   Laws. Jowlett Translation, Volume 2.
Polsky, Ned
1967   Hustlers, Beats and Others. Chicago: Aldine.
Price, W. H. et al.
1966   "Criminal Patients with XYY Sex Chromosome Complement" Lancet 1.
Quetelet, Adolphe Jacques
1842   Treatise on Man. Edinburgh: William and Robert Chambers.
Rains, Prudence
1971   Becoming an Unwed Mother. Chicago: Aldine.
Rosehan, David L.
1973   "On Being Sane in Insane Places." Science 179 (January):250–58.
Rosen, George
1968   Madness in Society. New York: Harper Torchbooks.
Rubington, Earl
1973   "Variations in Bottle-Gang Controls," in Earl Rubington and Martin S. Weinberg, eds., Deviance: The Interactionist Perspective. New York: Macmillan.
Rushing, William A.
1971   "Individual Resources, Societal Reaction, and Hospital Commitment." American Journal of Sociology 77 (November):511–26.
Sagarin, Edward and Robert J. Kelly
1975   "Sexual Deviance and Labelling Perspectives," in Walter R. Gove ed., The Labelling of Deviance: Evaluating a Perspective. New York: Sage Publications.
Sarbin, Theodore R. and Jeffrey E. Miller
1970   "Demonism Revisited: The XYY Chromosomal Anomaly." Issues in Criminology 5 (Summer):195–207.
Scheff, Thomas J.
1964   "The Societal Reaction to Deviance: Ascriptive Elements in the Psychiatric Screening of Mental Patients in a Midwestern State." Social Problems 11 (Spring):401–13.
1966a   Being Mentall Ill: A Sociological Theory. Chicago: Aldine.
1966b   "Typification in the Diagnostic Practices of Rehabilitation Agencies," in Marvin B. Sussman, ed., Sociology and Rehabilitation. American Sociological Association. Washington, D.C.
1975   "Labelling Theory of Mental Illness." American Sociological Review 39:444–542.
Schuessler, Karl, ed.
1973   Edwin H. Sutherland on Analyzing Crime. Chicago: University of Chicago Press.
Schur, Edwin M.
1971   Labeling Deviant Behavior: Its Sociological Implications. New York: Harper & Row.

Schwartz, Richard D. and Jerome Skolnick
1962 "Two Studies of Legal Stigma." Social Problems 10 (Fall):133–42.

Scott, Marvin B. and Stanford M. Lyman
1970 "Accounts, Deviance, and Social Order," in Jack D. Douglas, ed., Deviance and Respectability. New York: Basic Books, pp. 89–119.

Seligman, Kurt
1948 Magic, Supernaturalism and Religion. New York: Pantheon Books.

Sellin, Thorsten
1938 Culture Conflict and Crime. New York: Social Science Research Council, Bulletin 41.

Shah, Saleem A. and Loren A. Roth
1974 "Biological and Psychophysiological Factors in Criminality," in Daniel Glaser, ed., Handbook of Criminology. Chicago: Rand McNally.

Shaw, Clifford
1930,
1938 The Jack-Roller. Chicago: University of Chicago Press.

Shaw, Clifford R. and Earl D. Meyer
1929 "The Juvenile Delinquent," in The Illinois Crime Survey. Illinois Association for Criminal Justice, p. 662.

Shaw, Clifford R. and Henry D. McKay
1931 "Social Factors in Juvenile Delinquency." Report on the Causes of Crime, National Commission on Law Observance and Enforcement Report No. 13. Washington, D.C.: U.S. Government Printing Office.
1942 Juvenile Delinquency and Urban Areas. Chicago: University of Chicago Press.

Sheldon, William H.
1949 Varieties of Delinquent Youth. New York: Harper & Bros.

Short, James F. and Fred L. Strodtbeck
1965 Group Process and Gang Delinquency. Chicago: University of Chicago Press.

Simmel, George
1955 Conflict and the Web of Group Affiliations. Translated by Kurt H. Wolff and Reinhard Bendix. New York: Free Press.

Simpson, George
1963 Emile Durkeim. New York: Crowell.

Snodgrasse, Richard M.
1951 "Crime and the Constitution Human: A Survey." Journal of Criminal Law, Criminology and Police Science 42 (May/June):18–52.

Strauss, Anselm
1964a "Introduction," in George Herbert Mead on Social Psychology. Chicago: University of Chicago Press, Phoenix Edition.

Strauss, Anselm, Leonard Schatzman, Rue Bucker, Danuta Ehrlich, Melvin Labshin
1964b *Psychiatric Ideologies and Institutions.* Glencoe, Ill.: Free Press.

Suchar, Charles S.
1972 The Social Organization of Child Therapy. Northwestern University: unpublished PhD Dissertation.

Sudnow, David
1965   "Normal Crimes: Sociological Features of the Penal Code." Social Problems 12 (Winter):255–70.
Summers, Montague
1956   The History of Witchcraft and Demonology. New York: University Books.
Sumner, William Graham
1906   Folkways: A Study of the Sociological Importance of Usages, Manners, Customs, Mores and Morals. Boston: Ginn and Company.
1963   Social Darwinism: Selected Essays. Englewood Cliffs, N.J.: Prentice-Hall.
Sutherland, Edwin H.
1951   "A Critique of Sheldon's Varieties of Delinquent Behavior." American Sociological Review 16 (February):10–13.
Sutherland, Edwin H. and Donald R. Cressey
1934,
1974   Criminology. Philadelphia: Lippincott.
Sykes, Gresham and David Matza
1957   "Techniques of Neutralization: A Theory of Delinquency." American Sociological Review 22 (December):664–70.
Szasz, Thomas S.
1970   The Manufacture of Madness. New York: Harper & Row.
1973   The Age of Madness. Garden City; N.Y.: Doubleday Anchor.
Tannenbaum, Frank
1938   Crime and the Community. Cincinnati: Ginn and Company.
Taylor, Ian, Paul Walton, and Jock Young
1973   The New Criminology: For a Social Theory of Deviance. London: Routledge & Kegan Paul.
Temerlin, Maurice K.
1968   "Suggestion Effects in Psychiatric Diagnosis." Journal of Nervous and Mental Disease 147 (4):349–53.
Thio, Alex
1973   "Class Bias in the Sociology of Deviance." The American Sociologist 8 (February):1–12.
Thomas, W. I.
1923,
1967   The Unadjusted Girl. Boston: Little, Brown; New York: Harper Torchbooks.
Thomas, W. I. and Dorothy S. Thomas
1928   The Child in America. New York: Knopf.
Thomas, W. I. and Florian Znaniecki
1958   The Polish Peasant in Europe and America. New York: Dover Publications.
Thrasher, Frederic
1927,
1967   The Gang (abridged version). Chicago: University of Chicago Press.
Time Magazine
1975   May 19, p. 38.
1975   May 5, p. 82.
Tittle, Charles R.
1975   "Labeling and Crime: An Empirical Evaluation," in Walter R. Gove, ed., The Labelling of Deviance. New York: Sage Publications.

Warren, Carol A.
1974   Identity and Community in the Gay World. New York: Wiley.
Warren, Carol and John M. Johnson
1972   "A Critique of Labeling Theory from the Phenomenological Perspective," in Robert A. Scott and Jack D. Douglas, eds., Theoretical Perspectives on Deviance. New York: Basic Books.
Weber, Max
1947   The Theory of Social and Economic Organizations. Translated by A. M. Henderson and Talcott Parsons. Glencoe, Ill.: Free Press.
Weinberg, George H.
1972   Society and the Healthy Homosexual. New York: St. Martin's Press.
Weinberg, Martin S. and Colin J. Williams
1974   Male Homosexuals: Their Problems and Adaptations. New York: Oxford University Press.
Wenger, Dennis L. and C. Ritchard Fletcher
1969   "The Effect of Legal Counsel on Admissions to a State Mental Hospital: A Confrontation of Professions." Journal of Health and Social Behavior 10 (June):66–72.
Wheeler, Stanton, ed.
1969   On Record: Files and Dossiers in American Life. New York: Russell Sage.
Whyte, William Foote
1943   Street Corner Society. Chicago: University of Chicago Press.
Wilde, William A.
1968   "Decision-Making in a Psychiatric Screening Agency." Journal of Health and Social Behavior 9 (September):215–21.
Wilson, James Q.
1975   Thinking about Crime. New York: Random House.
Wirth, Louis
1926   The Ghetto. Chicago: University of Chicago Press.
Wiseman, Jacqueline P.
1970   Stations of the Lost: The Treatment of Skid Row Alcoholics. Englewood Cliffs, N.J.: Prentice-Hall.
Wolfgang, Marvin
1963   "Uniform Crime Reports: A Critical Appraisal." University of Pennsylvania Law Review 111 (April):708–13, 725–36.
Zeitlin, Irving
1968   Ideology and the Development of Sociological Theory. Englewood Cliffs, N.J.: Prentice-Hall.
Znaniecki, Florian
1934   The Method of Sociology. New York: Farrar and Rinehart, Inc.
Zorbaugh, Harvey W.
1927   The Gold Coast and the Slum. Chicago: University of Chicago Press.

INDEX